Modern Sexism

Blatant, Subtle,
and Covert Discrimination

DISCARDED

Modern Sexism

Blatant, Subtle, and Covert Discrimination

Nijole V. Benokraitis
University of Baltimore

Joe R. Feagin
University of Texas at Austin

PRENTICE-HALL
Englewood Cliffs, New Jersey 07632

Library of Congress Cataloging-in-Publication Data

Benokraitis, Nijole V. (Nijole Vaicaitis)
    Modern sexism.

    Includes index.
    1. Sex discrimination against women—United States.
2. Sexism—United States. I. Feagin, Joe R. II. Title.
HQ1426.B428 1986   305.4'2'0973   85-28256
ISBN 0-13-597634-0

Cover photo: Lou Odor Photography
Cover design: Diane Saxe
Manufacturing buyer: John B. Hall

© 1986 by Prentice-Hall
A Division of Simon & Schuster, Inc.
Englewood Cliffs, New Jersey 07632

Printed in the United States of America

10 9 8 7 6 5 4

ISBN 0-13-597634-0   01

Prentice-Hall International (UK) Limited, *London*
Prentice-Hall of Australia Pty. Limited, *Sydney*
Prentice-Hall Canada Inc., *Toronto*
Prentice-Hall Hispanoamericana, S.A., *Mexico*
Prentice-Hall of India Private Limited, *New Delhi*
Prentice-Hall of Japan, Inc., *Tokyo*
Prentice-Hall of Southeast Asia Pte. Ltd., *Singapore*
Editora Prentice-Hall do Brasil, Ltda., *Rio de Janeiro*
Whitehall Books Limited, *Wellington, New Zealand*

This book is dedicated

To Vitalius, my best friend, and to my parents, Ona and Pijus Vaicaitis.

N.V.B.

and

To all those women who still suffer from the actions of my gender, with the hope that they will continue to organize to stop such actions once and for all.

J.R.F.

Contents

Preface

Recently, seven executives—six men and a woman—were in a brainstorming session to come up with incentives for salespeople at a large Silicon Valley semiconductor company. One serious proposal was "to offer them a woman as a prize."

As this example suggests, blatant sex prejudice is alive and well. So is sex discrimination. Sex discrimination has changed during the past decade, however, and now includes less openly discriminatory behavior and practices. Even conservative business journals are beginning to admit that discriminatory barriers are not as visible as they were in the past. A recent article in *Fortune* stated that women in business now face "hidden obstacles" that are difficult to overcome. Although the article provided a few insightful examples of the hidden obstacles, most of the discussion focused on blatant sex discrimination.

However inadvertent, the shift from subtle to blatant sex discrimination in the *Fortune* article and elsewhere is not surprising. On the one hand, there is still so much blatant sex prejudice and discrimination, and some of it is so outrageous (as illustrated by the Silicon Valley example above), that it is difficult to ignore open sex inequality or to resist documenting it. On the other hand, subtle sex discrimination is difficult to define and measure. Even when it is not hidden, subtle discrimination is not immediately obvious. For example, a young couple is jubilant that the firstborn is a son because he will "carry on the family name" and be a "protector" of a little sister in the future. A father leaves work early to get to his ten-year-old son's soccer game on a Tuesday afternoon but "doesn't have time" to attend his sixteen-year-old daughter's regional basketball tournament on a Saturday morning. A mother willingly pays a teenage boy $20 an hour to mow the front lawn but complains about paying a teenage girl $1.50 an hour to babysit because "she doesn't do anything." Two college students are having difficulty in a calculus course; the mathematics professor advises the female student to drop the course but encourages the male student to get a tutor, work harder, and ask questions in class. *People,* the popular and self-professed "family" magazine, runs full-page liquor ads that exploit women's sex.

We are born into, grow up in, and grow old in a society that teaches us that the democratic phrase "all men are created equal" does not include women. As the above examples suggest, sex discrimination encourages and reinforces sex inequality. Whether intentional or unintentional, the values, attitudes, and behaviors generated by nonovert sex discrimination are harmful not only to men and women as individuals, but also to such basic institutions as the family, the economy, education, and the political system.

This book is about blatant, subtle, and covert sex discrimination. We describe and illustrate several types of sex discrimination, show how and why sex discrimination practices have changed during the past decade, suggest how and why women are sometimes complicit in discriminatory behavior, examine the consequences of all forms of sex inequality, and propose remedies for diminishing and eradicating sex discrimination in the future.

Modern Sexism has been written for a large audience. The book is relevant for students in the social sciences, the humanities, women's studies, public and business administration, social work, communications, and human relations. Much of the interview data, which come from individuals in a variety of occupations, should be interesting to the general public, affirmative action officers, policy makers, community planners, corporate executives and managers, counselors and personnel managers in industry, defense contractors, administrators, criminal justice staff, and educators at all levels.

We are planning to pursue the research on subtle and covert sex discrimination in the future and would be pleased to receive additional information on these topics from readers for future publications. As this book shows, all responses are confidential and data are presented anonymously.

ACKNOWLEDGMENTS

We are indebted to many people who have helped produce this book. The most important contributors were the more than 300 men and women who agreed to be interviewed or who sent in written comments about their experiences. Although sometimes painful, the responses were thoughtful and insightful. They provided the illustrative material for several chapters of this book.

A number of readers offered valuable suggestions on drafts of particular chapters. These readers include the late Devy Bendit, Kathy Block, Rose Brewer, Derral Cheatwood, Marie Crane, Minna Doskow, Jeri Falk, Diana Kendall, Ron Lippincott, Melanie Martindale, Richard Swaim, and Susan Zacur.

Randall Beirne, Wanda Breitenbach, Barbara Gibbs, Michelle Gilligan, Dorothy Heim, Carroll Heim, Frederick Kelly, Sheila Litzky, Lou Luchsinger, Susan Marshall, Doris Powell, Beatrice Robbins, and Liucija Vaicaitis provided insightful observations that influenced our thinking and writing. Catherine Gira has been a treasured colleague and friend. She has contributed valuable editorial assistance, years of stimulating dialogue, and continuous encouragement of this project.

We are grateful to Anna Alfaro-Correa, Achaempong Amoeteng, Lucy Azanolue, Cathy Crawford, Clairece Feagin, Eileen Gibb, Marie Mulvenna, and the reference staff at the University of Baltimore's Langsdale Library for their research and reference help.

Special thanks go to Gloria Schroeder, Allison Grooms, Portia McCormick, and Dana Campbell for spending many hours deciphering hundreds of handwritten pages and typing several drafts of the manuscript. Nijole Benokraitis is grateful to the Yale Gordon College of Liberal Arts at the University of Baltimore for providing a sabbatical leave and a faculty research grant during the early stages of the research.

At Prentice-Hall, Susan Taylor first encouraged this project in its embryonic stages. More recently Bill Webber has been a helpful and resourceful editor. The constructive criticism of the Prentice-Hall reviewers helped us clarify our perspective and arguments. We thank Louise Comfort (California State University at Hayward), Verta Taylor (Ohio State University), Susan Tiano (The University of New Mexico), and Charlene A. Urwin (Texas Christian University) for their challenging questions, useful comments, and helpful suggestions. We are grateful to Peggy Gordon, our production editor, and to Barbara Bernstein, Carol Ayres, and the other staff members at Prentice-Hall for their contributions in the last stages of the book's production. Brief sections of Joe Feagin's *Social Problems* textbook (second edition) are used here with the permission of Prentice-Hall.

Andrius and Gema Benokraitis have been mature and responsible beyond their young ages throughout the last five years of this project. They served as receptionists and word-processing advisors, photocopied stacks of articles in numerous libraries, scrubbed floors, baked for school functions, gave up important social activities, changed their plans at the last minute, did homework in parked cars and outside of unfamiliar offices during long interviews, and accepted unrealistic parental demands. When things got tough, they got tougher, but were always instrumental in keeping life in perspective. Vitalius Benokraitis is a very rare man. He was practicing sex equality long before it was fashionable to even talk about it and chuckled at the resulting criticisms. He continues to be supportive, encouraging, thoughtful, understanding, and patient. Most importantly, he never loses his temper or his sense of humor. Michelle and Trevor Feagin have also been supportive in this enterprise and have taught by their lives that optimism about a less sexist future is well justified. Clairece Booher Feagin has not only been supportive and encouraging, but has also contributed substantial material and insights to this book, making it better than it otherwise would have been.

Modern Sexism
Blatant, Subtle, and Covert Discrimination

Introduction:
Sex Discrimination in the 1980s

During a recent college class, a management professor spent the period explaining the differences between male and female managers. Among other things, he encouraged the students to "think twice" before hiring or promoting women to management positions in the future:

> Women work hard. They're good in detail, doing the necessary research, follow-up, following orders and are more willing than men to do almost any job they're asked to do. Women don't complain as much as men, are more reliable and don't sit around telling dirty jokes or war stories. . . . But you have to be careful. . . . You don't want them in really high-powered positions because it's not in their nature. Research shows that women want to mother, not lead. They want everyone to be friendly and feel good. . . . They're not very good in giving orders, kicking ass, or firing subordinates. Women are good for building morale, not profits.

The student who recounted this experience was asked how the class reacted. He replied, "After class some of the women were upset. They thought he was a sexist. Even a few of the guys were surprised. . . . But Professor [X] said his conclusions were based on research, so we all just took notes. Who's going to argue with an expert? [Laugh.] Besides that, would *you* disagree with someone who's giving out grades in a few weeks?"

Recently, one of the authors attended a meeting convened by a president of a university to update the faculty and staff on the activities, accomplishments, and progress of the different offices and academic departments. The president introduced the male deans and directors briefly and formally and used their appropriate titles. One of the deans, about halfway through the program, was an attractive young woman. In introducing this dean, the president made some loud asides about whether she should be addressed as "Dean" or "Mrs." and finally said, "Well, just come on up here, [Sue], and show everybody what you've got." The predominantly male audience burst into guffaws, applause, and knee-slapping. The dean, clearly embarrassed, proceeded to give her report over the lingering laughter of the audience.

Last year, a thirty-three-year-old, single, female store manager lost her job because the business was sold to another company. Whereas she was given two weeks' salary, a male manager who had been dismissed previously was given two months' salary. The company rationale was that the male employee had house payments and serious financial obligations. The woman's employer said that because she was single, had few financial burdens, and could stay with her parents until she found a new job, she didn't need a larger termination salary.

In 1982 one of the authors submitted a grant proposal to the federal government's Women's Equity Act Program (WEAP) to study sex discrimination in the labor force. Although all reviewers said that the proposal was well written and could be successfully implemented, two of the three reviewers rejected the proposal because "sex discrimination doesn't exist anymore" and recommended that the WEAP not fund projects that focus on "dated issues." (The proposal wasn't funded.)

Most people would probably not go so far as to argue that sex discrimination no longer exists. However, many people—including many of the women we interviewed—believe that "things have really changed" or that, personally, they would not be victims of sex discrimination. Even among those who said that they are discriminated against, a surprisingly large number blamed themselves or felt that it was only a "temporary condition" that they expected to change depending on a variety of "whens"—for example, "when I get a college degree," "when we get a new boss," "when I get a promotion," "when I find another job," or "when I pass the law boards."

As this book documents, sex discrimination is *not* an illusion. *Quite to the contrary, it is at least as robust as it was in the 1950s, 1960s, and 1970s.* Why, then, are many men and women today so accepting of sex inequality and so complacent about the future?

WHY AMERICANS ARE OPTIMISTIC

A majority of people are convinced that sex inequality is no longer a high-priority problem. This conviction is based, first and foremost, on a lack of information. Most Americans rarely see or pay attention to statistics that show that sex discrimination abounds. Even when such statistics are provided, the initial reaction is denial or skepticism: "That was last year. What about statistics for this year?" "Even national data aren't accurate." "But anyone can lie with statistics." Or, people point to exceptions: "My neighbor just got a job in construction, and she says she's getting the same salary as the men." "But the music industry is different. Look at all the money people like Cindy Lauper, Tina Turner, and Loretta Lynn are making."

Besides an ignorance of the facts and a focus on exceptions, another reason for our complacency is probably that the potentially explosive national and international problems during the 1970s and 1980s turned people's attention away from sex inequality issues.

1. During the 1970s Americans experienced Watergate, a spiraling inflation rate, a recession, threatening forecasts of another depression, unparalled unemployment, and severe energy shortages. Since the late 1970s national and international terrorism has reached unprecedented heights. American and European embassies have been bombed; civilians have been killed or taken hostage; there have been a number of attempted or successful assassinations of national leaders (President Reagan, Pope John Paul II, Indira Gandhi, Anwar Sadat); violence in Northern Ireland and Poland has escalated. In the United States, the Three Mile Island accident sparked widespread fears of nuclear disasters and environmental contamination, entire communities were relocated because of chemical pollution, and the Reagan administration's "Star Wars" statements led to generalized fears that a worldwide holocaust was not unlikely. Compared to these and other social and political problems, sex discrimination—"if it exists"—has been seen as a low-priority issue.

2. A number of surveys show that Americans are expressing more accepting attitudes toward women. For example, a 1979 national Harris Poll concluded that "the American male shows variety along the entire spectrum from traditional to innovative responses about work, the family, religion, leisure, marriage, and sex." The implication was that there are many liberated men who accept women as equals.[1]

A 1980 Roper Poll found that college-educated women, especially, were fairly confident that they were getting equal treatment in all job-related areas. More than 60 percent felt that they had an equal chance in promotions, with the same salaries and work responsibilities as men.[2]

These and other opinion polls reflect attitudes rather than behavior. Most people equate attitudes with behavior and then conclude that behavior toward women has changed. Also, opinion polls rarely differentiate between actual and expected values and behavior. Most people assume that how things should be are synonymous with how things really are.

3. The mass media continue to emphasize superficial changes in terms of equal sex roles. This has led many people to conclude, as one of our students put it, that "sex discrimination is only a minor problem." On the national level, for example, the media have played up women's "firsts"—first Supreme Court justice, first astronaut, and first Vice-Presidential candidate. Even at the local level, the mass media are quick to publicize the first female executive of a bank, the first female college chancellor, the first female district court judge, or the first female chair of

an important political committee. Emphasizing such "firsts" gives the impression that women have, indeed, made great strides and even that women are "taking over." Moreover, many people believe that such "firsts" are numerous, widespread, and representative across all institutions. Very few people realize that our ability to point to "firsts" reflects women's exclusion from most activities. There is little evidence, furthermore, that the "firsts" move beyond entry-level steps.

Many Americans assume that the mass media reflect real social changes and reality. Avid TV watchers point to the occasional anchorwoman and to the glamorous female physician or powerful woman executive on soap operas as evidence of gender equality. However, such shows mirror the media's perception of women as tokens. Also, the portrayal of women and their relationships with men is romanticized, trivialized, or treated in typically sex-stereotypical, simplistic ways. In "Partners in Crime," for example, the two female private investigators have "inherited" the agency from the same late ex-husband. They mince around in very high heels, very tight, short skirts, and very revealing dresses. True to Hollywood's perception of women, they spend more time changing hairstyles and wardrobes than investigating crimes. In such supposedly egalitarian TV shows as "Scarecrow and Mrs. King," Mrs. King is cute but empty-headed, talks in questions, whimpers a lot, and helps her male partner solve crimes only accidentally. In such female-dominated shows as "One Day at a Time," "Facts of Life," and "Gimme A Break," most of the themes revolve around sex and love, and the women and girls spend a lot of time worrying about their sexuality or looks, trying to figure out how to get or keep a man or how to make him happy. In both daytime and evening soap operas ("All My Children," "Dynasty," "Falcon Crest"), the rich, strong, powerful, and successful women are invariably cast as villains. The "good" women are helpless, sacrificing, loyal, naive, sweet, and easily manipulated. The message is that only "bad" women challenge or succeed in nontraditional female roles. A few TV shows, such as "Cagney and Lacey," "St. Elsewhere," "Cheers," and "Hill Street Blues" do portray women as strong, interesting, and intelligent personalities. Such shows, however, are not standard fare.

Many people believe that the greater display of female nudity and more "women's films" are proof of "women's liberation." However, there is little discussion of female nudity as pornography rather than art. Also, there is little recognition of the fact that many of the "women's films" still present women in traditional sex-stereotypical roles—as shrews, dumb housewives, sex symbols, domestic martyrs, or clinging vines. Even when the heroine starts out as an intelligent and interesting person, she invariably ends up committing suicide, dying, or being "done in" or rescued by a man. For example, in *Terms of Endearment* the wife of a cuckolding husband dies from cancer and leaves the kids to the grandmother because the father doesn't want the responsibility of raising children. He's too busy "finding himself" and chasing women. In *Sophie's Choice,* the heroine commits suicide and dies in the arms of her psychotic boyfriend rather than going off with the more "normal" man. The "woman as self-sacrificing martyr" is seen in *Kramer vs. Kramer,* where the wife gives up custody of the son even though the father has shown little interest in the boy in the past. In a rare portrayal of role reversal, where the husband loses his job and becomes a househusband while the wife finds a job and becomes an instant success in the business world, *Mr. Mom* still presents both roles in simplistic and sex-stereotypical ways. Both characters are "rescued," in the end, by going back to their traditional roles in the family and the workplace. In *The Bostonians,* an attractive, articulate, and intelligent young feminist becomes immobilized minutes before delivering a public talk that will catapult her into national recognition, and falls—pale, fainting, and helpless—into the arms of a handsome, barely verbal, macho Southern gentleman who has finally convinced her that "real women" find happiness only in the kitchen and the bedroom. What these and other films are saying to audiences, over and over again, is that only traditional sex roles bring men and women happiness and satisfaction. And, in a large number of films, for example, *An Officer and a Gentleman, Flashdance,* and *Romancing the Stone,* the women succeed only with the man's help or are totally dependent on men for survival and happiness.

During the 1950s and 1960s, most teenage films presented teenagers as little more than simple-minded kids who spent most of their time surfing, having beach parties, and playing adolescent cat-and-mouse courtship games. Such portrayals of teenagers were flattering compared to more recent films. In the typical teenage film of the 1970s and 1980s (*American Graffiti,* the *Nerds* and *Porky* films, *Tuff Turf, 16 Candles, Heavenly Bodies,* and *Mischief*), the teenage viewer is told that crude and vulgar behavior is hilarious, that sex is the only thing that is important in life, and that violent and manipulative sex is fun and funny. In the few instances in which adult women are presented at all, those who have authority are cast in particularly demeaning and degrading roles. Although a few teenage films, such as *The Outsiders* and *The Breakfast Club,* grapple with such adolescent problems as insecurity and peer pressure, most teenage films reflect little more than middle-aged male producers' and directors' somewhat pathetic sexual fantasies about teenage girls.

4. The mass media's (especially television's) recent dramatizations of such taboo and controversial topics as incest, rape, spouse abuse, and homosexuality have led many people to conclude that we are *really* open about women's issues and sex-related problems. But the mass media touch new topics only briefly and then move on, avoiding depth.

The media have generated or publicized numerous books and workshops, at local and national levels, that advise individual women how to "get ahead," find a job, get promoted, dress for success, handle an office affair, use cosmetics, get invited to a business lunch, sue for divorce, travel alone, locate child care, write a resumé, keep in shape, hide wrinkles, and so on. Most of the magazines are aimed not just at women, but at individual, middle-class working women. Almost all the covers show happy, smiling, attractive, fashionably dressed and well-groomed women who have fairly interesting jobs outside the home. The shopper standing in the checkout line at the local supermarket sees vivid pictures of "real change" in the roles of women and assumes that all women "have come a long way." Few people wonder why women, but not men, need the workshops, magazines, and advice on how to survive in the marketplace—especially since more than one-third of the labor force has been made up of women since 1940. Even fewer people recognize that many of the magazines and books portray fantasies about, not realities of, working women.

5. Another reason for the view that sex inequality has diminished is the greatly publicized fact that only a small number of women have been upwardly mobile since the launching of the women's movement in the late 1960s. These women, found almost exclusively in the professions and low-level management positions, are often touted as evidence of sex equality. Students often point to a female professor, their neighborhood female physician, or a policewoman to prove that "things have really changed." What is ignored, however, is the fact that such changes are highly skewed and represent an extremely small fraction of working women. As this book shows, even the few women in professional and nontraditional occupations face barriers in obtaining equitable promotions and salaries.

6. Many of us rely exclusively on our personal observations and experiences to generalize about the world at large. We assume, erroneously, that such generalizations are valid. If we have not *personally* discriminated or been discriminated against, we may assume that there is no sex inequality. Yet, we would be appalled at such illogical reasoning on other issues. Imagine denying the existence of suicide because we have never attempted to kill ourselves or arguing that there is no unemployment problem because we, our families, and friends have never been unemployed. We may not recognize such inconsistencies in our logic because, compared to problems like suicide and unemployment, sex discrimination is more acceptable, is not always blatant, or is not immediately visible.

7. Finally, many of us assume that sex discrimination is "not really a problem" because it is *illegal*. Some types of sex discrimination are illegal, but so are shoplifting, homicide, rape, aggravated assault, robbery, kidnapping, and a variety of other abuses. Unlike many other offenses, however, annual statistics on sex discrimination are not collected or published. Even data that are available—like the number of sex discrimination complaints or lawsuits filed—are not publicized or readily available. Many of us are not aware (or made aware) of the scope and severity of sex discrimination.

WHY AMERICANS SHOULD BE ANGRY

This Polyanna view of American reality is contradicted by the facts. By way of opening the discussion, consider women's dismal progress in employment, a presidential administration that has spearheaded anti-civil rights activities during the 1980s, and a male backlash evident in violence against women.

Employment. Those who argue that sex discrimination is disappearing typically rely on two indicators of change—the high labor-force participation of women and the increased entry of women into some professional graduate programs. In the last decade, the percentage of women entering some traditionally male-dominated areas has increased—from 12 to 39 percent in law schools, 11 to 29 percent in medical schools, and 2 to 20 percent in dental schools.

While it is true that women now make up more than half of the work force, *women's employment patterns in the mid-1980s are virtually the same as they were in 1960*. That is, women dominate occupations that are low-paying and considered "dead end" in terms of career mobility. Women still earn only 62 percent of what men earn, and the earnings gap increases as educational level increases.

Will women entering professional schools graduate and secure salaries comparable to those of men? The data on employment in higher education show no correlation between the availability of qualified women and the success of women in academic employment. Quite to the contrary, the data show that the women who received Ph.D.s in the early and mid-1970s have *not* been promoted, paid, or tenured at the same levels or rates as men. These differences exist even when comparisons are between men and women who are similar in terms of such characteristics as marital status, number of children, job longevity, discipline area, prestige of the Ph.D.-granting institution, and number and quality of publications. The percentage of women in (full) professor ranks is about the same in 1985 as it was in 1970—despite the increased number of women who received Ph.D.s in the early 1970s! In a recent study of 45 men and 45 women who earned M.B.A.s at Columbia University between 1969 and 1972, Devanna found that although men and women were paid comparable beginning salaries, there was a significant difference a decade later. Ten years after job entry, women earned less than men even though both men and women were in similar jobs, had comparable work experience, and were equally highly motivated.[3] Women graduates of professional programs in medicine, dentistry, law, and veterinary sciences will undoubtedly suffer similar fates.

What *has* changed since 1970 is that more women work "double days" (one shift at work and one shift at home), live in poverty, are single heads of households, and are increasingly victimized by a variety of violent crimes inside and outside their homes. Moreover, those few women who have been upwardly mobile are encountering different, rather than less, discrimination.

The federal government. Many of the gains that women made during the 1970s have been eroded in the 1980s. In terms of affirmative action, the Reagan administration attacked existing legislation and cut the budgets and staffs of already-weak enforcement agencies. In 1983, for example, the Justice Department called for a diluted interpretation of Title IX that would legalize sex discrimination in a number of programs in higher education. Title IX of the Education Amendments of 1972 barred discrimination in "any education program or activity receiving federal financial assistance." In 1984 the Supreme Court restricted this broader interpretation considerably by ruling in *Grove City College* v. *Bell* that only a specific program receiving federal aid—rather than the entire institution—was barred from discrimination. After the ruling, some lawmakers introduced legislation to amend Title IX to show that Congress intended the law to be applied more broadly than the Supreme Court's narrow interpretation in *Grove City College* v. *Bell.* If such new legislation fails, some forms of sex discrimination that are now illegal will once again be legal:

> Should the Reagan administration's point of view prevail, Title IX would be gutted—despite the fact that the law itself would not be amended. For example, institutions could bar women from crowded classes or deny women athletic opportunities and still receive federal funds. *Many of the discriminatory policies that have been abolished would once again be legal* [emphasis added].[4]

The few programs (such as the WEAP) that received modest funds for sex discrimination research during the 1970s barely survived into the 1980s. Some agencies, including the National Science Foundation and the National Institute for Mental Health, which used to earmark a small percentage of monies for sex inequality-related research in the 1970s, shifted most of those funds to research on defense, science, and engineering in the 1980s. By the mid-1980s, the directors and grant proposal reviewers for civil-rights-related research had been replaced by non-academics whose backgrounds demonstrate not only a lack of training and experience to evaluate proposals but also long histories of anti-civil rights activities.

Finally, more than half of the members of the Commission on Civil Rights (the federal government's civil rights "watchdog") were replaced in the early 1980s by individuals (including reactionary minority women) who publicly supported and promoted anti-affirmative action attitudes and efforts. These members actually canceled reports and articles commissioned by prior appointees. While the new appointees were proud of the commission's "balanced" (i.e., right wing) hearings and publications, which opposed such issues as comparable worth and supported discriminatory seniority systems, numerous organized civil rights groups promoting women's and minorities rights were so dismayed by the committee's anti-equal rights activities that they advocated eliminating the commission altogether.

The Reagan administration's view and treatment of women have also been instructive. For example, during a 1983 convention of the International Federation of Business and Professional Women in Washington, D.C., a long-scheduled tour of the White House was canceled because of administrative snafus. In his apology for the cancellation, the president asserted his "recognition of women's place": "I happen to be one who believes that if it wasn't for women, us men would be walking around in skin suits carrying clubs." Thus, according to the president, women's place is in the home—civilizing and supporting their "menfolk" and keeping the cave clean and cozy.

In 1984, during the Walter Mondale-Geraldine Ferraro campaign* against Ronald Reagan, top government officials (and their wives) used sexist slurs and

---

*In 1984 the Democratic party's nominees were Walter Mondale for President and Geraldine Ferraro for Vice-President; their counterparts in the Republican party were Ronald Reagan and George Bush.

made derogatory statements about Ferraro and women's issues without fear of re-crimination. Vice-President Bush said of the Bush-Ferraro debate: "We tried to kick a little ass." Mrs. Bush described Ferraro as a "$4 million _____ " (and it rhymes with "witch"), and one of Bush's aides publicly described Ferraro as "too bitchy." In 1984 White House economist William Niskanen described the concept of com-parable pay as "a truly crazy proposal," and Clarence M. Pendleton, Jr., Chairman of the Civil Rights Commission, called comparable worth "the looniest idea since 'Looney Tunes' came on the screen." While public and political pressure forced Democratic candidate Jesse Jackson to apologize for an anti-Semitic remark, there was no comparable public outrage or pressure to make these prominent officials apologize for the numerous offensive and demeaning comments made about women.

In the early 1980s there was a growth of conservative political and religious groups that endorsed traditional sex roles. During the 1984 presidential campaign, for example, Ferraro was publicly criticized by Catholic Church officials for her political pro-abortion views even though she said that, personally, she would never have an abortion because it was forbidden by the Catholic Church. Reagan's divorce was accepted without comment. There was an intensive investigation of Ferraro's personal and business background and her husband's finances without a parallel scrutiny of the Bushes' backgrounds. Many women voters did not vote the Mon-dale-Ferraro ticket in 1984 even though, a year earlier, two influential Republican women—the chief of the National Women's Political Caucus and a member of the Federal Trade Commission—described President Reagan as a "dangerous man" who had created a climate that "exposes the shallowness of our nation's commitment to [sex] equality." As the 1984 presidential election results showed, however, most men and women were not disturbed by the Reagan administration's endorsement of sex inequality.

Violence.   Another troubling indicator of sex inequality has been the escala-tion of violence against women. About 95 percent of the victims of sexual child abuse are girls, and rape statistics increase annually. In terms of our most recently discovered crime—spouse abuse—more than 2 million American women are severely beaten in their homes every year, 20 percent of the visits by women for emergency medical services are caused by battering, and one out of every four female murder victims is killed by her husband or boyfriend.[5] Since between 40 and 60 percent of all crimes against women are not reported, the above statistics are severely under-estimated. Many cases of physical violence are never reported by women because they expect and accept violence in interpersonal relationships. For example, a social worker who gives talks on domestic violence to high school students recently said that many young women see physical violence as "normal":

A number of the girls said that being slapped, hit or punched by their boy-friend shows that he "really cares" about her. . . . That he's just "setting her straight. . . ." Even girls who come from non-abusive homes accept being hit because they feel it's better than being ignored by the guys.

Some male politicians are still using euphemisms to describe wife abuse. In 1985, for example, the wife of the enforcement chief of the Securities and Exchange Commission sued for divorce alleging that during their eighteen years of marriage, she had been the victim of periodic beatings by her husband, which had left her with a broken eardrum, wrenched neck, several black eyes, and many bruises. The husband "strongly contested that he was a wife beater" and referred to the beatings as "occasional highly regrettable episodes."

The film industry has been especially enthusiastic in depicting women in roles where they are hurt, maimed, mutilated, terrorized, or brutally murdered (for example, *Looking for Mr. Goodbar, Tattoo, Klute, Dressed to Kill,* and *Deep Throat*). Horror movies aimed at teenage audiences typically depict the female as a victim. And, the brightest, most independent, and most attractive girls/women are the ones who are most likely to be terrorized or brutalized (for example, *Are You Home Alone?* and *Nightmare on Elm Street*). X-rated adult films in which women are raped, disemboweled, sodomized, mutilated, and tortured abound. Some rock music and many rock videos reinforce the idea that sex and female victimization go together. The rock song "Eat Me Alive" describes a girl being forced to commit oral sex at gunpoint. The typical rock video shows women as seductresses, as murder victims, being locked in cages, dressed in fishnet and leather, and enjoying sadistic sexual intercourse.[6] More than half of the Music Television videos (MTVs) feature or suggest violence, present hostile sexual relations between men and women as commonplace and acceptable, and show male heroes torturing and murdering women for fun.[7] In a recent study of rock videos, Shorr concluded that through their music, teens and young adults "continue to live in a society in which males perceive females to be little more than sex objects."[8] Especially grim is the fact that such films and videos portraying women as victims are extremely popular among both teenagers and adults.

The most recent expression of violence against women has been the attacks on and bombings of abortion clinics. Even though abortion has been legal since the early 1970s, there were more than thirty bombings of planned parenthood clinics between 1982 and early 1985. Of the few individuals arrested in early 1985, almost all were young, white, middle-class males who have been active in anti-abortion organizations and activities. Of the three men arrested most recently for bombing at least eight abortion clinics in Maryland, Washington, D.C., and Virginia, one was a minister. At least in some men's minds, there is no religious or philosophical contradiction in destroying private property or in killing people who disagree with the pro-life platform. This may be the case because the majority, if not all, of the victims would be women. While some men use violence to keep women "in their place," there is little comparable interest in promoting women's rights in such areas as child support, wife abuse, rape, or women living in poverty. The conservative political climate of the 1980s may have legitimated the use of violence to keep women "in their place."

In summary, there is a great deal of evidence showing that sex inequality is not a "minor problem." In some cases, overt and blatant sex discrimination has increased. In other cases, sex inequality has taken subtle forms. *Sex discrimination has not diminished; it has only changed.*

PURPOSE AND ORGANIZATION OF THE BOOK

The purpose of this book is to explore the broad range of sex discrimination. Although we will discuss overt sex inequality, we will emphasize the less blatant and less visible types of discrimination—in other words, subtle and covert sex discrimination. Our discussion will focus on the dynamics, processes, and consequences of sex inequality.

Chapter Two provides an overview of women's subordinate place in a sexist society on the individual, organizational, and societal levels. Among other topics, we document the political backsliding on sex discrimination issues, the media's presentation of women as second-class citizens, men's unwillingness to share institutional power with women, and the resurgence of individualistic ideologies that emphasize women's responsibility to the home, to men, and to traditional expectations about femininity.

Chapter Three suggests an analytical typology for examining sex discrimination. The research on overt sex discrimination is reviewed. The main focus, however, is on the importance of understanding and uncovering subtle and covert sex discrimination. We define basic concepts of sex discrimination, provide examples, discuss conceptual and measurement problems, and describe the major dimensions of sex discrimination.

Chapter Four presents a summary of findings on overt discrimination and provides evidence of continuing sex inequality at individual, organizational, and institutional levels. General and specific instances of domestic and employment sex discrimination are described in both formal and informal situations. We show that overt sex discrimination has been institutionalized and internalized and continues to operate to keep women in unequal statuses and positions.

Chapter Five provides evidence of nine types of subtle sex discrimination processes: condescending chivalry, supportive discouragement, friendly harassment, subjective objectification, radiant devaluation, liberated sexism, benevolent exploitation, considerate domination, and collegial exclusion.

Chapter Six documents six types of covert sex discrimination: tokenism, containment, manipulation, sabotage, revenge, and co-optation. Also discussed are the effects of formal and informal merit procedures in reinforcing and proliferating covert sex discrimination.

Chapter Seven deals with the special plight of minority women as victims of overt, subtle, and covert sex discrimination. We discuss the double jeopardy that minority women encounter in employment, education, and the domestic area and examine the reasons for the estrangement of minority women from the women's movement.

Chapter Eight studies the negative effects of overt, subtle, and covert sex discrimination on the individual, organizational, and societal levels. Sex inequality at all three levels has resulted in a number of negative consequences for both men and women. Some of these negative consequences include emotional, psychological, and health problems; a suppression of talent; lowered productivity; reduced creativity; and a disruptive impact on families. Also discussed are the negative consequences of social policies on the work and family lives of both men and women.

Chapter Nine suggests remedies for overt, subtle, and covert sex discrimination at individual, organizational, and societal levels. In addition to summarizing remedies that have been offered by other authors, we suggest several new and different solutions for the old problem of sex inequality.

NOTES

1. *The Playboy Report on American Men,* Playboy Enterprises, 1979, p. 58.
2. Roper Organization, *The 1980 Virginia Slims American Women's Opinion Poll,* 1980, p. 41.
3. Mary Anne Devanna, "Male/Female Careers, The First Decade: A Study of MBAs," New York: Columbia University Graduate School of Business, 1984, mimeographed paper.
4. Bernice R. Sandler, "The Quiet Revolution on Campus: How Sex Discrimination Has Changed," *The Chronicle of Higher Education,* February 29, 1984, p. 72.
5. See CIStems, Inc., Cultural Information Service, New York, 1984.
6. Bill Barol, "Women in a Video Cage," *Newsweek,* March 4, 1985, p. 54.
7. National Coalition on Television Violence, "Rock Music and MTV Found Increasingly Violent: Sexual Violence Predominates," NCTV Press Release, January 10, 1984.
8. Jonathan L. Shorr, "Rock Videos and Values: A Content Analysis" (paper presented at the 15th annual Popular Culture Association meetings, Louisville, Kentucky, April 1985), p. 11.

2

Woman's Place in a Sexist Society: Society, Organizations, and Individuals

Early in 1984 the *Wall Street Journal* featured a front-page story about a New York City group called the Baker Street Irregulars, prominent men dedicated to reliving the adventures and spirit of Arthur Conan Doyle's detective Sherlock Holmes. They hold annual dinner parties for men only, with a pre-dinner toast to "the woman," a woman specially chosen for the occasion, who after the toast is sent away. These male aficionados of Holmes, the bachelor, believe that Holmes had a distaste for women. Heading its story with "To a Sherlockian, Coolness to Women is an Elementary Canon" and providing a critical insight into yet another good-old-boy ritual, the *Wall Street Journal* article both demonstrated and reinforced the anti-female aspects of much male togetherness in this society. The sex discrimination faced by women is a critical feature of a society that is so male dominated that few analysts, journalists, or researchers can fathom its deep roots.[1]

We have noticed a disturbing trend in the thinking of many Americans over the last decade. Many students who enter our college courses are convinced that sex discrimination is no longer a serious problem in the United States. Invariably, even the most informed students become visibly impatient when we introduce such "ancient history" as sex discrimination and male domination. After all, students argue, things have really changed since the 1960s. "My boss has told me several times that the company has to hire more women." "If there were sex discrimination, I wouldn't have been accepted into the management training program." "Some of the most successful accountants I know are women." "My husband was very supportive when I said I wanted to go back to school." "I can be an engineer if I want to be."

This view of the world is not surprising, for it can be found among such prominent writers and advisers to U.S. presidents as George Gilder and Phyllis Schafly. Indeed, in *Wealth and Poverty* the influential Gilder has argued that there is no need for affirmative action because (1) it would seem genuinely difficult to document the idea that America is still oppressive and discriminatory, and (2) discrimination has already been effectively abolished in this country.[2]

Sex discrimination is explicitly described by Gilder as a "myth." Affirmative action is seen as unnecessary. Gilder suggests that affirmative action for women is a "mockery" that victimizes black men, the "true" victims of discrimination. Even though this argument about black men contradicts Gilder's argument that discrimination for blacks has been abolished and in spite of the undocumented character of many of Gilder's arguments, his book became the "bible" for many in the Reagan administration and in conservative business circles in the 1980s.

Phyllis Schafly, the prominent right-wing advocate, has argued vigorously in recent years that sexual harassment is not a problem in this country, because "virtuous women" do not suffer sexual harassment in the work place. Schafly has been successful in fighting against the liberation of women from male dominance; she articulates the American dream of the ideal husband-centered family. Her Ozzie-and-Harriet family image, with the woman at home with the kids and the man bringing home the paycheck, is still a strong American ideal, even though it is declining rapidly as an American reality. Indeed, in recent years only 28 percent of American families fit the dream family Schafly vigorously defends. Even Schafly's own life as a touring lecturer and writer contradicts the dream she preaches.[3] Schafly has also attacked such progressive changes as federal affirmative action regulations, which she views as hurting the traditional mother in the ideal family by allegedly giving her husband's job to a woman and by "obsoleting the role of motherhood."[4]

Although the views of Gilder and Schafly are among the most reactionary of the views on changes in sex roles, many Americans, both the powerful and the rank and file, share them. We shall now examine these reactionary views more closely at the societal, institutional, and individual levels.

THE SOCIETAL LEVEL

The momentum of the late 1960s and early 1970s, which was directed toward expanding employment and educational opportunity for women, slowed significantly in the late 1970s and 1980s. Governmental policymakers and private sector decision makers became preoccupied with matters other than sex discrimination. It was only a century ago that a decade or two of great progress in expanding opportunities for black Americans (1865–85), often called the Reconstruction period, was followed all too soon by a dramatic resurgence of white conservatism and control, a reaction period. While there are major differences between then and now, just two decades after public policy shifted significantly in favor of expanded opportunities for women and minorities, we again see significant movement in a reactionary direction.

The presidential level. We have seen this reaction at the presidential level. In the early 1980s, President Ronald Reagan publicly opposed the Equal Rights Amendment (ERA). And in late 1983, President Reagan intentionally destroyed the U.S. Commission on Civil Rights, an organization long effective in the fight for better conditions for America's women and minorities. He replaced two moderate members of the commission with a male-dominated group sympathetic to extreme right-wing views on the role of women and minorities in U.S. society. Reagan's right-wing commission has abandoned its traditional role of studying federal government programs to see if they are discriminatory. Mary Berry—a prominent historian, former dean at the University of Maryland, and a member of the liberal minority on the commission—reviewed the studies proposed by the new majority and argued that the new commission was becoming "the President's Commission for the further advancement of white males."[5] This right-wing coup, coming on the heels of similar actions rolling back anti-discrimination actions by the Equal Employment Opportunity Commission (EEOC) and the Department of Justice, clearly signaled an era of reaction at the federal level in the 1980s.

That Reagan's stance on various issues, including the ERA, was extreme can be seen in opinion polls. By 1982, for the first time in opinion-polling history, a significant sex difference in the job-approval rating of an American president had developed. In April 1982 only 42 percent of women approved of Reagan's job performance, compared to 61 percent of men, according to an ABC-*Washington Post* poll.[6] Reagan's position on the ERA and other equal rights issues, as well as his emphasis on a massive military buildup and on military involvement to solve world political problems, may be the major reasons for some women's disenchantment with the Reagan administration.

The courts. We see also reaction, or a slowing of progress, in the federal court system. For example, a 1978 report by the U.S. Commission on Civil Rights found that 800 sections of the U.S. legal code still had examples of sex bias or sex-based terminology that were in conflict with the ideal of equal rights for women. Many state laws are similarly sex biased.[7] The report argued that the failure to incorporate the Equal Rights Amendment into the U.S. Constitution perpetrated sex bias in U.S. law. By the 1980s an increasingly conservative Supreme Court had demonstrated a halting move away from equal rights. In 1984 the Supreme Court ruled that an entire college is not subject to civil rights laws protecting women, even if one of its programs receives major federal aid.[8] Grove City College, a private college in Pennsylvania, argued that it should not be covered by Title IX of the 1972 Education Amendments (banning sex discrimination) because the only federal aid it received went directly to students. Grove City College said it did not discriminate in any programs against women.

The Court ruled that the college was covered by Title IX, but only for the aid program itself. (The Reagan administration had backed this narrow interpretation of the *Grove City College* case.) This decision signals a backing away from broad protection of women in educational institutions. Title IX of the 1972 Educational Amendments prohibits sex discrimination in "any educational program or activity receiving federal financial assistance." This language had been broadly interpreted prior to the Supreme Court decision as prohibiting sex discrimination in all programs at a college that received any significant federal aid. In his dissent to part of *Grove City College* v. *Bell* (1984), Justice William Brennan noted that the legislative intent of Title IX was clear: to prohibit sex discrimination across the board in colleges receiving federal aid. Because in this case the federal aid received by Grove City College's students benefited the general operating budget of the entire college, Brennan argued that sex discrimination in all its programs should be banned.

The *Grove* ruling is already preventing or justifying the inaction of government agencies after the discovery of sex discrimination. For example, after an investigation of complaints at University of Maryland's College Park campus, the Office of Civil Rights sent the university a letter stating that disparities had been found between the men's and women's athletic programs in such areas as recruitment, support services, travel, and competitive opportunities. Three weeks after the *Grove* ruling, however, the university received a letter saying that the Office of Civil Rights was dropping the charges because it had concluded that it did "not have jurisdiction to pursue this matter."[9]

Affirmative action.   The 1980s brought a marked backing away from positive programs designed to upgrade women in U.S. society. From the late 1960s through the mid-1970s, legislation, judicial decisions, executive orders, and administrative guidelines generated requirements for "result-oriented" programs that would promote qualified women and minorities in employment. Called "affirmative action," these programs suffered from much heated attack. Many debates centered on these action programs. Many people still assume that "goals" and "quotas" are synonymous, that "preferential treatment" is being given to unqualified women and minority job applicants, and that affirmative action programs violate promotions based on tradition, "merit," and seniority.[10]

Much of this debate has been misplaced. Officials often drew up "paper tiger" plans that could not be implemented or enforced and that could be easily challenged.[11] The affirmative action guidelines were vague, the interpretations were highly discretionary and varied even within an organization. Because many affirmative action officers were poorly trained, lacked enforcement powers, and were not supported by the higher echelons, affirmative action officers were rarely taken seriously.

Such "paper tiger" programs may lead to a poorly constructed affirmative action plan issued with fanfare but weakly enforced. A top Sears executive has complained about negotiations with the government: "We are forced to create mounds of paper to prove that people aren't available instead of creatively and innovatively developing techniques to make sure people are available."[12] Whether he would aggressively pursue the development of new techniques to find qualified women if he did not face the paperwork is open to question. But a number of observers of organizations, assessing organizational reactions to affirmative action, have noted that too much of the effort often goes into paperwork, both statistical and legal, and too little into aggressively finding women for nontraditional positions. In a recent article two veteran management consultants have concluded from their experience not only that too much corporate effort is aimed at winning the statistical battle, but also that hostile overreactions, little budget money, and poor management have created "mongrel" affirmative action plans that are weak.[13] Weak efforts may bring in or upgrade a few women, but at the same time they alienate many white males who can then blame their own problems on affirmative action.

One problem is the failure to link patterns of discrimination to the need for remedies. Apart from a few words about sharp declines in discrimination, most critics of affirmative action focus on the operation and effects of the programs and ignore the background and context of sex discrimination. An adequate defense of affirmative action requires a thorough problem-remedy approach, since it is the discriminatory problem that requires the remedy. Discrimination is the *problem* for which affirmative action is the *remedy*. Equal opportunity and affirmative action efforts make sense only if we understand the problems of individual and institutionalized discrimination.

Few who attack affirmative action believe that massive discrimination still exists. So we have prominent white males such as George Gilder who not only reject most affirmative action efforts but also argue that discrimination has already been effectively abolished in this country. There is no consensus on affirmative action as a remedy because there is no consensus on the character and persistence of discrimination in the United States. Some decline in blatant sexist attitudes and the decline in some blatant forms of sex discrimination are taken by many commentators as signs that discrimination is dead—or so near death as to require little further societal or governmental intervention.[14]

The bottom line on evaluating change in conditions for women is that two decades into equal opportunity and affirmative action programs, few systematic or fundamental changes can be seen in most major institutional sectors of this society. White males overwhelmingly dominate upper-level and middle-level positions in most major organizations, from the Department of Defense, to General Motors, to state legislatures, local banks, and supermarket chains. The dominant national concern has shifted away from patterns of sex (and race) discrimination. Those hurt most by the shift have been those people who have long suffered from traditional institutionalized discrimination—women and minorities.

The resurgence of the beauty standard. Beyond the governmental level we also see a broad trend in the direction of reemphasizing the traditional aspects of woman's place in a patriarchal society. In their analysis of fashion, Lauer and Lauer show that, historically, women's fashions changed, in large part, in response to men's perceptions of feminine beauty. To accentuate a small waist and a large bosom, nineteenth-century women corseted themselves even though corsets crushed the ribs, deformed the breasts, weakened and diseased the lungs by making breathing difficult, twisted the spinal column, and crowded the liver, heart, and stomach so badly that sometimes they ceased to function properly.[15] In the 1850s, the "bloomer" gained appeal because it encouraged a woman to move freely in performing household tasks. However, the appeal was short-lived:

> It was 'bad fashion,' unattractive and inappropriate to the women of the Republic. Opponents . . . pointed out that the Bloomer was one of those styles that uglified rather than beautified. . . . It magnified large feet and was unflattering to short women, and one of the functions of fashion is to cover the defects of beauty.[16]

From the early 1900s to the late 1960s, fashion showcased women's bodies, sexuality, and femininity. During the 1920s and 1930s, "flappers" showed a lot of leg, thigh, and arm. During the 1950s, billowy skirts, several layers of petticoats, ruffles, tiny waists, and cleavage were "in." The mini-skirts of the 1960s showed more body than clothing.

During the late 1960s, activist women in the newly emerging "women's liberation movement" reacted negatively to male and female definitions of beauty that were based solely on physical appeal; many refused to wear cosmetics, endorsed more "natural" hairstyles that did not necessitate monthly visits to the beauty salon, and wore pants and baggy clothes that did not accentuate their bodies.

Since the mid-1970s there has been a great deal of renewed emphasis on women looking "beautiful." Most women are still judged primarily by their beauty or attractiveness, whereas men are judged primarily in terms of their achievements. We still live in a society where more money is spent on women's looks than on social service programs. In 1970, for example, Americans spent over $10 billion on cosmetics and personal hygiene products alone. These expenditures on physical attractiveness do not include the costs of "beauty books," cosmetic plastic surgery, designer clothes and accessories, beauty spas, and video exercise tapes and books. Ironically, of the nation's largest firms, five of the ten headed by women are in the beauty business and have very healthy assets—Estee Lauder ($1 billion), Mary Kay Cosmetics ($304 million), Jockey International ($250 million), Christian Dior New York ($215 million), and Diane von Furstenberg ($200 million).[17]

Being attractive to men is still a major goal of most women. Because a woman's looks are treated as her primary (perhaps only) asset, the older a women gets, the more anxious she becomes about aging. As the baby boom cohorts are approaching their forties, the cosmetics industry is launching campaigns that create the "older woman's" need to be beautiful and glamorous and is promoting products that will meet those needs: "Johnson & Johnson, whose no-tears shampoo was second only to Dr. Spock in bringing up the 1950s baby, has now introduced Affinity, a shampoo 'for hair over 40.'"[18] "Looks" have a major impact in this society, even though many Americans might admit that talent, intelligence, achievements, and effort should be accorded more importance in assessing the contribution of a woman.

The mass media. Another sign of nonprogress at the societal level is the treatment of women in the mass media. Essential to modern capitalism is advertising, with sexist ads being so commonplace they cannot be avoided. Women still appear less frequently in ads than men, are much more likely to be seen in home rather than work settings, and are more likely to be in ads for food, home, beauty, and clothing products. A recent study of 2,000 ads in *Time, Vogue, Ladies' Home Journal,* and *Playboy* found that between 1960 and 1979, both men and women were very likely to be portrayed in the traditional roles (women as housewives, men on the job). And they found *no* significant change in the emphasis on traditional sex roles in the ads over this period. Many writers have emphasized the growing numbers of women who have moved into the work place, but there has not been a corresponding increase in the occupational portrayals of women in magazine ads. Ads for women continue to accent the beautiful-body theme (modeling, fashion, cosmetics, beauty aids) and the housewife theme (parenting, cleaning, cooking).[19] The mass media briefly gave some attention in the 1970s to women other than housewives and secretaries. Some advertising presented models in pantsuits or pin-striped business suits who looked like the stereotype of the "new business women." Yet, by the 1980s advertising had moved away from this changing emphasis to more traditional models, such as women in gowns dancing at discos.

A related issue is how the news media present the social situation of women. There is subtle discrimination in the way issues are defined and presented in the news media. For example, celebrated sex discrimination cases are discussed for a while, but on an episodic basis. Cumulative patterns of discrimination, the deep problems of discrimination for women, are ignored—as though the media also accept the view that women no longer suffer from sex discrimination. An example is the case of Christine Craft, a woman newscaster who sued a Kansas City TV station that fired her because station researchers said local viewers saw her as too old and unattractive and "not deferential enough to men" when on the air. In January 1984, after a long court battle, she was awarded $325,000 by a Missouri jury. Her case received extensive national publicity for a few days now and then, over several months, but no systematic analysis of women *in* the news media was conducted *by* the new media. In June 1985, a federal appeals court overruled the jury decision and rejected Craft's sex discrimination charge. The appeals court ruled that the TV station had not defrauded Craft by promising "no makeover or substantial changes" in appearance when she was hired but then requiring her to spend hours with clothing and "appearance" consultants. The appeals court ruled that Craft had to *prove* that her employers intended to change her appearance.[20]

THE ORGANIZATIONAL LEVEL

At the level of organizations, some progress in upgrading women has taken place, but major problems remain. And there has been significant backtracking. Recent nationwide opinion polls have shown that male decision makers in organizations, including top managers and executives, are often willing to hire women, but only in token numbers and primarily at entry levels.

Old-boy networks and the male viewpoint. A key problem is that those who rule in organizations, both private and governmental, like to perpetuate their own kind. Diana Kendall has suggested that there may be a weird "sociobiology of organizations where a person wants to foster another person who will assist him while he is still in the organization and will carry on just as he did when he retires, dies, etc. This may be a way in which people leave their 'mark' on an organization—by leaving someone else there who is very much like themselves. The woman and/or minority group member does not fit this model that rules organizations."[21] This pattern is still strong in many organizations.

Women and minorities somehow fall outside the critical old-boy networks. Dorothy Gregg, a vice president of a New York forecasting firm, spoke at a Federation of Women's Clubs convention in Florida in 1983. Gregg termed corporations "paramilitary bureaucracies" in which it is "useful to have attended Yale, Harvard, or Princeton and even more useful to have been an officer of the U.S. Navy." She noted that corporations are still dominated by the good-old-boy network, the modern equivalent of primitive tribalism. An example of this can be seen in the results of a recent education study:

> Research assistantships are assigned by individual faculty members who have the support for this type of appointment. Male faculty members tend to favor male graduate students as research assistants for various and sundry reasons ("because they play squash together") with the result that few women are selected and hence more become teaching assistants by default.[22]

Old-boy networks function both during and after work hours. Women employees are often handicapped by not being part of after-hours events, such as drinks at a bar or a golf outing. At these times, important advice is passed along to rising young employees about how organizations work. Because women are often not part of these informal networks, they may not get the critical information necessary for advancement in an organization. One analyst of organizations notes that an executive might say: "Hey, Phil, if I were you I would consider making a lateral move into marketing. No one here at B & B makes it to the top without a couple of solid years in marketing."[23] As a result of their exclusion from informal networks, women do not plan their careers and career moves as well as men, and the like-reproduces-like feature of organizations remains paramount.

Another dimension of this like-breeds-like situation can been seen in the limited experience many top male decision makers have had with women on their own professional or business level. A widespread problem is that the wives of most top-level male decision makers do not work outside the home, are active in volunteer work, travel the "luncheon circuit," or spend three days a week at the local health/beauty spa. Hence, these male decision makers have limited contact with career women who have occupational goals similar to those of men. As a result, they may have trouble relating to women different from their wives. While a male executive may not openly let a professional woman know he views her as "odd" or "different," this way of viewing professional women becomes an organizing model of thought in his hiring, promoting, or relating interpersonally to professional women. An example of this can be seen the 1980–83 study of the wives of college and university presidents by the American Association of State Colleges and Universities.[24] An image of wives joining the work force in increasing numbers was not borne out in this study. Only 32 percent of these top-level wives were employed on a full-time or part-time basis in 1982–83. Both those wives working and not working outside the home maintained a schedule of forty or more hours a week in entertaining and volunteer work. One analyst commented that the survey's findings show, in part, that "the first flush of the feminist movement, with its emphasis on working for money, is past."[25] Not only does this suggest that many wives of top executive and professional men are, as the same analyst put it, "finding outlets for their executive talents and managerial competencies in the role of the president's wife" rather than in their own careers, but also that male presidents have the most contact with women who organize their lives in this manner. It is thus probable that the men's way of thinking about career women they encounter, hire, or consider for promotion is affected by constantly seeing women in a domestic position. This thinking helps to reproduce organizations as male-centered dynasties.

The like-reproduces-like feature of organizations is supplemented by other problems as well. Women moving into organizational worlds where few have gone before are often more honest and forthright than men and expect the business world to be "fair." It is difficult for many women to accept the dishonesty and unfairness of the business world, such as the cases where the boss takes credit for a woman's work or where the boss promises a woman subordinate a promotion that he really does not intend to give. Lawrence Schwimmer has noted that women believe that hard work is the route to success, but such is "only true if you are meeting the boss's definition of hard work."[26]

Another example of subtle discrimination at the organizational level has been documented in a study by Harlan and Weiss, who found that middle-level managers tend to promote older, less aggressive women and women who "don't rock the boat" in middle-management positions. At many levels, boat-rockers do not do well in modern corporations. As Schwimmer puts it, "if management perceives you to be a boat-rocker, you may never get the opportunity to move up to the higher ranks."[27] Yet in some companies, top executives have passed over these middle-level women when looking for senior managers, because they were looking for more dynamic and aggressive managers. Regardless of the level of promotion, both types of women, the aggressive and the nonaggressive, have encountered significant discrimination in the "man's world."

Some women who have tried to move up the organizational ladder have been rejected ("burned"). They then send out negative messages to other women in the organization and, through interviews in the mass media, to women outside the organization. Since they become "fed up" with trying to make it in an organization, they communicate negative feelings to other women, including friends and relatives. This in turn reduces the motivation of other women to try to penetrate the corporate system.

Blatant discrimination in organizations. Blatant sex discrimination and sex prejudice have by no means disappeared from organizations in this society. Chauvinistic attitudes of male executives remain a major barrier to women in business and other sectors. One problem in the business sphere is that male managers resist sending single female employees with married male employees on business trips. Another is the male assumption that women cannot handle technical fields as well as men. One researcher reported, in a survey of 1,000 women executives, that one-fifth of the women said they had encountered serious sexual harassment on the job.[28] A key aspect of sexual harassment on the job is its reinforcement of other types of discrimination. Work becomes a prize men give to women if women permit harassment. Like wife battering and rape, sexual harassment at work is now coming out of the closet. And, like rape, this harassment is pervaded with stereotypes of working women as sex objects, including the notion that most women intentionally invite the harassment. Sexual harassment has been defined by Farley as "unsolicited nonreciprocal male behavior that asserts a woman's sex role over her function as a worker."[29]

A recent survey of women college seniors at the University of California (Berkeley) found that 80 out of 269 respondents—nearly one in three—reported unwanted sexual harassment by teachers during their college career. Including multiple instances, the 80 students reported 100 examples of unwanted sexual contact, leers, or lewd suggestions from instructors. Most of the examples involved explicit sexual propositions, touching, fondling, or leering. Most of the students, out of fear of retaliation, did not confront the instructors directly or complain. Many in the group were harmed by the harassment. They reported a loss of self-confidence or a disillusionment with academia.[30]

THE INDIVIDUAL LEVEL

The success ethic. At the level of individual women and men we see continuing problems. Today many women and men are less informed about sex inequality, and many seem to be more conservative about sex role expectations than in the recent past. In recent years popular books have emphasized a variety of individualistic themes, views that take the blame off the patriarchal social system. Thus many women have been so bombarded with the individualistic success ethic proclaimed in many best-seller books that they have accepted the proposition that their own failure or success is primarily of their own making. Held back by blatant and informal discrimination, these victims are now told they have only themselves to blame if they do not succeed. Numerous books tell women that, if they don't make it in U.S. society, it is their own fault; their problem is not the fault of sex discrimination or sexual harassment.

In *Having It All: Love-Success-Sex-Money*, Helen Gurley Brown, the creator of *Cosmopolitan* magazine, gives fairly conventional advice to women: dress "pretty," diet to be sexy, loving clothes is not a sin, love his entire body, get a job in order to get in touch with the better type of man, starting as a secretary is a good way to make it, "nice" girls finish first, don't be aggressive, sexual harassment isn't so terrible (tolerate it if you can), try to be a woman, and don't be afraid of having sex with the boss. A basic theme in the book is that being successful is up to the woman; that barriers such as sexual harassment are not very serious; that if women don't succeed, they should try and try again; and that if women fail, it is probably their fault. Success comes from diligent efforts, working hard over many years. While Brown does write for women with careers outside the home, she is simply packaging the traditional individualistic ethic for women who work outside the home.[31]

This renewed emphasis on the individualistic ethic for women is based on the fundamental individualistic ethic dominant in this society since the eighteenth century. This individualistic ideology today includes the following beliefs:

1. That each individual should work hard and strive to succeed in competition with others
2. That those who work hard should be rewarded with success (seen as wealth, property, prestige, and power)
3. That because of widespread equal opportunity those who work hard will in fact be rewarded with success
4. That economic failure is an individual's own fault and reveals lack of effort and other character defects

The second half of the nineteenth century was a major era of rapid capitalistic expansion in the United States, with an unprecedented exploitation of natural and human resources and the development of new industries. The evolutionary perspective of Charles Darwin, as applied to human society by the social Darwinists, was compatible with this aggressive expansion in its two main themes—the "struggle for survival" and the "survival of the fittest." Social and economic life was considered to be nature's life-and-death struggle, in which the best individual competitors both should and would win out over others. Moreover, the hierarchical structure of society and its social divisions, including distinctions between the rich and the poor and between men and women, were thought to be the result of the operation of basic laws of nature. Closely linked to these beliefs was the idea that the competitive struggle should not be tampered with by government, lest all manner of social ills result. Today social Darwinism persists in individual values about the subordinate "place" of women in the society and also in the view that women who fail have only themselves to blame for their lack of success.[32]

In the book *Equality,* William Ryan suggests that our historical emphasis on individualism was based on, and encouraged, the accumulation of resources by individuals who did not have such societal handicaps as skin color and sex. The large nonwhite and female segments of the population did not have access to these resources. They have been told to seek "equal opportunity" but are excluded from sharing in "equal results." Thus, (white) men can embrace the egalitarian rhetoric without a significant sharing of the basic resources and rewards.[33]

The resurgence of femininity. In the last decade we have seen a renewed emphasis on femininity. Susan Brownmiller has noted the new emphasis, especially among many better-off women, on baubles and beads, on high heels, makeup, and dresses. Brownmiller raises questions about the new emphasis on femininity in the 1980s, which she attributes in part to the failure of women to get good jobs outside the home and to intensified competition among women for the "available men." In the competition for men, women undergo expensive, painful, unnecessary, and sometimes unsuccessful aesthetic surgery to improve physical characteristics that appeal to men. In 1984, nearly half a million Americans had cosmetic surgery for such things as eye tucks, face-lifts, and fat removal. Over 80 percent of the patients were women. The most popular operations were breast-related: 95,000 for breast augmentation and 16,200 for breast lifts. By comparisons, there were only 4,500 hair transplant cases.[34] The resurgence of concern among women and among advertisers with feminine clothing—dresses, hose, and high heels—is perhaps symbolic of the retreat from progress for women. While concern with clothes can have its positive side, excessive concern reinforces the sexist roles in society. Brownmiller notes that "to care about feminine fashion, and do it well, is to be obsessively involved in inconsequential details on a serious basis. There is no relief."[35] Clothing reinforces societal sex role divisions. Who is who is clear from grouping men in pants and women in skirts—this *seems* to be the *natural* order of things. Brownmiller further notes the basic contradiction in the femininity syndrome:

> The world smiles favorably on the feminine woman: it extends little courtesies and minor privileges. Yet the nature of this competitive edge is ironic, at best, for one works at femininity by *accepting restrictions,* by limiting one's sights, by choosing an indirect route, by scattering concentration and not giving one's all as a man would to his own, certifiably masculine, interests.[36]

Individualistic femininity means vulnerability, the need for protection, dependence on, and subordination to men.

This renewed femininity can be seen in the work place. A recent study of fifty young women in the professions and arts with six-figure incomes found that most attributed their success to such female personality traits as getting along well with people, understanding, and being deferential. Older professional women have ascribed their success to technical skills, competence in the job, and independence. Given the fact that top male decision makers have wives and daughters who do not work outside the home in professional positions, these decision makers may *reward* the women who "fit in," those who get along well with other people, those who are interpersonally sensitive and feminine.[37] A successful female vice-president in a music and fine arts college, for example, was very proud of the "feminine" characteristics that, she believes, helped her be upwardly mobile:

> When I was on the faculty, I purposely negotiated between the faculty, especially the men, who are always squabbling. . . . I'd comfort the losers and

praise the winners. . . . I made sure, too, that I never aligned myself with the feminist faculty. . . . Giving a lot of small, classy parties didn't hurt.

CONCLUSION

Why did the progress for women that began in the 1960s slow down by the 1970s and even regress during the 1980s? There are a number of reasons. They include a false sense of security among women and sympathetic men about the achievements of the 1970s. Some cite the weakening leadership in some women's organizations. But more important has been the resistance of the male-centered society to sex role changes on the scale required. The right-wing political groups that rose to power in the late 1970s and 1980s intentionally rolled back some gains made by women and minorities. Moreover, the difficulties encountered in trying to penetrate a male-dominated society have significantly reduced the expectations of many women. Some women have accepted limited progress in nontraditional employment. Others have retreated from the male world, some into extreme femininity. They have lowered their expectations and have accepted more traditional sex roles because they are powerless to do otherwise, *not* because they prefer subordinated sex roles. Many of the battles won in the late 1960s and 1970s were limited or temporary victories.

Many organizations and institutions did become less sexist under pressure from protesting women and active national leadership for women's rights. But organizations and institutions are *so* male oriented and male dominated that many of these changes have been modest and too easily reversed. Men who control organizations do not have to work hard to perpetrate sex discrimination when the organizations and institutions have been structured that way for centuries. Women may have penetrated some entry positions in organizations, but it is much harder for them to get into the top positions, the core, the "inner sanctum."

Virginia Woolf wrote that "women have served all these centuries as looking glasses possessing the magic and delicious power of reflecting the figure of man at twice its natural size."[38] Women have challenged and are challenging their looking-glass function in this society, but they are a long way from shattering the glass.

NOTES

1. Lee Barton, "To a Sherlockian, Coolness to Women Is Elementary Canon," *Wall Street Journal,* January 6, 1984, p. 1.
2. George Gilder, *Wealth and Poverty* (New York: Basic Books, 1981).
3. How Long Till Equality?" *Time,* July 12, 1982, p. 29.
4. Spencer Rich, "Schafly: Sex Harassment on Job No Problem for Virtuous Women," *Washington Post,* April 22, 1981, p. A2.
5. Charles Farrell, "Aide to Civil-Rights Commission Proposes Study of Effects of

Affirmative Action on Companies," *Chronicle of Higher Education,* January 1, 1984, p. 1.

6. Dick Kirschten, "The Presidential 'Gender Gap' Looms as a Major Political Problem for the GOP," *National Journal,* August 21, 1982, p. 1,457.
7. Tristam Coffin, "Women's Lib: The Revolution at the Gates," *Washington Spectator,* March 1, 1983, p. 2.
8. "Supreme Court Rules Anti-Sex Bias Law Covers Only College Programs that Get Direct U.S. Aid," *Chronicle of Higher Education,* March 7, 1984, pp. 1, 19–25.
9. "U.S. Refuses to Act on Sex-Bias Charge at University of Maryland," *Chronicle of Higher Education,* March 21, 1984, pp. 1, 16.
10. For a discussion of the pros and cons of the affirmative action debates, see Nijole V. Benokraitis and Joe R. Feagin, *Affirmative Action and Equal Opportunity: Action, Inaction, Reaction* (Boulder, Colo.: Westview Press, 1978), pp. 171–191.
11. See ibid., pp. 44–56, 95–115, 154–168, for descriptions of "paper tiger" programs in industry, business, higher education, and government.
12. Max Benavidez, "The Sears Interview: Ray Graham," *Forum,* October 1980, p. 16.
13. Gopal C. Pati and Charles W. Reilly, "Reversing Discrimination: A Perspective," *Labor Law Journal* (January 1978), p. 23.
14. Cf. Nathan Glazer, *Affirmative Discrimination* (New York: Basic Books, 1975).
15. Robert H. Lauer and Jeanette C. Lauer, *Fashion Power: The Meaning of Fashion in American Society* (Englewood Cliffs, N.J.: Prentice-Hall, 1981), pp. 209–215.
16. Ibid., p. 251.
17. Cited in George Spencer and Nicole Flewellyn, "Female Executives Foresee Gains," *Fortune,* December 1984, p. 49.
18. "The Look of a 'Certain Age'," *Newsweek,* January 28, 1985, p. 64.
19. Teresa Gardner and Paula England, "Sex Role Portrayals in Magazine Advertisements, 1960–1979" (unpublished paper, University of Texas, Dallas, 1981).
20. Joseph A. Reaves, "Fired Announcer Taps Grass-roots Support," *Austin American Statesman,* January 15, 1984, p. A6; "Woman TV Announcer Loses Jury Award," *Austin American Statesman,* June 6, 1985, p. E1.
21. This was suggested to us by Diana Kendall (personal correspondence, March 1984).
22. Roberta M. Hall and Bernice Sandler, "The Classroom Climate: A Chilly One for Women?" (Washington, D.C.: Association of American Colleges, Project on the Status and Education of Women, 1982), p. 10.
23. Cited in "Women Executives: What Holds So Many Back?" *U.S. News and World Report,* February 8, 1982, p. 63.
24. Beverly T. Watkins, "Most Presidents' Wives Do Not Have Jobs, Survey by State-Colleges Group Finds," *Chronicle of Higher Education,* December 7, 1983, p. 23.
25. Ibid.
26. "Women Executives," p. 63.
27. Ibid., p. 64.
28. Ibid., p. 63.
29. Lin Farley, *Sexual Shakedown* (New York: McGraw-Hill, 1978), pp. 14–15.
30. Donna J. Benson and Gregg E. Thomson, "Sexual Harassment on a University Campus," *Social Problems* 29 (February 1982), pp. 240–250.
31. Helen Gurley Brown, *Having It All: Love-Success-Sex-Money* (New York: Simon and Schuster, 1982), pp. 16–60.

32. Joe R. Feagin, *Subordinating the Poor* (Englewood Cliffs, N.J.: Prentice-Hall, 1975).
33. William Ryan, *Equality* (New York: Random House, 1981), pp. 8–10.
34. "New Bodies for Sale," *Newsweek*, May 27, 1985, pp. 66–67.
35. Susan Brownmiller, *Feminists* (New York: Simon and Schuster, 1983), p. 81.
36. Ibid., pp. 15–16.
37. "Femininity Gets Credit for Success," *Austin American Statesman,* December 19, 1983, p. A18.
38. "How Long Till Equality?" p. 29.

3

Overt/Subtle/Covert Sex Discrimination: An Overview

Consider the following examples of a management meeting where both male and female managers are present:

Situation 1: Women are routinely addressed as "honey," "babe," or "gorgeous," and hear sexist stories, jokes, and vulgar language. They are expected to take notes and listen. Active participation is discouraged.

Situation 2: Off-color stories are typically not told. Or, if they are, they are interrupted with the warning "there are ladies present." Men speak differently to women than they do to men—they are more formal, polite, deliberate, and long-winded.

Situation 3: Only a few women are present. Women's input is minimal or guarded. While their comments are often overlooked, the women are also encouraged to participate because they represent "the other women."

Although the content of interaction varies, all three cases illustrate sex inequality. In all three examples, women are treated like women, not managers. In situation 1, language is openly sexist and derogatory (overt discrimination). In situation 2, the somen are treated like "ladies" rather than co-workers (subtle discrimination). In situation 3, women are overlooked or set apart as symbols (covert discrimination).

Such terms as "covert discrimination," "subtle discrimination," and "unintentional discrimination" are beginning to appear with greater frequency in common parlance, newspapers, textbooks, and feminist articles. There has been an increased awareness of the importance of addressing non-overt sex discrimination. For example, the 1980 Report of the President's Advisory Committee for Women stated that "covert biases are equally as detrimental to accomplishing educational equity as overt discriminatory practices."[1] In a study of sex roles in organizations, Forisha and Goldman stressed that "probably the gravest problem that women face is sexism . . . not . . . sexist practices which are overt but . . . the pervasive and relatively inaccessible, non-conscious value that women are not men and men are better than women."[2] Most recently, the U.S. Commission on Civil Rights stated that productive approaches toward eliminating discrimination must emphasize "an informed awareness of the form, dynamics, and subtleties of the process of discrimination."[3]

Despite the agreed-upon importance of understanding covert and subtle sex discrimination, theoretical and research efforts in this area have been embryonic. The analytical focus on sex discrimination has not changed significantly since the 1950s. For the most part, almost all of the research on sex discrimination still examines only overt sex discrimination.

TYPES OF SEX DISCRIMINATION:
DEFINITIONS AND ILLUSTRATIONS

For the purposes of this book, sex discrimination refers to the unequal and harmful treatment of individuals or groups because of their gender. Although both men and women can be targets and victims of sex discrimination, a vast literature indicates that being a woman is frequently a better predictor of inequality than such variables as age, race, religion, intelligence, achievements, or socioeconomic status.[4] That is, although some men may be discriminated against because of their education, religion, race, or political affiliations; for example, they are not treated unequally simply because they are men. Quite to the contrary, being a man may neutralize or override racial, age, or religious discrimination. Women, on the other hand, will be treated unequally simply because they are women and regardless of other variables.*

Current examinations of sex discrimination, however valid, are inadequate and incomplete because they emphasize overt discrimination and pay minimal,

---

*We recognize, however, that in a broader analysis gender discrimination cannot be separated from issues of race and class (capitalism). We will focus on the race issue in Chapter Seven and will touch on matters of class in a number of contexts. Since this book focuses on contemporary patterns of discrimination and is not intended as a comprehensive theoretical treatment of sex roles in their complex economic, social, and political frameworks, we will not discuss the differing theoretical frameworks, such as liberal feminism and socialist feminism, as they attempt to deal with the relationships between gender, race, and class stratification. Readers wishing to probe these important theoretical issues should consult the work of Zillah Eisenstein (for example, *Capitalist Patriarchy and the Case for Socialist Feminism*, Monthly Review Press, 1979) or Angela Davis (*Women, Race and Class*, Random House, 1981).

if any, attention to subtle and covert discrimination. This results in understanding only a portion of the dynamics and characteristics of sex inequality.

After providing some working definitions and examples, we will summarize the state of the literature in the areas of overt, subtle, and covert sex discrimination; suggest some dimensions across which sex discrimination varies; and discuss women's complicity in discriminatory practices.

Overt sex discrimination. Overt sex discrimination refers to an unequal and harmful treatment of women that is readily apparent, visibile, and observable and can be easily documented. Examples of overt sex discrimination include sexual harassment, sexist language and jokes, physical violence and violation (rape, incest, wife abuse), and other forms of unequal treatment in the family, employment, politics, religion, and other institutional sectors. For instance, inequality in the economic sector includes unequal salaries in comparable jobs, lack of promotion opportunities, and sex-segregated labor markets.

Overt discrimination can be (and has been) documented by examining the disparate distribution of rewards by sex. Nationally, for example, women's salaries are still 59 percent of those of their male counterparts (lower than the 1969 figure of 61 percent). In 1980 women with a college degree earned about the same as men who had completed only elementary school ($16,417 and $15,709, respectively), and women in managerial/administrative positions had a median income of $12,936 compared to $23,558 for men at these occupational levels.[5]

All of the anti-discrimination legislation passed since the 1963 Equal Pay Act has been aimed at dismantling overt sex discrimination. Thus, we have laws prohibiting sex discrimination in employment (Title VII of the 1964 Civil Rights Act), education (Title IX of the Education Amendments Acts), housing, credit, and law. Clearly, the passage of anti-discrimination laws has not resulted in sex equality. Such legislation has been functional, however, both in recognizing that sex discrimination exists and providing men and women with some of the tools to fight blatant sex discrimination.

Subtle sex discrimination. Subtle sex discrimination refers to the unequal and harmful treatment of women that is visible but often not noticed because we have internalized sexist behavior as "normal," "natural," acceptable, or customary. However liberated we might like to be, most of us—men and women alike—feel that women are *really* not as good, capable, competent, and intelligent as men, especially in prestigious, competitive, and traditionally male-dominated jobs. For example, when a male faculty member becomes chairperson of a department, he is congratulated, encouraged, and reinforced in his "mobility." A female faculty member, on the other hand, is quite likely to get such spontaneous (and sincere) comments as, "Didn't anybody else [i.e., men] in the department want the job?" "Are you an Acting Chair?" or "Won't this interfere with your kids' schedules?" Sometimes, of course, men also get such comments. However, the tone and message are quite different. For men, there is a playful ribbing about taking an administrative position (for example, he has joined the ranks of "the enemy" or has abdicated from the important role of teaching to "push paper"). Despite the teasing, the man is supported and reinforced. For women, however, the comments are negative because they raise questions about her administrative competence, ability, or priorities. Thus, whereas men are kidded because "Aren't you *too good* to be doing administration?" the message to women is "Are you *good enough* to be doing administration?" Similar experiences have been reported by women administrators and managers in the profit sector.

In terms of characteristics, subtle sex discrimination can be innocent or manipulative, intentional or unintentional, well intentioned or malicious. As Chapter Five will show, subtle sex discrimination, although it *can* be documented, is not as easy to prove as overt sex discrimination because most of us do not perceive subtle sex discrimination as "real" discrimination. Consequently, subtle discrimination processes are often not seen as discriminatory because they have become acceptable—through tradition, custom, religious interpretations (or misinterpretations), mythologies, folk beliefs, "scientific" theories (as biological determinism), and laws.

Both because subtle sex discrimination is not part of our consciousness and because it may be unintentional, subtle sex discrimination can provide a semblance of sex equality because there is an absence of overt sex discrimination. For example, having a woman chair an academic department, especially if it is male dominated, may be seen as an "objective" measure of sex equality. If, however, her appointment/election is not taken seriously because of her gender (i.e., subtle sex discrimination) by students, secretaries, faculty, and administration and if she accepts such reactions, her effectiveness will be neutralized or undermined. Objectively, the department would be applauded for its progressive treatment of women and would be seen by such groups as the EEOC as fulfilling goals of promoting women in higher education. In reality, however, she would be little more than a figurehead, a puppet, or a token.

Covert sex discrimination. Covert sex discrimination refers to the unequal and harmful treatment of women that is hidden, clandestine, maliciously motivated, and very difficult to document. As will be discussed later, there are several forms of covert sex discrimination. Regardless of the form it takes, covert sex discrimination refers to behavior that consciously, purposely, and skillfully attempts to ensure women's failure, whether this is reflected in promotions, retention, and hiring or in such less tangible reactions as not taking women seriously.

One of the most common and successful methods of keeping women in their "place" internally in organizations is to impose responsibilities that are impossible to meet and then castigate women for not fulfilling the duties. For example, giving women last-minute jobs that are impossible to complete by the assigned deadline can, when nothing else (gossip, sexual harassment, and ridicule) succeeds, ensure a woman's lack of promotion or salary increase. A major problem, as will be discussed in Chapter Six, is that covert sex discrimination is very difficult to prove or document.

Summary. The three types of sex discrimination can be seen as lying along a continuum and varying on such dimensions as visibility, intent, degree of harm, documentation, and remedies. (See Table 3.1.)

Table 3.1 suggests several generalizations. First, although the three types of discrimination (overt, subtle, covert) can be seen on a continuum, there is some overlap of characteristics across the categories. For example, overt and subtle discrimination can be both intentional and unintentional.

Second, a single discriminatory act may represent several types of inequality. Since its passage in 1976, several large financial institutions, such as Household Finance Corporation, have been sued for violating the Equal Credit Opportunity Act. Some of the violations—requiring the spouse's approval for a loan, for example—have been blatantly discriminatory. Other loan and credit violations have been much more subtle.[6] Some financial institutions do not inform their applicants that if the applicant volunteers information on income received through alimony, child support, or public assistance, the applicant will probably be defined as being financially unstable and rejected as a "bad risk." Not telling consumers that they are not required to give information on sex, marital status, and some sources of income is a covert form of sex discrimination. Using the information to screen out women who are not supported by men's "stable" income represents subtle sex discrimination.

Because subtle and covert discrimination are more difficult to see, document, and remedy, they may well last longer. Thus, it is especially important to understand both of these types of inequality. As will be discussed, however, there are still some serious gaps even in our understanding of how overt sex discrimination works.

Despite the documentation of the existence and persistence of overt sex discrimination and *despite* national anti-discrimination legislation (for example, affirmative action, the Equal Pay Act, and Title IX), why is sex inequality alive, well, and flourishing? There are several possible answers.

TABLE 3.1. Sex Discrimination Typology

	OVERT	SUBTLE	COVERT
	X————————————X————————————X		
VISIBILITY	HIGH	LOW	VERY LOW
Intent	Intentional and unintentional	Intentional and unintentional	Intentional
Degree of harm	Very severe–mild	Severe	Severe–very severe
Can be documented	Always	Often	Seldom
Can be remedied (legislation, norms, bureaucratic rules)	Definitely	Probably	Rarely

As we discussed in Chapter One, the Reagan administration's dismantling and diluting of sex equity legislation, organizations, and research agencies have fueled a widespread backlash against women's liberation activities. Also, such best-sellers as *The Total Woman, The Cinderella Complex,* and *Having It All* either glorify women's subservience or blame women for their subordinate position. Finally, our discriminatory processes have become more sophisticated. Like the chameleon, sex discrimination is evolutionary, adaptable to change and new environments. In other words, *as overt and visible barriers began to be challenged during the late 1960s and early 1970s, they were replaced by subtle and covert sex discrimination in the 1980s.*

This is not to say that subtle or covert sex discrimination did not exist prior to the 1970s. They did—especially in those upper-level occupations where women tried to compete with men for power, wealth, or status. However, because overt sex discrimination was accepted, unquestioned, or normative, alternative discriminatory strategies were less necessary.

As greater numbers of women enter the labor force and compete with men— especially in such lucrative positions as management, the professions, "high tech," and the crafts—subtle and overt sex discrimination techniques will become more common and sophisticated. A handful of researchers have noticed this change and have begun to address issues related to subtle and covert sex discrimination. The analyses, however pioneering, have been modest and incomplete.

RESEARCH ON SUBTLE AND COVERT SEX DISCRIMINATION

If one searches the literature diligently, it is possible to find a few indirect references to or examples of subtle and covert sex discrimination. For example, Korda cautions corporate women not to be "taken in" by flirtation, flattery, and seductive innuendos and to be suspicious of chivalry because "deference to a woman becomes a means of excluding her from the group."[7] Schrank, although he does not describe the processes, emphasizes that when their power is threatened, vested groups of men will pull any woman down for "tinkering with their interest."[8] In a study of employment agency referrals, Pifer shows that minorities are given job referrals but are told about fewer job openings, less desirable jobs, and only the lowest-paying jobs.[9] Examining criminal justice systems, Feinman found that policewomen and women corrections officers faced barriers that are not immediately visible—for example, tougher job requirements and different training and promotion procedures.[10] And, in a case study of upwardly mobile elementary school principals, Ortiz found that one of the key barriers to moving into upper-echelon high school administration was exclusion from male-dominated informal groups that wield influence with superintendents, board members, and community leaders.[11]

Although these and other studies provide insights into understanding subtle and covert sex discrimination, there are a number of limitations: the inference of process from consequences, an absence or ambiguity of definitions, an inconsistent usage of concepts, and a focus on very specific populations.

Inferring process from consequences. A number of authors infer the presence of subtle/covert processes from statistics showing discriminatory consequences. For example, Astin, in her study of women doctorates, suggests that subtle discrimination must be present because a prospective employer was disinterested in pursuing an apparently qualified woman's job inquiries and because professional women felt isolated from collegial relationships.[12] Thus, Astin documents the low percentage of female Ph.D.s in academia but infers rather than shows the presence of subtle discrimination. It is probably true that academic departments do not hire women (despite competitive credentials) because women are believed to have a "dampening" effect on male camaraderie; for example, women are expected not to be interested in discussing football, wars, or male sexual adventures. However, not being hired *(consequence)* does not explain the mechanisms *(process)* used to disqualify women. Similarly, Frieze attributes a series of sex inequalities—in training, job failure, male and female expectations—to covert discrimination without defining the term or showing how covert discrimination produces such inequalities in the criminal justice system.[13]

Absence/ambiguity of definitions. Definitions of subtle/covert sex discrimination are rarely given. For example, a recent study of "chilly classroom climates" states only that "subtle biases in the way teachers behave toward students may seem so 'normal' that the particular behaviors which express them often go unnoticed."[14] Although some processes are described (for example, praising the responses of men but not of women), definitions of subtle sex discrimination are not provided.

Where definitions are given, they are unclear. The most elaborate definition available characterizes covert discrimination as having three sets of attributes: hidden, malicious, surreptitious, and intentional; unconscious, subconscious, and unintentional; and as resulting from marital status because the married woman is "under cover, authority, or protection of the husband."[15] The examples of covert sex discrimination include women faculty members being excluded from informal departmental decisions, being routinely given the responsibility of performing clerical chores, and having to choose between raising a family or pursuing a successful career.[16] There is no explanation, however, of how covert sex discrimination "results" from marital status.

Inconsistent usage of concepts. Prejudice and discrimination are sometimes used interchangeably to describe both covert and subtle discrimination. Analytically, prejudice refers to attitudes, whereas discrimination refers to acts. Yet, several writers use these terms synonymously. For example, Smith refers to discrimination as both "adverse actions and attitudes."[17] Frieze's article on covert discrimination focuses almost exclusively on attitudes rather than acts,[18] and Kendall and Feagin, despite their emphasis on acts and behavior, sometimes infer subtle sex discrimination from prejudicial attitudes and stereotypes.[19]

Similarly, the terms "subtle" and "covert" are sometimes used interchangeably and ambiguously. For example, in defining covert discrimination as the "hidden set of assumptions about how men and women should behave and the goals that they set themselves," Ramaley also describes covert discrimination as being subtle and rarely conscious.[20] This suggests that the two concepts—subtle discrimination and covert discrimination—are overlapping or interchangeable. Even when only the covert discrimination concept is used, its usage is imprecise, vague, and often inconsistent. That is, can covert discrimination be both surreptitious and unconscious since surreptitiousness implies conscious planning?[21] Also, can covert discrimination be surreptitious, intentional, *and* unintentional?[22]

Although Pottker implies that covert discrimination is different from overt discrimination (without defining either term), her examples of covert discrimination are not dissimilar from examples of overt discrimination.[23] For instance, Pottker describes nepotism as "one of the most visible and structured ways a university can discriminate against women" employees.[24] If nepotism is visible, however, why is it an example of covert discrimination?

Focus on specific populations. The handful of available studies on subtle and covert sex discrimination focus almost exclusively on women in higher education, on students (and often only on minority women students), and on a few subtle barriers (such as hiring). For example, Kendall and Feagin found that minority women medical students experienced such discriminatory barriers as tokenism, the absence of sanctions against overt discrimination, the absence of role models and mentors for minority women, and evaluation procedures that reflected white male attitudes and values.[25] However interesting the findings, the study does not define covert discrimination and focuses only on minority women in higher education. In a study that also was limited to students in higher education, Hall and Sandler recently described some of the subtle ways in which women students experience inequality in the classroom.[26] For example, instructors call more often on men than women, respond more extensively to men's comments, use classroom examples that reflect sex-stereotypical ideas about social roles, and address the class as if no women were present (for example, "When you were a boy . . . ."). Again, the study does not define subtle discrimination and describes only female students in higher education.

Goodwin offers one of the most insightful descriptions of how covert discrimination actually works in excluding women (and minority men) from employment in higher education: for example, offering candidates unacceptable salaries and increasing the salaries after the candidates have rejected the job offers; delaying signing the contract until, faced with meeting deadlines from other institutions, the candidates are "forced" to remove themselves from consideration; and discouraging women (and minorities) from accepting job offers by telling them that they received the offers because of affirmative action requirements rather than on their own merit.[27] Goodwin's observations are limited to discussions of hiring barriers and only to those in higher education.

To summarize, there have been a number of attempts to define and examine non-overt sex discrimination. However, these studies have not had clear conceptual frameworks and have been limited to very specific populations.

LEVELS OF SEX DISCRIMINATION

Besides the three types of sex discrimination (overt, subtle, covert), sex inequality operates at four levels—individual, organizational, institutional, and cultural.

At level one—individual discrimination—the unequal behavior occurs on a one-to-one basis. It may be direct, interpersonal, and face-to-face or indirect and impersonal. It may be motivated by prejudice or operate independently of prejudice. In terms of the latter case, a supervisor may not promote a woman not because he is prejudiced but because he knows she will not be accepted by her peer group of male managers.

At level two—organizational discrimination—the unequal behavior occurs because of practices, rules, and policies that are different for each sex. For example, a female physician employed at a nationally known pharmaceutical company noted that in interdepartmental memos and introductions to outsiders, women physicians are often called by their first name (or even "Miss" and "Mrs.") while the men are addressed as "Dr." Activities that are geared toward women routinely receive smaller budgets and attention than those that serve men. In universities and colleges, women's studies programs have very low budgets and few resources, while men's athletic programs garner generous budgets, facilities, and support.

Individuals inside and outside organizations can discriminate. Discrimination within organizations can be less visible because sex inequality has been built into the rules, procedures, policies, routine practices, and philosophies of an organization. According to Kravetz, for example, women social workers and women clients encounter sex discrimination because sexism is built into the social work curriculum. Kravetz maintains that "stereotypical views of female development, anti-women bias in personality theories, and traditional sex-role standards provide the theoretical framework for much social work knowledge. . . . Sex bias and sex-role stereotyping pervade clinical theories and literature."[28] Some discriminatory organization rules and practices are more direct and formalized. For example, because military regulations and procedures prohibit women from combat roles, women face severe career mobility obstacles.[29] Without combat experience, promotions to the highest military levels are impossible.

Also, organizational practices discriminate by not providing equal opportunities regardless of sex. In a study of retail sales clerks, for example, Talbert and Bose found that women's wages are lower than those of men because women are not given the opportunities to increase their salaries.[30] That is, women are generally segregated into jobs that are highly routinized and outside of locations that have high salaries (specialty stores, suburban stores, and departments servicing high-status customers). Also, the hiring of men into "big ticket" departments means that women are excluded from positions that result in high commission rates. For example, women sell pots and pans, while men sell refrigerators, stoves, and kitchen cabinets; women sell such accessories as lamps, throw pillows, and sheets, while men sell furniture.

At level three—institutional discrimination—the unequal behavior is established and deeply internalized by participants who share expectations across family, political, economic, educational, military, and religious institutions. There has been a great deal of research showing that the American nuclear family structure victimizes women and children (for example, high incidences of child abuse, wife abuse, mental health problems of wives) but provides benefits for men. According to Doyle, husbands gain a maid and a socioemotional bridge (the wife deals with the husband's family, the children, and the community) and profit by having better physical health care because "many wives express concern over their husband's physical health, often prompting him to take better care of himself."[31] In contrast, wives suffer losses:

> Housework is neither interesting nor creative; in the expressive phrase of the women's movement, it is "shit work." For those with the talent and interest, decorating and gourmet cooking are creative and fun. But most housework consists of mopping floors, washing dishes, and cleaning toilet bowls. Not only is it boring, it is repetitive and never ending.[32]

Political institutions, similarly, reflect an internalization of men as leaders and women as interlopers. After Geraldine Ferraro was named as Walter Mondale's running mate in the 1984 presidential election, Ferraro underwent a series of harassing incidents that were not true of her male counterparts regardless of political party. For example, her income tax returns were extensively scrutinized and publicized, and her family background was rigorously investigated while her opponent, Bush, got "kid glove treatment." Also, Ferraro was the only vice-presidential candidate, historically, who encountered repeated questions about her "qualifications."

At level four—cultural discrimination—sex inequality is built into our literature, art, music, language, morals, customs, beliefs, and ideology. In art, we see women as seductresses (Bellini, Titian), as sex objects (Rubens, Renoir), as masses of distorted sex organs (Picasso), and as grotesque molls (Lindner).[33] In an examination of how popular culture has distorted the images of women in fiction, television, motion pictures, fashion, magazines, and advertising, Weibel found that women have been portrayed primarily in domestic, housewifely, and consumer roles over the past century and a half despite women's increasing participation in the labor market.[34] Weibel's predictions of the future are not optimistic:

> Since men have the controlling positions in most popular arts today, it seems safe to conclude that they will continue to portray women in the manner

that's easiest, most profitable, and maybe most interesting for them—as the opposite of, and refuge from, the power struggle in the world of work, that is, as domestic and compliant to the point of self-sacrifice.[35]

There is no evidence that the ideologies of men and women are changing to parallel changing work roles. In a recent national survey, nearly two-thirds of the 3,000 women interviewed said they thought that "the decline of traditional male and female roles in society would result in more children having identity and adjustment problems."[36] Women are so wedded to traditional cultural sex stereotypes, they are already beginning to blame themselves for possible future problems instead of changing expectations about men's and their own roles in the family and the economy.

It should be noted, finally, that the three types of discrimination (overt, subtle, covert) are present at each level of discrimination (individual, organizational, institutional, cultural). As discussed earlier in this chapter, most of the research, writing, and thinking on sex discrimination has focused primarily on overt discrimination at all four levels. In this sense, a large portion of discriminatory behavior still remains unexamined.

DIMENSIONS OF SEX DISCRIMINATION

Overt, subtle, and covert discrimination can vary on five dimensions: structural or situational, cumulative or episodic, deliberate or accidental, public or private, and formal or informal.

Structural or situational. Sex discrimination is often built into organizational rules, procedures, and institutional structures. For example, because of women's historical exclusion from a number of professional areas (science, engineering, medicine, law, and business), their labor-force participation in these areas has been low. Rules regarding seniority, rank, and tenure have effectively limited the competition to men. Because the family is often structured in ways that include the full-time attention of one adult to children for many years, it is difficult for women—the family caretakers—to participate in other institutional areas (for example, political and economic systems).

Sex discrimination can also be limited to specific situations. Thus, male nurses complain that they are sometimes treated as men rather than nurses; women patients will ask for a female nurse when they need help with a bedpan or bathing. In the same situation, although female nurses technically have the same institutional rights and privileges as male nurses within the organization, they report being excluded from certain professional experiences in which male nurses are encouraged to participate (for example, having lunch with physicians or attending informal consultations about patients).

Cumulative or episodic. Some discriminatory barriers grow and snowball, while others flare up and subside on a short-lived basis. In terms of the former, for example, Frasher et al. found that school superintendents' sex-role stereotypes have long-term and incremental implications.[37] That is, because women are expected to perform family responsibilities, they will be excluded from consideration in jobs that are "financially rewarding, have prestige, or may be critical for professional advancement." Rejecting women from such jobs will affect their future long-term salaries and promotions.

Episodic discrimination may be situation-specific but does not have to be limited to only one type of situation. For example, management might institute dress codes for women (but not men) and only in certain positions (for example, for receptionists but not for women working in mail rooms). Although it may be situation-specific, episodic discrimination does not imply an absence of widespread sex inequality. Quite to the contrary, episodic discrimination is a symptomatic reaction to pervasive and deep-rooted sex inequality even though the behavior is not incremental. For example, a maintenance department (staffed predominantly by men) may refuse a secretary's request to shampoo the office rugs because "the guys are too busy" (or may respond only if the secretary is attractive or seen as potentially sexually accessible). If the issue is pursued by the secretary's supervisor, the secretary is told by the maintenance supervisor that "I'm tired of you secretary-types always telling me what to do."

Deliberate or accidental. There are many accounts of consciously motivated, malicious, and deliberate discrimination—especially against women in traditionally male-dominated jobs—in both blue-collar and professional occupations. Women's participation has been discouraged through unionized sabotage, practical jokes, sexual harassment, social isolation, open hostility, hazing, vulgar teasing, wrong directions/instructions, and exclusion from training programs.[38]

Even more common (and sometimes more harmful) is accidental discrimination that may be due to ignorance, insensitivity, provincialism, misinformed kindness, or misguided favors. In terms of the last two behaviors, for example, most women faculty members are often automatically assigned women-related responsibilities that impede their professional progress and development. Thus, they are given extracurricular sex-stereotyped tasks (for example, counseling women students, providing community service on women's issues, and being a "women's representative" on a myriad of faculty committees) that infringe on the time needed for research, publications, and professional growth. Such assignments are especially detrimental professionally for female faculty members who are not feminists and are not doing research on women's issues. For example, a female physiologist who is doing research on the aging process will find "feminist assignments" distracting and professionally debilitating—especially if she is already working in inadequate facilities and has minimal, if any, research support from colleagues and administration.

As one of our male readers pointed out, an organization that assigns these tasks to men and not women will also be criticized as being "sexist" by feminists. The point, however, is that such assignments are *rarely* given to men despite men's abilities, talents, interests, and strengths. On the other hand, many women are *automatically* expected to perform a variety of extra duties just because they are women.

Public or private. A number of our respondents noted that public and private stances on discrimination are sometimes radically different:

> Our office manager has told several of us, in private conversations, that she gets very angry when the men refer to secretaries as "girls." She also makes a big point of correcting some of us when we say "he" rather than "he or she." But she's never done this with any of the bosses. She just smiles, nods, and says, "Yes, sir." (Secretary in manufacturing)

Similarly, men may be private feminists and public chauvinists:

> One of my best friends at work is the chair of the communications department. He's the first, when a bunch of us are talking informally, to correct men about comments like "Can we invite our wives (rather than "spouses") to the dinner?", to criticize male faculty for their leering and sexist asides about coeds, and to use "the student," "the faculty member," and "they" instead of "he," "him," or "his." When we're at public functions, though, and especially if male administrators are present, he never corrects the deans or the president, laughs heartily at dirty jokes (even when women faculty are present), and talks about his wife and daughter in very derogatory, demeaning ways. (Female faculty in an English department)

A public-private schism may reflect an individual's political motivation. By castigating discriminatory behavior in a closed group and participating in discrimination publicly, individuals may be trying to play both sides—especially if the group membership does not overlap. Although some men and women are personally "liberated," they are unwilling or unable to fight public battles because they want to avoid conflict, are afraid to be classified as "bra burners" or "wimps," or to be excluded from all-male (or all-female) discussions and recreational activities.

Formal or informal. Sex inequality can be formalized through laws, executive orders, judicial decisions, constitutional amendments, and administrative or organizational procedures. Some current sex discrimination reflects past legislation that has defined women as "things" and "property" rather than as individuals. We still have sex-based inequalities in such areas as pension payments, insurance rates, and prosecution of sex crimes. Even in the one area that is considered almost exclusively the responsibility of women—childbearing and childrearing—women are legally controlled through a variety of restrictive laws on abortion, childbirth, and custody of children.

Sex inequality can be formalized within organizational structures and procedures. Higher education institutions establish formal and "legitimate" hiring criteria requiring credentials (such as having a Ph.D.), publications, or relevant professional experience that will formally screen out many women applicants. For example, law school search committees often look at the prestige of the law degree, experience, a law review editorship, and clerkships (especially at appellate federal levels) in hiring prospective faculty. At face value, such criteria appear valid and reasonable. They are exclusionary, however, because many women feel that they must reject acceptances from prestigious law schools because of family responsibilities, because they have been historically excluded from law review experiences, or because they are hired as court clerks on a token basis.[39]

Even when formal discrimination is illegal and declining, informal discrimination can be rampant. That is, in colleges and universities, women (regardless of marital status) are typically excluded from male networks; are appointed jointly to a traditional and a women's studies department, creating competing time demands and marginality in both departments; and during tenure, merit, and promotion decisions, have publications (on women) deemed "irrelevant" in comparison to male faculty research (on men).[40]

In summary, measuring subtle and covert sex discrimination is not as simple as gauging the presence or absence of discrimination. Because sex discrimination varies on such dimensions as structure, cumulativeness, deliberateness, level, and degree of formality, there is a great deal of variation in the character of discrimination. Despite these variations, however, sex inequality would be considerably less widespread if it were not accepted by both men and women.

ACCEPTANCE OF INEQUALITY

Sex inequality is deeply embedded in our culture. Both men and women have deeply internalized a belief in the appropriateness of women's deference and subordination. Groups outside the family (peers, friends, community organizations, work structures, and the government) support and encourage gender inequality and reinforce men's and women's beliefs about women's "innate" inferiority and responsibility to serve others.

Internalization of sex inequality. A number of studies have found that the socialization of children remains traditionally sex typed. Even when mothers are employed outside the home, there is an early and strong socialization in terms of work segregation by sex. According to White and Brinkerhoff, for example, women's employment "sinks their daughters even deeper into the domestic role," and the older children get, the more stereotypical become their work assignments.[41] This is consistent with Huber and Spitze's findings that "married couples are remarkably resistant to changing household norms and behaviors."[42]

Women's acceptance of sex inequality and discrimination is evident in their participating in sex-segregated activities, self-denigration, and reluctance to "toot their own horn." In a speech given at the New York Academy of Sciences more than a decade ago, Beryce MacLennan stated that "women frequently collaborate in their own subordination"; for example, they accept jobs below their grade rating, do not fight for salaries and promotions, gladly take on new responsibilities without demanding additional pay, are shy about publicizing their achievements, are more interested in interpersonal relationships rather than upward mobility, and do not think strategically and politically.[43] More recently, in a national study of first-level managers in organizations, Deaux found striking differences of self-evaluations by sex. Male managers—in contrast to women managers—viewed themselves as performing better than women in equivalent jobs and as having more ability and higher intelligence; they believed that their success was due to ability rather than luck or chance.[44]

Apparently, many women's frustration in not being rewarded and acknowledged for accomplishments is lower than their acquiescence in propping up male egos.[45] This acceptance of the status quo may be due, in part, to women's fear that sharing their domestic power with men might diminish their importance/status in the home (many women's *only* source of authority). More importantly, many women experience guilt feelings because they are not living up to traditional sex role expectations,[46] and they accept as "inevitable" the fact that "women bear the main brunt of child care and domestic organization" because this is "what a woman's supposed to do."[47] They want to avoid conflict because "the wife perceives that her husband's preference is for her to stay at home when an infant is present,"[48] and they are anxious about current and prospective criticism from friends, peers, and relatives that disengagement from domestic duties reflects a neglect of husband and children. Finally, women (and men) are discouraged from changing sex role expectations by outside sources.

Encouragement of sex inequality. One of the most informative and striking examples of employed women's subordination to traditional and repressive sex roles is the literature documenting the lack of sex role changes in dual-earner families.[49] Generally, males who share in homemaking activities are ridiculed or ostracized: "Men may down-grade the efforts of other men to contribute to homemaking and pressure them to spend more time and effort on the job or in the peer group."[50]

Besides friends and peers, relatives may not be supportive of working wives because the husband's relationships with his family may be curtailed. Working wives "have tended to experience difficulty in persuading their mothers-in-law that social occasions must be rationed and carefully scheduled."[51] Also, there is little support from the community-at-large for nontraditional sex roles within the family. One recent article suggests that mothers are wholly responsible for parenting since "few would debate the *almost mystical significance of the mother-infant bond* [emphasis added]."[52]

Finally, both government and industry have discouraged fathers from parenting and mothers from working outside the home:

> Mothers who are employed outside the home experience discrimination in many areas: difficulty in locating child care, lack of flexible work schedules, limited opportunity for part-time careers and the expectation that they will assume, in addition to employment, responsibility for child care and housework. Few public policies offer support for maternal employment.[53]

The internal and external pressures to maintain rigid sex stratification within and outside the home are functional for men and the business industry. For men, sex discrimination results in less competition in the work place, a greater availability of leisure time, and an avoidance of stressful domestic and work responsibilities within families.

Business and industry profit from sex discrimination in several ways. Wives donate much free time, effort, and energy to the company by doing supportive work that allows husbands to give most of their time to the company. Second, persuading women that their work is not important justifies paying them low wages and salaries. Finally, sex-segregated labor markets ensure male dominance in the economic sector, which, in turn, influences men's and women's unequal participation in religious, legal, military, and political sectors.

The next three chapters discuss how this dominance works through overt, subtle, and covert sex-discriminatory mechanisms.

NOTES

1. President's Advisory Committee for Women, *Voices for Women* (Washington, D.C.: Government Printing Office, 1980), p. 31.
2. Barbara Forisha and Barbara Goldman, *Outsiders on the Inside: Women and Organizations* (Englewood Cliffs, N.J.: Prentice-Hall, 1980), p. 113.
3. U.S. Commission on Civil Rights, *Affirmative Action in the 1980s* (Washington, D.C.: Government Printing Office, 1981), p. 15.
4. See, for example, Jo Freeman, ed., *Women: A Feminist Perspective* (Palo Alto, Calif.: Mayfield Publishing Co., 1984); Laurel Richardson and Verta Taylor, eds., *Feminist Frontiers: Rethinking Sex, Gender, and Society* (Reading, Mass.: Addison-Wesley Publishing Company, 1983); and Nona Glazer and Helen Y. Waehrer, eds., *Women in a Man-Made World: A Socioeconomic Handbook* (Chicago: Rand McNally, 1977).
5. U.S. Bureau of the Census, *Current Population Reports*, series p-60, no. 132, table 51.
6. See Leslie Maitland Werner, "Loan Company Settles U.S. Bias Case," *New York Times*, November 1, 1984, p. 23.
7. Michael Korda, *Power! How to Get It, How to Use It* (New York: Ballantine Books, 1975), pp. 261, 267.
8. Robert Schrank, "Two Women, Three Men on a Raft," *Harvard Business Review* 55 (1977), pp. 100–108.

9. Alice Pifer, "Wanted: Employment Agencies that Don't Discriminate," *Civil Rights Quarterly Perspectives* 12 (1980-81), pp. 16-23.
10. Clarise Feinman, *Women in the Criminal Justice System* (New York: Praeger, 1980), pp. 52-58.
11. Flora Ida Ortiz, "Scaling the Hierarchical System in School Administration: A Case Analysis of a Female Administrator," *Urban Review* 3 (1979), pp. 111-126.
12. Helen S. Astin, *The Woman Doctorate in America* (New York: Russell Sage Foundation, 1975), p. 100.
13. Irene H. Frieze, "Psychological Barriers for Women in Sciences: Internal and External," in *Covert Discrimination and Women in the Sciences*, ed. Judith A. Ramaley (Boulder, Colo.: Westview Press, 1978), pp. 65-95.
14. Roberta M. Hall and Bernice R. Sandler, *The Classroom Climate: A Chilly One for Women?* (Washington, D.C.: Association of American Colleges, Project on the Status and Education of Women, 1982), p. 2.
15. Elske Smith, "The Individual and the Institution," in *Covert Discrimination and Women in the Sciences*, ed. Judith A. Ramaley (Boulder, Colo.: Westview Press, 1978), pp. 7-8.
16. Ibid., pp. 8-17, 22-24.
17. Ibid., p. 7.
18. Frieze, "Psychological Barriers," pp. 65-95.
19. Diana Kendall and Joe R. Feagin, "Blatant and Subtle Patterns of Discrimination: Minority Women in Medical Schools," *Journal of Intergroup Relations* 9 (Summer 1983), pp. 6-9.
20. Judith A. Ramaley, ed., *Covert Discrimination and Women in the Sciences* (Boulder, Colo.: Westview Press, 1978), p. 3.
21. Smith, "The Individual and the Institution," pp. 7-8.
22. J. Brad Chapman, "Male and Female Leadership Styles: The Double Bind," in *Covert Discrimination and Women in the Sciences*, p. 98.
23. Janice Pottker, "Overt and Covert Forms of Discrimination against Women," in *Sex Bias in the Schools: The Research Evidence*, ed. Janice Pottker and Andrew Fishel (Cranbury, N.J.: Associated University Press, 1977), p. 23.
24. Ibid., p. 392.
25. Kendall and Feagin, "Blatant and Subtle Patterns of Discrimination," p. 16.
26. Hall and Sandler, "The Classroom Climate," pp. 8-9.
27. James C. Goodwin, "Playing Games with Affirmative Action," *Chronicle of Higher Education* 24 (1975).
28. Diane Kravetz, "Sexism in a Woman's Profession," *Social Work* 21 (1976), p. 424.
29. Juanita M. Firestone, "Sexist Ideology and the Evaluation Criteria Used to Assess Women's Integration into the Army," *Population Research and Policy Review* 3 (1984), pp. 77-95; Esther B. Fein, "The Choice: Women Officers Decide to Stay In or Leave," *New York Times Magazine,* May 5, 1985, pp. 32-46.
30. Joan Talbert and Christine E. Bose, "Wage-Attainment Processes: The Retail Clerk Occupation," *American Journal of Sociology* 83 (1983), pp. 403-424.
31. James A. Doyle, *The Male Experience* (Dubuque, Iowa: Wm. C. Brown Company Publishers, 1983), pp. 271-272.
32. Howard J. Sherman and James L. Wood, *Sociology: Traditional and Radical Perspectives* (New York: Harper & Row), p. 65.
33. Marie Richmond-Abbott, *The American Woman* (New York: Holt, Rinehart and Winston, 1979), pp. 71-95.
34. Kathryn Weibel, *Mirror Mirror* (Garden City, N.Y.: Anchor Books, 1977). See also Angela G. Dorenkamp, John F. McClymer, Mary M. Moynihan, and Arlene

C. Vadum, *Images of Women in American Popular Culture* (New York: Harcourt Brace Jovanovich, 1985).

35. Weibel, *Mirror Mirror*, pp. 225–226.
36. Roper Organization, *The 1980 Virginia Slims American Women's Opinion Poll*, p. 104.
37. J. Frasher, R. Frasher, and F. Wims, "Sex-Role Stereotyping in School Superintendents' Personnel Decisions," *Sex Roles* 8 (1982), p. 267.
38. See, for example, Terry Metherby, ed., *Conversations: Working Women Talk about Doing a Man's Job* (Milbrae, Calif.: Les Femmes Publishers); Gena Corea, *The Hidden Malpractice: How American Medicine Treats Women as Patients and Professionals* (New York: William Morrow and Co., 1977); and Brigid O'Farrell and Sharon L. Harlan, "Craftworkers and Clerks: The Effect of Male Co-Worker Hostility on Women's Satisfaction with Non-Traditional Jobs," *Social Problems* 29 (1982).
39. D. Kelly Weisberg, "Women in Law School Teaching: Problems and Progress," *Journal of Legal Education* 30 (1979), pp. 226–248.
40. Robert J. Menges and William H. Exum, "Barriers to the Progress of Women and Minority Faculty," *Journal of Higher Education* 54 (1983), pp. 123–144.
41. Lynn K. White and David B. Brinkerhoff, "The Sexual Division of Labor: Evidence from Childhood," *Social Forces* 60 (1981), pp. 170–181.
42. Joan Huber and Glenna Spitze, "Wives' Employment, Household Behaviors, and Sex-Role Attitudes," *Social Forces* 60 (1981), pp. 160–161.
43. Beryce W. MacLennan, "Women's Part in Institutional Sexism" (speech given at the New York Academy of Sciences, January 10, 1973, mimeographed).
44. Kay Deaux, "Self-Evaluations of Male and Female Managers," *Sex Roles* 5 (1979), pp. 571–580.
45. Cynthia F. Epstein, "Ideal Roles and Real Roles: Toward a Theory of Gender Inequality" (paper presented at the 1983 American Sociological Association meetings, Detroit, Mich.).
46. L. A. Gilbert, C. K. Holahan, and L. Manning, "Coping with Conflict between Professional and Maternal Roles," *Family Relations* 30 (1981), pp. 419–426.
47. N. A. Heckman, R. Bryson, and J. B. Bryson, "Problems of Professional Couples: A Content Analysis," *Journal of Marriage and the Family* 39 (1977), pp. 329–330.
48. G. D. Spitze and L. J. Waite, "Wives' Employment: The Role of Husbands' Perceived Attitudes," *Journal of Marriage and the Family* 44 (1982), p. 120.
49. The discussion in this section is adapted from Nijole Benokraitis, "The Father in Two-Earner Families," in *Dimensions of Fathering*, ed. Frederick W. Bozett and Shirley Hanson (Beverly Hills, Calif.: Sage Publications, 1985), pp. 243–268.
50. L. Lein, "Male Participation in Home Life: Impact of Social Supports and Breadwinner Responsibility on the Allocation of Tasks," *Family Coordinator* 28 (1979), p. 492.
51. D. St. John-Parsons, "Continuous Dual-Career Families: A Case Study," in *Dual-Career Couples*, ed. J. B. Bryson and R. Bryson (New York: Human Sciences Press), pp. 30–42.
52. B. L. White, "Should You Stay Home with Your Baby?" *Educational Horizons*, 59–60 (1980–82), p. 59.
53. A. M. Farel and A. W. Dobelstein, "Supports and Deterrents for Mothers Working Outside the Home," *Family Relations* 31 (1982), p. 285.

4

How Overt Sex Discrimination Works

Overt sex discrimination includes those discriminatory actions directed against women that are quite obvious and visible. Many such discriminatory actions have been institutionalized in U.S. society.

OBVIOUS DISCRIMINATION BEGINS AT HOME

Most adult Americans get married at some point in their lives, although many also get divorced. In all family systems there are critical roles and sets of rights and duties tied to specific positions in families. Wife and husband, mother and father, are social roles with specific expectations. In U.S. society a woman as wife is expected to act in certain subordinate ways as a consequence of her role. She has certain traditional and legal duties and rights, many of which reflect clear-cut discrimination. There are exceptions, of course, with a growing number of women and wives filling nontraditional roles, such as college professor and telephone repairperson, but most women still must play out traditional sex roles in their lives, inside and outside the home.

Making decisions. Decision making in the U.S. family is still typically patriarchal, in spite of jokes about women "wearing the pants." A major study of decision making in families by Blood and Wolfe showed that the husband's desires prevail in regard to the most important decision for many families—the character and location of the husband's job. This typically determines the family's location and life-style. In addition, husbands' desires prevail more often than do wives' in decisions about the car, whereas decisions about food and which doctor to call are more likely to reflect the wives' desires. Another study of family decision making asked couples, "When there's a really important decision on which you two are likely to disagree, who usually wins out?" *Not one* of the middle-income housewives reported that they usually had more influence than their husbands. Half said the husband had the greater influence; the other half said the influence was about equal.[1]

Marriages are set within a larger society with its conventional female and male roles stratified in terms of power, resources, and benefits. Most women come to marriage with substantially less in the way of employment and political resources than men. Existing research indicates that the husband's power in the family derives to a substantial extent from his job and income position in the outside world.

Who gets the burden of child rearing?   One feature of family life that accents the unequal power of the husband is the childbearing cycle. Gillespie notes that "many women stop working [outside the home] during this stage and, in doing so, become isolated and almost totally dependent socially, economically, and emotionally upon their husbands, further eroding any strength they may have gained due to earning power (as workers outside the home) or participation in organizations."[2] Having to quit work reduces the resources, and thus the leverage, of wives.

Child rearing is an important aspect of family life that has been delegated primarily to the wife-mother role. Child care originally came under the auspices of the wife because of her biological role in bearing and breastfeeding infants. But, with bottle feeding, it has become possible for men to take over the total child rearing function, although most have not done so. Even today taking responsibility for child care is still a major aspect of the prevailing definition of a woman's family role. This means that, just when many women are no longer hemmed in by frequent childbirth or the need to nurse infants, they are pressured by sex-typed role definitions to remain in the home as the major socializers of the children.

Sexuality.   Perhaps the most taboo-ridden dimension of the traditional woman's role is sexuality. In regard to sexual intercourse, husbands have had a legal or traditional "right" to insist on intercourse, and a wife has a duty to submit. Even though twenty-four states now have laws allowing charges of spousal rape, it is difficult for a husband to be convicted for forcibly raping his wife because of the traditional view of his right to sexual intercourse. Women are often treated as sexual objects, as things or commodities. The commodity character of women can be seen in the language many men use, for example, such terms as "bird," "chick," and "my woman." Television programs, mass media advertising, and the cosmetics industry present women as sex objects, to be manipulated for the pleasure of men:

Consequently sexual sensation is packaged, and delivered confined and synthesized in prevailing notions of sexuality—sugar sweet or black leather and net. . . . Sexuality is communicated in the media in a series of images. A hand stroking hair, legs walking into summer, clean-washing-crisp housewives, children with cereal spoons and oral brand satisfactions.[3]

There has been evidence, recently, that women may be beginning to see the ancient rite of sexual intercourse itself as a form of male self-gratification rather than as an expression of affection. For example, in November 1984, nationally syndicated columnist Ann Landers asked her women readers, "Would you be content to be held close and treated tenderly and forget about 'the act'?" Of the 90,000 respondents, 72 percent said yes. The response was interesting because it suggests, among other things, that some women are not getting love or affection during or apart from sexual intercourse. Even more interesting was the reaction to the survey. Male critics especially—from syndicated columnists to professional sexologists—ridiculed Landers and her "methodology" and implied that many women are prudes.

Such hostile reactions by men are not surprising. Since we socialize men to define their masculinity and identity in terms of economic success and sexual prowess, a woman's disinterest in sexual intercourse can be an ego-shattering experience.

VIOLENT DISCRIMINATION AGAINST WOMEN

It is women who, disproportionately, suffer from violence by men in the United States.

Husbands target wives. Physical force is important in giving many men power over their wives. Official statistics on wife abuse are not kept regularly, but a general picture can be culled from the data available.

1. Typically one third of women homicide victims are killed by their husbands.
2. In a Cleveland survey of 600 wives, 37 percent cited physical abuse as a cause of the divorce.
3. In 1974 in wealthy Fairfax County, Virginia, there were 4,000 family disturbance calls. (Most family disturbance complaints are made by female victims).
4. A nationwide Louis Harris Poll found that 25 percent of the males in the sample approved of a husband slapping his spouse, with the proportion higher among the college educated than those with a grade school education.[4]

In addition, in the 1970s New York's family courts in one year dealt with more than 14,000 wife-battering cases. One expert has estimated that there are at least 1 million cases of wife beating in the United States each year.

The widespread problem of wife beating has been severely neglected in large part because of prevailing male attitudes that wife beating is a good thing or see such husband-wife relations as a private matter beyond the reach of the law. Violent wife abuse is sometimes openly rationalized in U.S. culture, as can be seen in advertising. In a mid-1970s *Vogue* magazine piece, a male and female model are shown fighting, then caressing. In one scene the woman shows pain on her face from the man having hit her. The woman's clothes, the ad says, can "really take the heat." And a bowling center ad in Michigan said, "Have some fun. Beat your wife tonight. Then celebrate with some good food and drink with your friends."[5]

Rape outside and inside the home. Forcible rape is defined by the police as sexual intercourse forced by a man upon a woman against her will. In the mid-1980s there were almost 80,000 forcible rapes reported by the Federal Bureau of Investigation. This figure was up sharply from the 1967 figure of 28,000. The rate per 100,000 population also climbed faster than any other violent crime, from 14.0 per 100,000 people in 1967 to 33.6 per 100,000 people in 1982.

There are many cultural myths about rape, myths that typically blame rape on the victims:

> All women want to be raped.
> She was asking for it.
> No woman can be raped against her will.

These views come not only from the lips of average men (and some women) but also from the writings of some academic specialists. The view that male and female sex roles "naturally" mean sexual submission leads easily to the view that a woman cannot be raped against her will. And romanticized views of rape suggest that rape is something women secretly enjoy. Some movies, such as *A Clockwork Orange, Straw Dogs,* and *Passage to India,* have dramatized and glorified the rape and brutalization of women in the guise of cinematic art. This sexist orientation is also seen in the pornography industry, which is designed to profit from making women even more dehumanized sex objects; in some pornographic magazines and movies, women are the targets of cruelty, violence, and murder. Moreover, the view of rape as something most women want is a blatant lie. Indeed, there are hundreds of rape-murders each year.[6]

Rape can happen to any woman; a five-year study in a Washington, D.C., hospital found that those treated for rape ranged from a fifteen-month-old girl to an eighty-two-year-old woman. Indeed, the sexual abuse and rape of girls by close relatives—fathers, uncles, and brothers—is a widespread problem in the United States, a problem that has not yet come "out of the closet." Incest is usually a matter of a male relative forcing a girl to submit to sexual abuse or rape. Rape is a problem inside *and* outside the home. (Boys and men face rape much less often, except in some U.S. prisons, where rape is commonplace as a way of subordinating some prisoners to the more dominant inmates.)

Most rape victims are of the same race and income level as the rapist. Teenage females and women who live in poor, high-crime areas run the greatest risk, but almost one-third of all rape cases occur in the victim's own home. Force is commonplace in rape cases. A study in Boston found that half of eighty rape victims interviewed had been threatened with a weapon and that another twenty-one had been physically coerced in some way. Nearly one-fifth of all rapes are committed by two or more assailants. About one-fifth of all rape victims are between twelve and fifteen years old. Rape occurs even though almost 90 percent of the victims use such self-protective measures as physical force, trying to get help, or threatening the offender.[7] As these statistics suggest, women are raped despite protective and preventive efforts.

Most recently, researchers are finding that "date rape" or "acquaintance rape" is commonplace, especially on college campuses, but it is rarely reported because the experience is not defined as a rape. There is resistance to defining sexual violence by a date as a rape because of the "ideal image" of college dating, a romantic involvement with the perpetrator, cultural acceptance of male aggression during courtship, false stereotypes about rapists (a stranger attacking late at night in an isolated place), and the embarrassment of educational institutions to deal with the issue of date rape.[8]

Rape and law enforcement.   Police reactions to rape victims have often been skeptical or even hostile. Susan Brownmiller reports that at a training session for New York police lieutenants the male police officers nearly unanimously felt there was no such thing as rape, suggesting that women themselves desired to be attacked or attracted attackers by their dress or behavior. Today most male police officers often harbor the same stereotypes about women and rape that prevail in the larger society. One research study by Feild found that police officer attitudes toward rape were actually similar to the attitudes of convicted rapists on a number of dimensions. Often it is to these unsympathetic police officers that a female victim must go to report the violent crime of rape.[9]

Once a woman victim gets to court, she may find that she is also on trial. Defense attorneys may raise questions about her sexual history, although most states prohibit such questioning unless relevance is shown. Some state courts have required extensive corroboration of the victim's story and specific evidence that force was used in the rape. Not surprisingly, then, relatively few rapists have ever been convicted. A mid-1980s analysis by the National Council on Crime and Delinquency reported on the likelihood of prosecution for rape in California based on three studies. One study of 881 rapes found only 14 percent were prosecuted; another study of 260 rapes found that 17 percent were prosecuted; and the largest study of 12,300 rapes found that only 3 percent resulted in prison sentences for the rapists. A research study by Diana Russell of 900 San Francisco women found that 44 percent had at some point in their lives been the victims of rape or attempted rape, but that only 10 percent had ever reported the events to the police. Informed estimates suggest that 20 to 50 percent of all rapes are never reported. This amazing statistic is ironic in that the common belief in the male culture is that women rush to false accusations of rape against men, a belief used to justify the excessive evidence requirements in rape cases. Yet a victim of assault or robbery does not, under the law, have to prove that he or she resisted or that the act involved the use of physical force. The fear of men that unsatisfied women freely accuse their men of rape is not supported by careful research studies.[10] A New York City study found that only 2 percent of rape accusations were unfounded, about the same proportion as for other violent crimes. Other recent research indicates that the proportion ranges from 2 to 9 percent.[11] Nonetheless, in a 1985 midwestern case a woman who admitted that she falsely accused a man of rape made national headlines for weeks, but the same national media did no articles of comparable significance on the 1500 women who were raped each week during that period.

Recently, under pressure from women's rights groups, numerous state legislatures have changed their rape laws. Since the early 1970s some state laws have been changed to get rid of the requirement that women prove they "fought back" physically or the requirement that extensive evidence corroborating the woman's story be presented. In some states the term "rape" has even been replaced by "sexual assault" to make it easier for victims to report what has happened to them. Many states have also passed "shield" laws preventing the prior sexual experience of the rape victim from being introduced as evidence in a trial. Yet these changes have come slowly and on a piecemeal basis. In many cases the problem still lies in the lack of vigorous enforcement of the laws. It is still clear that rape victims have less than adequate recourse solely because they are predominantly girls and women. If men were the primary victims of rape, one can be certain rape would be taken *much* more seriously as a crime.

Rape and the sexist society.   Numerous rape studies have demonstrated that rape is frequently not a crime of sexual passion but a crime of violence directed against women. Such violent actions are a logical, if extreme, extension of the values of a sexist U.S. culture that has encouraged in males, young and old, a "macho" orientation toward subordinating women sexually. A surprising finding about rape is that rapists as a group are normal males in level of intelligence, personality type, appearance, and sexual drive. Rapists are not male oddballs, but, as Herman puts it, their behavior "evolves out of a situation in which 'normal' males feel a need to prove themselves to be 'men' by displaying dominance over females."[12]

Rape in turn creates a fear for many women that infects their daily lives. "Every woman knows the fear of being alone at home late at night or the terror that strikes her when she receives an obscene phone call. She knows also of the 'mini-rapes'—the pinch in the crowded bus, the wolf whistle from a passing car, the stare of a man looking at her bust during a conversation."[13] The fear engendered in women by the threat of rape is similar to the fear of wife beating. Both fears have broader social consequences in pressuring women to accept subordination and degradation across a number of institutional areas. Sexism is manifested in many areas of a girl's or a woman's life.

DISCRIMINATION IN EMPLOYMENT
OUTSIDE THE HOME

Segregating women workers: institutionalized discrimination. The proportion of women in the work force has risen systematically for several decades. By the mid-1980s more than 40 percent of the total civilian labor force was composed of women. Yet women in the labor force outside the home are employed primarily in traditional women's occupations. Most occupations are sex typed; they are predominantly male or female in composition. The segregation of job categories by sex reflects to a substantial degree institutionalized patterns of overt discrimination. For example, in a typical office building of a typical corporation workers tend to fall into four broad categories:

1. The managers—almost entirely male
2. The clerical staff—almost entirely female
3. The technical staff—mixed-sex with better-paying positions dominated by males
4. The janitorial staff—dominated by minorities, many of them minority women.

Sex segregation is commonplace in all types of private capitalistic and public sector organizations, so much so that it seems the "natural order of things." Yet it is not a natural order, but an unnatural order reflecting the historical and contemporary institutionalization of sex discrimination. Job categories have been intentionally segregated. For example, as late as 1920 the majority of clerical work was done by men; as recently as 1950 about 40 percent of clerical employees were male. By 1980, however, only 20 percent of all clerical employees were male.[14] Much of the direction of this trend was intentional, and one result was a decline in wages paid to (women) clerical employees. Today men work in far more types of occupations than women, who are heavily concentrated in just 30 of the 400 to 500 major job categories in the United States.

The occupational gap. Table 4.1 shows the percentage of women workers in selected major occupational categories charted by the U.S. Bureau of Labor Statistics among employed persons in 1982.[15] While there have been increases in the proportions of women in nontraditional job categories in the last decade (for example, engineers), the longitudinal data show slow changes in most job segregation. The proportions of females remain low among engineers, lawyers, physicians, dentists, corporate managers, craft workers, and transport workers. Moreover, a number of studies show that women hold less than 1 percent of top-level management positions, 1-2 percent of the directorships of corporations, and about 6-7 percent of middle-level executive positions. Women are rare among top capitalists and in the middle and upper managerial levels.[16]

In recent years many commentators have suggested that women are moving up rapidly and are thus closing the occupational gap with men. Yet the gap is closing very slowly, in part because the movement of women into traditionally male

TABLE 4.1. Percentage of Women Workers
in Selected Major Occupational
Categories (1982)

OCCUPATIONS	PERCENTAGE OF WOMEN
Engineers	5.7
Lawyers and judges	15.4
Librarians	80.7
Physicians and dentists	14.6
Registered nurses	95.6
Elementary, secondary teachers	70.7
Managers, administrators	28.0
Sales managers	25.9
Retail sales clerks	70.0
Wholesale salespersons	13.9
Clerical workers	80.7
Craft workers	7.0
Transport workers	8.9
Food service workers	65.7
Private household workers (maids, servants)	96.9

jobs has been exceeded by the movement of new women workers into the traditional female-typed jobs. Thus, in the mid-1980s about 60 percent of all women workers still worked in clerical, retail sales, and service jobs. Most women work in jobs that are at least 75 percent female. Few women are found in the traditionally male categories with the highest earnings. Moreover, some statistics that suggest progress are misleading. About 70 percent of white males and 17 percent of white women work in the Census Bureau's category of "professional and technical" jobs. These figures imply equality; however, a close examination of the fifty detailed jobs in that broad occupational category reveals that a majority of the women work in only *five* of the fifty jobs. As one might expect, men dominate most of the better-paying professional and technical jobs.[17]

Local studies of private and governmental organizations have also found clear-cut job segregation. For example, recent in-depth analysis of the work force of the city government in Chicago looked closely at the sex segregation of jobs. Women made up 19 percent of the work force, but held only 0.1 percent of the skilled craft jobs, 2 percent of the service and maintenance jobs, and 4.3 percent of the protective service jobs. Yet they held 82 percent of the clerical jobs. (Women were proportionately represented in the broad categories of managerial and professional jobs, but it is likely that they were in the lower-paying jobs.) The study found that "men's jobs" paid considerably more on the average than "women's jobs." About 80 percent of the women workers earned less than $20,000 annually, whereas 80 percent of the men earned more than $20,000 annually. Lower incomes are a major consequence of overt institutionalized discrimination against women.[18]

Comparable pay for comparable work? It is commonly said that market capitalism pays people what they are worth. Yet recent job evaluation studies looking at the skill, effort, responsibility, and productivity of jobs suggest that this is a myth. Regardless of their worth in terms of objective job evaluations, women's jobs are paid less than comparable men's jobs.[19] As shown in Table 4.2, women in jobs with similar or higher skill/responsibility ratings still earn less than men.

In defending this blatant inequality in pay many employers argue that they are not really discriminating, that women are paid less because they are simply less qualified in terms of education and experience. Yet when educational level is examined we find that it is actually the best-educated women who have the *worst earnings relative to men* (see Table 4.3). These 1980 data show the basic pattern for all full-time, year-round workers.[20] In no case do women do better than 63.7 percent, and that at the *lowest* level of education. Increased education does not increase women's equality to men in terms of income.

A recent University of Michigan study on family, work, and income examined the wage gap. Educational differences were found to account for only 2 percent of the wage gender gap; differences in self-imposed work restrictions and in continuity of employment also did not explain male-female differences. The only major factor that explained a significant (25–30 percent) part of the wage difference was accumulated full-time work experience, which, as one might expect, was greater on the average for men in the sample. The Michigan researchers concluded that sex discrimination in labor markets and in the socialization of girls in the home (to accept "pink-collar" jobs) accounted for most of the earnings differential between men and women workers. The study also found that male workers were more likely than women workers to get jobs that have authority in hiring and promotion of other

TABLE 4.2. Evaluations of Selected Jobs in Selected Regions

JOB	MONTHLY SALARY	JOB EVALUATION STUDY POINTS
Minnesota		
Registered nurse (female)	$1,723	275
Vocational education teacher (male)	2,260	275
San Jose, California		
Librarian I (female)	750	288
Street sweeper operator (male)	758	124
Senior legal secretary (female)	665	210
Senior carpenter (male)	1,040	210
Washington		
Laundry worker (female)	884	105
Truck driver (male)	1,493	97
Secretary (female)	1,122	197
Maintenance carpenter (male)	1,707	197

TABLE 4.3. Comparison of Incomes of Full-time, Year-round Male and Female Workers (1980)

EDUCATION	MEAN INCOME		WOMEN'S PERCENTAGE OF MALE INCOME
	MEN	WOMEN	
Elementary			
Less than 8 years	$13,183	$ 8,437	63.7
8 years	15,709	9,582	60.9
High School			
1–3 years	16,940	10,164	60.4
4 years	20,222	12,335	60.6
College			
1–3 years	22,517	14,185	63.3
4 years	28,306	16,417	57.6
5+ years	33,085	19,520	59.0

people. These men in authority see to it that, for the most part, men replace them in authority. The Michigan researchers conclude that "equalizing job skills" and "promoting education and training for women" will not eliminate much of the wage gap.[21]

A recent court decision. In December 1983 a federal district judge ruled that the state government of Washington had discriminated against women employees who received lower wages and salaries in female-typed job categories than men received in male-typed jobs with similar skill and knowledge levels. Women were found to be paid 20 to 30 percent less than men in comparable jobs; the judge ordered $828 million in back pay and raises to be awarded to women. This case has created a controversy across the nation over the "comparable pay for comparable work" principle.[22]

However, even the opponents of this principle seem to admit that it is the "prevailing market" in the United States that sets lower wages and salaries for women. Because this differential is so widespread, they argue, it cannot be "discrimination." Yet differential pay for the same work is by definition sex-related discrimination of the most overt and harmful type. This is so readily apparent and overt that (male) employers refuse to accept it as discrimination they must remedy. Indeed, their main argument is that it would be too costly to pay women a fair wage equal to comparable male-typed jobs. A new employer or an employer expanding operations usually accepts the prevailing "market wage rates" for women and the prevailing "market segregation" of jobs. In other words, employers accept and perpetuate the sex discrimination long built into job markets. Overt discrimination yesterday means overt discrimination today. One of the major reasons for the development of affirmative action programs was to fight such historical perpetuations of inequality.

SPECIFIC DISCRIMINATORY PRACTICES
IN EMPLOYMENT

Occupational and unemployment data clearly reflect inequalities among men and women. But we can go further to describe some of the specific discriminatory mechanisms that help shape the subordination of women in the job sphere. We will deal with subtle and covert examples in the next two chapters. Here we will examine some of the more blatant and visible discriminatory mechanisms.

Recruitment practices. Women have faced a number of important discriminatory barriers in the area of recruitment. The persistence into the last decade of sex-segregated job advertising—a newspaper format with columns of female jobs and columns of male jobs—has resulted in a number of court cases in which judges have equivocated on banning this ingrained practice because of the apparent conflict with the First Amendment's guarantee of freedom of the press were such a job advertising format to be prohibited. Whatever the legal status of such practices, they are clear-cut examples of intentional institutionalized discrimination. The negative impact of such recruiting practices has been documented. One study by Bein and Bein clearly showed that sex-segregated ads discourage female applicants from inquiring about "male jobs." And while most newspapers have desegregated their ad columns in recent years, sometimes the language used in the ads—"attractive," "girl Friday"—continues to reflect intentional job market segregation.[23]

Much overt discrimination still occurs informally in hiring networks, such as through the use of employment agencies. In a midwestern city one researcher, posing as an employer, recently called a dozen employment agencies and asked for a saleswoman "with the right image who will fit in—someone attractive and under twenty-five." Nine of the twelve agencies violated the law by accepting this request to discriminate against older women. Similarly, agencies will take orders based on hair color ("get me a blonde") and "good looks." Another survey of women with five or more years in the work place found that one-third of those surveyed said they had not gotten at least one promotion because a younger person had been chosen. A part of today's most blatant sexism includes the "young woman" preference of male decision makers with authority. Women receive discriminatory treatment in this regard, because the bodies of men generally are not used as important hiring criteria.[24]

Screening practices. Employment interviews have become a particularly important part of the job screening process. Since screening criteria can be subjective—such as an evaluator's impressions of "intelligence," "appearance," and "emotional makeup"—the (male) personnel evaluator's stereotyped notions may lead to rejection. Widely accepted stereotyping can operate against women. Notions that "they lie about their age" or "have a high absenteeism rate" may lead to informal rules dictating the rejection of a woman.[25]

Stereotyped views of a woman's family responsibilities have kept women from employment in certain occupational settings. For example, the Equal Employment Opportunity Commission found one employer guilty of sex-based discrimination in refusing to hire a woman on the grounds that her husband's long-term illness involved family responsibilities that would interfere with her job performance. In *Phillips* v. *Martin Marietta Corporation* (1971), the Supreme Court held to be discriminatory under the law employment restrictions against women with preschool-aged children; denial of employment to unwed mothers has likewise been ruled discriminatory. The point here is that these women were differentially excluded because of an employer's view of their family or marital responsibilities. These discriminatory practices have persisted into the 1980s.[26]

In the 1980s overt discrimination against women may be more common than against minority men because employers and unions are more acutely aware of the illegality of blatant race discrimination than of blatant sex discrimination. Interestingly, most recent sex discrimination cases tried in federal courts have concerned overt discrimination, whereas most race discrimination cases have involved more subtle discrimination.[27] A number of recent gender discrimination cases have dealt with the blatant sexual harassment women suffer at numerous points during their employment experiences, from initial screening to promotion. And a number of important race discrimination cases have dealt with the effects of job layoffs on minority workers with less seniority than whites. In *Wygant* v. *Jackson* (1984), a case to be reviewed by the U.S. Supreme Court in the fall of 1985, under an affirmative action plan black teachers were laid off at proportionately the same rate as whites when the city of Jackson, Michigan, was faced with job layoffs. Some white teachers objected and sued, arguing that blacks should suffer more layoffs than white teachers because the latter have more seniority. Even though lower seniority is a result of blatant discrimination in the past, the white teachers are really arguing that subtle discriminatory practices that have been reinforced through seniority policies should continue to be implemented.

Ironically, the inclusion of the prohibition on sex discrimination in the 1964 Civil Rights Act was in part a ploy by southern representatives in Congress to prevent its passage. For those male legislators, and for many male employers, prohibitions on sex discrimination often were, and are, seen as a joke. And Title VII of the 1964 Civil Rights Act permits exceptions to the prohibition on sex discrimination in cases where sex is really a "bona fide occupational qualification." Some employers, when challenged, have defended blatant sex discrimination in such terms. Jobs such as commercial sales representative and railroad telegrapher have been defended by at least one company as "male jobs," whereas airlines have defended their position that women are best qualified to serve as stewardesses. Yet few jobs anywhere in the society seem to necessitate that sex be an occupational qualification.

Promotional practices. Some promotion, job progression, and transfer practices have had a differential and adverse impact on women. Discrimination in current promotion practices for women has been documented. One study found that half the employers in large firms surveyed (300 of *Fortune*'s top 750) openly admitted that discrimination against women was institutionalized in business and management; three quarters of a sample of 300 smaller firms surveyed also admitted to such discrimination. The practices cited included discrimination in promotions and pay. A survey of 144 women in management positions found 70 percent reporting overt, intentional discrimination, including salary inequalities and differential promotion criteria. There were numerous reports that women had to be extraordinary "superwomen" or "water walkers" to make it up into higher administrative levels.[28]

Studies have found that male executives and managers continue to harbor stereotyped views of women workers that can shape the promotion of women. Bass and his associates found that many men thought male workers would not work under women supervisors and that women workers were supposed to "serve" men. A study of a large industrial supply corporation found numerous examples of overt, intentional discrimination in promotion practices. Rationalizations given for not promoting qualified women included "She's likely to quit and get married" and "She has children and her family responsibilities will interfere with a higher-level job."[29]

The established structure of female-male white-collar jobs, such as women in clerical work and men in management, makes it difficult for many women in clerical jobs to get promotions to other types of positions. While recruitment from the outside varies from one company to another, it is generally the case that once a woman is locked into certain job tracks, such as secretarial or other clerical lines, it is difficult for her to move into most supervisory and management lines. Low-mobility job tracks in turn shape men and women workers' attitudes, particularly handicapping women by increasing their unwillingness to protest unfair treatment in promotions.

In addition, women clerical employees can be demoted or fired simply because of their subordinate tie to a particular male manager or professional. When a male boss leaves, his male replacement may fire his inherited secretary, preferring his "own woman." This type of managerial empire-building can also involve male employees, but because of the peculiarly patriarchal character of the manager-secretary relationship, women seem to be the most likely victims. For example, a very experienced and respected fifty-four-year-old secretary found the following situation when her boss changed:

> I liked my job and I worked hard, staying late to get things done. Everyone said how competent I was. My trouble began when I got a new boss, who began to pick at little things, saying I talked too much on the phone.... Finally I received a scathing memo from him which made it clear I'd have to quit. I was stunned. I had so much experience and knew so many things about that place.... It could have been my age, or the benefits I was getting because of my experience, or it could be he wanted a younger woman to chase around the desk."[30]

Job conditions: sexual harassment.   A major example of intentional, well-institutionalized sex discrimination can be seen in studies of harassment. Sexual harassment is widespread and usually intentional. Work becomes a prize men give to women if women permit a wide range of sexual harassment. Like wife battering and rape, sexual harassment and extortion at work are just now coming out of the closet. Sexual harassment has been portrayed by Farley as "unsolicited nonreciprocal male behavior that asserts a woman's sex role over her function as a worker."[31] The actual mechanisms and practices of harassment include touching, staring at, or making jokes about a woman's body, nonreciprocated requests for sexual intercourse, and actual rape at work. Verbal abuse is common. Derogatory language and jokes directed at women are examples of overt sexual discrimination. Examples drawn from women commenting about their college settings illustrate the power of words to hurt:

> Class time is taken up by some professors with dirty jokes which . . . often happen to be derogatory to women (i.e., referring to a woman by a part of her anatomy, portraying women in jokes as simpleminded or teases, showing . . . women as part of the 'decoration' on a slide).
>
> . . . in other classes they hear women described as "fat housewives," "dumb blondes," as physically "dirty," as "broads," "chicks," or "dames," depending on the age of the speaker.
>
> [I] saw a slide show in (Course X) on computers which had female models in bikinis standing next to computers and the narration of the film included comments such as "Look at those measurements," etc.[32]

More extreme verbal abuse can lead to physical abuse. A young file clerk reported that her boss regularly asked her to come into his office "to tell me the intimate details of his marriage and to ask what I thought about different sexual positions." The implications were serious. Physical contact ranges from repeated "accidental" contacts to actual rape. One woman worker noted that "My boss . . . runs his hand up my leg or blouse. He hugs me to him and then tells me that he is 'just naturally affectionate.'"[33] Blatant discrimination in many settings often includes the physical manipulation of women, as this comment by a woman medical student indicates:

> A dozen of our classmates walked out in mid-lecture after a Professor of Surgery pinched the breast prosthesis of a mastectomy patient and then the breast of a woman radiologist, saying, "I'd like to bump into either of you in an elevator any time!" From such examples we learned how doctors treat our women patients and colleagues, and how are we to view women any differently?[34]

Such overt discrimination on the basis of sex is not harmless, for it is damaging not only to the images women have of themselves but also to the educational process.

Sexual harassment is commonplace. A Cornell study of 155 women employees found that 92 percent felt sexual harassment was a serious problem for women. Half reported they had been the victims of physical harassment, while 70 percent said they had been the victims of repeated and unwanted sexual comments, suggestions, or physical contact. This male behavior hurts women of various income levels. A *Redbook* survey of 9,000 women found that 90 percent had encountered unwanted sexual harassment in their jobs. More than half felt this type of sexual discrimination was a serious problem.[35] A recent study of sexual harassment at Harvard University found that 34 percent of female undergraduates, 41 percent of female graduate students, and 49 percent of nontenured female faculty reported that they had been subjected to sexual harassment, ranging from sexist jokes and verbal abuse to sexual assault. Again, most said they had not reported these abuses because they feared reprisals or felt that nothing could be done.[36]

MacKinnon suggests there are two types of this sex discrimination. In some cases it is a question of quid pro quo, of sexual favors for an employment benefit. Retaliation for rejecting male advances can take the form of demotions, salary cuts, and pressure to resign. In addition to the quid pro quo mechanism of discrimination, there is the type of sex discrimination that is a routine feature of a job. As MacKinnon notes, "a woman worker may be constantly felt or pinched, visually undressed and stared at, surreptitiously kissed, commented upon, manipulated into being found alone, and generally taken advantage of at work."[37] Sexual harassment is part of a large system of employment discrimination. It does not exist in isolation as the peccadilloes of scattered males.

Tied to males. One study of secretaries and managers demonstrates that many secretarial situations in business are patrimonial; that is, the status and income of a female secretary are tied to those of her male boss. Kanter concludes from her study of a major industrial supply corporation that secretaries obtained many of their rewards not from skills they used but rather from the rank and promotions of their bosses. In particular, sexuality was found to be important in the promotability of a secretary. Kanter notes that secretaries were often sent to secretarial schools as much for posture, how to dress, and use of deodorants, as for typing and filing skills. Since secretaries are status symbols for their bosses, personal appearance and attractiveness are critical for success. Kanter quotes one corporate official: "We have two good secretaries with first-rate skills who can't move up because they dress like grandmothers or housewives."[38]

THE BOTTOM LINE

As we have already seen, traditional sex segregation and discrimination in employment patterns mean that women receive less pay than men. The income levels of women in the labor force (outside the home) are a bit more than half those of male workers. In the early 1980s the median income of full-time workers was $12,001 for women and $20,260 for men. It is sometimes said that the average earnings of women workers are catching up with those of men workers. Yet the data available suggest that the gap between men and women has actually widened since the 1930s. As shown in Table 4.4, the earnings for women workers, relative to men, peaked at

TABLE 4.4. Average (Median) Earnings of Full-time,
Year-Round Male and Female Workers
Since 1939

	ANNUAL MEDIAN EARNINGS		WOMEN'S WAGES AS PERCENTAGE OF MEN'S WAGES
YEAR	WOMEN	MEN	
1939	$ 863	$ 1,356	63.6
1946	1,710	2,588	66.1
1956	2,827	4,466	63.3
1961	3,351	5,644	59.4
1966	3,973	6,848	58.0
1971	5,593	9,399	59.5
1976	8,099	13,455	60.2
1981	12,001	20,260	59.2

the end of World War II at 66.1 percent, then declined to about 59–60 percent, a figure that has been relatively stable since 1960.[39] Since 1960 full-time women workers as a group have made no relative gains on male workers. More recent data for the 1980s show a similar pattern (see page 124).

OTHER EXAMPLES OF BLATANT DISCRIMINATION

We do not have the space here to go into much detail about the many other types of overt discrimination that women face in such areas as housing, law, and politics, but we can give a few examples.

Discrimination in housing. Discrimination against women in the housing arena has been commonplace. Intentional discrimination by real estate brokers against white married women is less common than in the case of minority persons because these women frequently seek housing with their husbands, either present or in the immediate background. However, when it comes to the growing number of single women, both white and nonwhite, seeking to buy housing with or without children, discrimination again rears its ugly head. Misconceptions exist in the real estate industry with regard to the effect of single female homeowners on property values (similar to the alleged negative effects of minority ownership). Single women are believed to be poor credit risks by many male decision makers in the housing industry. Women are stereotyped as having less business sense than men. Their incomes are thought to be unstable, and there is a pervasive fear that they will become pregnant and lose their jobs. A female real estate broker in San Francisco was told by the Equal Rights Committee of the California Real Estate Board, "Let's face it, you know women cannot take care of property like men can and they are more flighty and we have to understand that and that is a good basis for prudent lending practices."[40] For the prospective female home buyer, the initial screening for a mortgage loan is often done by male real estate brokers or bankers who are frequently reluctant to present a client whose eligibility for a loan appears to be "questionable" in conventional terms.

Women also suffer discrimination in rental housing. Many single women, including those separated or divorced, must depend on rental property because of their lower incomes and the difficulties they experience in obtaining mortgage loans. Within the rental market women face a variety of discriminatory practices, all rationalized as protecting the interests of the landlord. Sometimes women are simply told that a unit is not for rent to a single woman; a man is needed to "keep up the property." Some are quoted a higher price than a single male or a married couple, especially if they have children.

Discrimination in loan and credit practices.　The 1974 Equal Credit Opportunity Act makes it illegal to discriminate against women in many types of credit transactions. On paper this law looks good, and it has brought some important changes in loan practices. Still the law's penalties are weak, and the law is difficult to enforce because of the subtle and informal character of mortgage and other loan practices. In addition, the law was weakened by corporate and other business interests in the legislative process, as in the requirement that wives must request businesses to make family credit account arrangements in the names of both spouses and must request explanations for denials of credit. As a result, many women are not aware of their legal rights, or they face opposition from their husbands if they attempt to request their rights. As a result, there is still overt discrimination in the areas of lending and credit.[41]

CONCLUSION

Sex discrimination continues to take many forms, from blatant to covert, from individual to institutionalized, from economic to political and legal. All forms operate to keep a woman "in her place." We have seen in this chapter that overt sexist discrimination is still very much a part of a supposedly civilized America. Now we will turn to less obvious, but no less serious, types of subtle and covert discrimination.

NOTES

1. Robert O. Blood and Donald M. Wolfe, *Husbands and Wives* (New York: Free Press, 1963), pp. 20–22; D. M. Jeer, "Husband and Wife Perceptions of Family Power Structures," *Marriage and Family Living* 24 (February 1962), pp. 65–67.
2. Dair L. Gillespie, "Who Has the Power? The Marital Struggle," in *Women: A Feminist Perspective,* 1st ed, ed. J. Freeman (Palo Alto, Calif.: Mayfield Publishing Company, 1975), pp. 65–86.
3. Shelia Rowbotham, "Imperialism and Sexuality," in *Feminist Frameworks,*

ed. Alison M. Jaggar and Paula Rothenberg Strahl (New York: McGraw-Hill Book Company, 1978), pp. 316–317.

4. Del Martin, *Battered Wives* (New York: Pocket Books, 1976), pp. 12–15; see also Karen Durbin, "Wife Beating," *Ladies Homes Journal* (June 1974), p. 64.

5. Martin, *Battered Wives,* p. 11.

6. Susan Brownmiller, *Against Our Will* (New York, Bantam Books, 1975), pp. 346–349, 380–389.

7. U.S. Department of Justice, Bureau of Justice Statistics, *Criminal Victimization in the United States, 1982* (Washington, D.C.: Government Printing Office, 1984).

8. Thomas I. Meyer, "'Date Rape': A Serious Campus Problem that Few Talk About," *Chronicle of Higher Education,* December 5, 1984, pp. 1, 12.

9. Brownmiller, *Against Our Will,* pp. 408–409; H. S. Feild, "Attitudes toward Rape," *Journal of Personality and Social Psychology* 36 (February 1978), pp. 156–178.

10. M. Joan McDermitt, *Rape Victimization in 26 American Cities, Application of Victimization Survey Results Project* (Washington, D.C.: Government Printing Office, 1979), p. 1; Susan A. Basow, *Sex-Role Stereotypes* (Monterey, Calif.: Brooks/Cole Publishing Company, 1980), pp. 277–278; Timothy Harper, "Legal View of Rape," *Dallas Morning News,* May 18, 1984, p. C2.

11. Menachem Amir, *Patterns in Forcible Rape* (Chicago: University of Chicago Press, 1971); Diane Herman, "The Rape Culture," in *Women: A Feminist Perspective,* ed. J. Freeman (Palo Alto, Calif.: Mayfield Publishing Company, 1984), p. 23.

12. Herman, "The Rape Culture," p. 23.

13. Ibid.

14. Evelyn Nakano Glenn and Roslyn L. Feldberg, "Clerical Work: The Female Occupation," in Freeman, *Women* (1984), pp. 317–320.

15. Bureau of the Census, *Statistical Abstract of the United States: 1984* (Washington, D.C.: Government Printing Office, 1984), pp. 419–420.

16. Susan A. Basow, *Sex-Role Stereotypes,* p. 272.

17. Bureau of Labor Statistics, *Employment Earnings,* January 1983, Table 22.

18. American Federation of State, County, and Municipal Employees, "A Profile of the City of Chicago as an Employer of Men and Women," Washington, D.C., November 1982.

19. Hay Associates, State of Minnesota Report, March 1982; Hay Associates, City of San Jose, November 1980; State of Washington Study, *Public Personnel Management Journal,* Winter 1981–1982; we draw on summaries of these studies in National Committee on Pay Equity, *The Wage Gap* (Washington, D.C., 1983), p. 5.

20. Bureau of the Census, *Current Population Reports,* series P-60, no. 132, table 51.

21. The Michigan study is summarized in "Why Do Women Earn Less?" *ISR Newsletter* (Ann Arbor: University of Michigan, Spring/Summer 1983).

22. "Washington Women Win Raises in Wage Suit," *Austin American Statesman,* December 2, 1983, p. A5.

23. Pittsburgh Press Co. v. the Pittsburgh Commission on Human Relations, 413 U.S. 376 (1973); Brush v. San Francisco Newspaper Printing Co., 469 F.2d 89 (1972); Sandra L. Bein and Daryl L. Bein, "Sex-segregated Want Ads: Do They Discourage Female Job Applicants?" in *Discrimination Against Women,* ed. Catherine R. Stimpson (New York: R.R. Bowker Company, 1973).

24. Ellen Cassedy and Karen Nussbaum, *9 to 5: The Working Woman's Guide to Office Survival* (New York: Penguin Books, 1983), pp. 121–123.

25. Felix Lopez, "The Bell System's Non-Management Personnel Selection Strategy," in *Equal Employment Opportunity and the AT&T Case,* ed. Phyllis A. Wallace (Cambridge, Mass: M.I.T. Press, 1976), pp. 226–227; see Edgar S. Ellman, *Managing Women in Business* (Waterford, Conn.: National Sales Development Institute, 1963).

26. EEOC Decision No. 71-2613, 4 FEP Cases 22 (1971); Phillips v. Martin Marietta Corp., 400 U.S. 542 (1971); EEOC Decision No. 71-332, 2 FEP Cases 1016 (1970); Wygant V. Jackson Board of Education, 746 F.2d (October, 1984).

27. Marianne Ferber and Jane Loeb, "Performance, Rewards, and Perceptions of Sex Discrimination among Male and Female Faculty," *American Journal of Sociology* 78 (January 1973), pp. 995–1002; Barbara Babcock, Ann Freedman, Eleanor Norton, and Susan Ross, *Sex Discrimination and the Law: Causes and Remedies* (Boston: Little, Brown and Company, 1975), pp. 300–330.

28. Robert Tsuchigane and Norton Dodge, *Economic Discrimination Against Women in the United States* (Lexington, Mass.: Lexington Books, 1974), p. 54.

29. Bernard M. Bass, Judith Krussel, and Ralph Alexander, "Male Managers' Attitudes Toward Working Women," *American Behavioral Scientist* 18 (November 1971), pp. 228–229; Rosabeth Moss Kanter, *Men and Women of the Corporation* (New York: Basic Books, 1977), p. 67.

30. Cassedy and Nussbaum, *9 to 5,* p. 123.

31. Lin Farley, *Sexual Shakedown* (New York: McGraw-Hill Book Company, 1978), p. 14.

32. Roberta M. Hall and Bernice Sandler, "The Classroom Climate: A Chilly One for Women?" (Washington, D.C.: Project on the Status and Education of Women, 1982), p. 5.

33. Farley, *Sexual Shakedown,* p. 15; Catherine A. MacKinnon, *Sexual Harassment of Working Women* (New Haven: Yale University Press, 1979), p. 29.

34. Hall and Sandler, "The Classroom Climate," p. 3.

35. Farley, *Sexual Shakedown,* p. 20–21; MacKinnon, *Sexual Harassment of Working Women,* pp. 26–27; Claire Safran, *Redbook Magazine,* November 1976, pp. 149–219.

36. "Fair Harvard, Are You Fair?" *Time,* November 14, 1983, p. 109.

37. MacKinnon, *Sexual Harassment of Working Women,* p. 40.

38. Rosabeth Moss Kanter, *Men and Women of the Corporation,* pp. 74–76.

39. National Committee on Pay Equity, "The Wage Gap: Myths and Facts," Washington, D.C., 1983, pp. 3–4. (These data are taken from U.S. Department of Labor reports.)

40. U.S. Department of Housing and Urban Development, *Women and Housing: A Report on Sex Discrimination in Five American Cities* (Washington, D.C.: Government Printing Office, 1975), pp. 54–58.

41. Basow, *Sex-Role Stereotypes,* p. 278.

5

How Subtle Sex Discrimination Works

Because most of us are still almost exclusively concerned with documenting and identifying the more visible and widespread types of overt sex discrimination, we are inattentive to other forms of inequality. Subtle sex discrimination is a slippery concept, difficult to define and measure, but it is very real. And because it can shape organizational procedures, subtle sex discrimination is considerably more harmful than most of us realize. Subtle sex discrimination has the following characteristics: (1) It can be intentional or unintentional, (2) it is visible but often goes unnoticed (because it has been built into norms, values, and ideologies), (3) it is communicated both verbally and behaviorally, (4) it is usually informal rather than formal, and (5) it is most visible on individual (rather than organizational) levels and appears to be episodic and situational (rather than cumulative and structural).

Nine types of subtle sex discrimination mechanisms are discussed in this chapter: chivalry, discouragement, harassment, objectification, devaluation, sexism, exploitation, domination, and exclusion. Although these mechanisms are not exhaustive, they illustrate some of the ways in which subtle sex discrimination works.

CONDESCENDING CHIVALRY

Condescending chivalry refers to superficially courteous behavior that is protective and paternalistic but treats women as subordinates. This behavior ranges from simple, generally accepted rules of etiquette regarding sex (for example, opening doors for women) to more deeply entrenched beliefs that women are generally helpless and require protection and close supervision.

Chivalrous behavior implies respect and affection. That is, many men assume that referring to women as "little girl," "young lady," "little lady," and "kiddo" is a compliment—especially if the woman is over thirty. Some women may be flattered by such terms of endearment. Yet, comparable references to men ("little boy," "little man") are considered insulting, demeaning, or disrespectful because they challenge men's adulthood and authority. Thus, it is acceptable to refer to women, but not men, as children.

Even when women are clearly in positions of authority, their power may be undercut through "gentlemanly" condescension. For example, one women dean (who is responsible for, among other things, collecting, reviewing, and coordinating course schedules every semester) complained that some chairmen refuse to take her seriously. When chairs are late in submitting schedules and she calls them into her office, some emphasize her gender and ignore her administrative power: "They do things like put their arm around me, smile, and say, 'You're getting prettier every day' or 'You shouldn't worry your pretty little head about these things'."

Chivalrous, paternalistic and "protective" behavior also limits women's employment opportunities. According to Richardson, acting out such "feminine" and "masculine" ritual ceremonies as waiting for a door to be opened or a cigarette to be lit perpetuates male superiority and female inferiority in economic and not just social situations:

> Acting out . . . ritual ceremonies between the sexes . . . ensures that women will retain their second-class social citizenship and remain culturally defined as immature, incompetent and childlike. To want "equal pay for equal work" and at the same time to be treated "like a lady" are inconsistent and incompatible objectives.[1]

A number of women we talked to said they were automatically excluded from some jobs because men still assume that women won't want to travel, will be unwilling to set up child-care arrangements, and "don't want to be in the public eye." Or, when women already have jobs, they will be excluded from important meetings or not considered for promotions because they should be "protected." Consider the experience of a thirty-three-year-old, unmarried store manager provided by one of our respondents:

> [Mary's] male counterparts in the company frequently were invited to out-of-town business meetings and social functions from which she was excluded. These occasions were a source for information on business trends and store promotions and were a rich source of potentially important business contacts. When [Mary] asked why she was not invited to these meetings and social gatherings, the response was that her employer thought it was "too dangerous for her to be driving out of town at night by herself. . . ."

In most cases, it is still assumed that women need, want, or should want protection "for their own good." During a recent lunch with colleagues, for example, one of the authors was discussing prospective faculty who could fill a dean's position that was about to be vacated. The comments, from both male and female faculty, were instructive:

> Mary Ann is a very good administrator, but she plans to get married next year. I don't think she'll have time to be both a wife and a dean.
>
> Well, Susan has the respect of both faculty and administration but hasn't she been talking about having children?
>
> Tracy's been a great faculty leader and she's done an outstanding job on committees, but she's got kids. What if they get sick when important decisions have to be made in the dean's office?
>
> Sara has been one of the best chairs in the college, a good researcher and can handle faculty. [A pause.] On the other hand, now that her kids are grown, she probably wants some peace and quiet and wouldn't want to take on the headaches of a dean's office. . . .

In effect, every prospective female candidate was disqualified from serious consideration because it is generally assumed that women should stay in presumably "safe" positions where their femininity, motherhood, and ability to fulfill wifely duties will remain intact.

Whether well-intentioned or malicious, chivalrous behavior is dysfunctional because it reinforces sex inequality in several ways. First, treating women as non-adults stunts their personal and professional growth. "There are problems harder to put a finger on: . . . suggestions initiated by a woman are listened to, but always a bit more reluctantly than those initiated by a man. People, sure, will listen, but we are not urged to suggest. Women, very simply, are not actively encouraged to develop."[2]

Second, chivalry justifies keeping women in low-paying jobs. Some have argued, for example, that because some women (for example, nurses and cleaning women) are encouraged to work long hours or late at night, state protective laws do not represent progressive reform but have been designed to reduce competition from female workers and to save the premium overtime and better jobs for men.[3] Finally, chivalrous behavior can limit women's opportunities. Men's belief that women should be protected may result, for example, in men's reluctance to criticize women:

> A male boss will haul a guy aside and just kick ass if the subordinate performs badly in front of a client. But I heard about a women here who gets nervous and tends to giggle in front of customers. She's unaware of it and her boss hasn't told her. But behind her back he downgrades her for not being smooth with customers.[4]

Thus, not receiving the type of constructive criticism that is exchanged much more freely and comfortably between men can lead to treating women like outsiders rather than colleagues.

Interestingly enough, most of us do not recognize the fact that chivalry is specious, inconsistent, and exploitative. Women are seen as too helpless to open their own doors but quite capable of chairing difficult and unpopular committees. Or, women are "protected" from the stress and strain of management and supervisory positions but considered tough enough to train forty or fifty clerical workers or carry the entire student-advising burdens of a department. Thus, the traditions of chivalry "take credit for insulating [women] from the dirtier part of their environment, [but] take no pains to save them from the drudge and filth of their own work."[5] Gloria Steinem is reputed to have stated that she enjoys having a door opened for her, but it shouldn't cost her $5000 a year.

SUPPORTIVE DISCOURAGEMENT

Supportive discouragement refers to a form of subtle sex discrimination in which women receive mixed messages about their abilities, capabilities, intelligence, performance, or accomplishments. There are at least four types of supportive discouragement: the woman is encouraged but misdirected; encouraged but not supported or rewarded; encouraged but excluded; and encouraged but then used, manipulated, or exploited.

Encouraged but misdirected. In some cases, women are encouraged, on the one hand, to be ambitious and successful but are advised or mentored, on the other hand, to pursue dead-end, limited, or unchallenging educational and job avenues. A useful concept in this regard is the "cooling-out" process:

> Given [women's] impressive performance in elementary and secondary school, they could not be told abruptly that they should not have a career despite their prior academic accomplishments. Rather, they are accepted into college but then encouraged to segregate themselves within certain disciplines. While they may not be dismissed from the academy . . . they are nonetheless "dismissed" from any meaningful competition.[6]

Also, since women are believed to be less than serious in college, the cooling-out process encourages women to doubt their abilities and purpose and emphasize their limitations. For example, it is acceptable to do poorly in math and science because of the belief that women are in college only to find husbands. Finally, women are led to believe that a lack of commitment to a college education is acceptable, normal, and reasonable—and a result of the woman's own decision:

> The "cooling out" process of gently lowering ambitions seems to be peculiarly applicable to all women in academe regardless of their original commitment or overall ability. . . . Individuals must come to their own conclusion seemingly through their own initiative. . . . The mother may influence her daughter to opt for a "feminine career"; alternatively, the father may serve as coolant by refusing to subsidize his daughter in what he perceives as nonsocial objectives.[7]

Such misdirected encouragement can also be seen outside of higher education. For example, a study of displaced homemakers found that (well-intentioned) counselors routinely encouraged displaced homemakers' participation in workshops that set very high goals (for example, supervisory and management jobs) but that actually trained women to occupy only low-level, low-paying positions (for example, clerical, domestic, service).[8]

Another example of misdirected encouragement involves supporting women to compete at a high level but evaluating only sex-stereotypical characteristics that exclude them from serious job consideration. For example, a middle-level (GS-10) female federal employee, a computer programmer in the Army, said she was denied a promotion because the (all-male) evaluation team focused on her stereotypically female high evaluations of being "supportive," "following directions," and being "thorough" while ignoring such nonfemale characteristics (on which she was also evaluated highly) as leadership, innovation, and original contributions to the division.

One of the authors has also seen a number of situations in which reentry women were encouraged to pursue a college degree but discouraged from doing so in stereotypically male fields.[9] For example, reentry women are routinely encouraged (especially by male faculty) to pursue graduate degrees in social work, teaching, and nursing rather than in business, engineering, and computer science because "you've got a real knack for dealing with people."

Encouraged but not supported/rewarded. A second type of supportive discouragement is one in which women are encouraged but not supported or rewarded for nontraditional achievements. In *How to Suppress Women's Writing,* Russ suggests several subtle ways by which women are encouraged but not supported in writing:

> I remember a writing student weeping in my office not because her family opposed her writing but because they thought it would keep her busy until she got married. "Nobody takes it seriously!"
>
> A contemporary of mine, who has now published two novels, said bitterly that her father was more impressed by her hobby of macrame (which "takes the brains of a flatworm") than by her first book.[10]

A number of interviewees reported similar instances of general encouragement but lack of support in specific situations. For example, a female assistant professor of economics said her (all-male) department was continuously encouraging her to finish her dissertation and promised to provide all necessary support. When, however, her Ph.D.-granting institution offered her a year's contract—during which she could both teach and finish her dissertation—her department refused to allow her to take the year's leave of absence. According to her department, they could not spare any of the full-time faculty. However, since she was the top teacher in her department (in which all of the other full-time faculty males had terrible teaching reputations) and one of the most popular instructors at the university, her department was willing to encourage her professional development only if it didn't interfere with the department's reputation and student enrollment figures.

In a study of 449 middle-level managers (217 men and 232 women) working in a newspaper circulation department, Ogan found, similarly, that although women were encouraged to succeed, they were neither supported nor rewarded in terms of job responsibilities.[11] For example, women were less likely than men to be nominated for management training seminars, had fewer subordinates ("perhaps because [men] are frequently perceived as [more] capable of holding positions of high responsibility"), and had less secretarial assistance and less control over the budget. Thus, women were not provided the resources (routinely given to men) that would support their credibility, experience, and upward mobility.

Encouraged but excluded. A third form of supportive discouragement is to encourage women but to exclude them from job consideration, as well as from active participation and decision making on the job. One reason for this explanation is that when a situation is unclear, relying on sex-stereotypes provides predictability about expected behavior. For example, in a study of sixty-four mid-level managers of a manufacturing company, Gerdes and Garber found that when the job environment was ambiguous because the job was incongruent with traditional sex rules (that is, either men or women could perform the necessary job but adequate information on individual competence was lacking), "evaluators assumed that the (male) candidate possessed the required skills, and the female candidate lacked these stereotypically masculine skills."[12] Thus, female candidates are excluded from consideration because the male evaluators do not know how to evaluate women.

There are many ways by which women are encouraged to participate in a variety of activities, but are in fact excluded from equal participation. For example, some universities formally encourage women's athletic programs but discourage women's participation by not providing competent coaches, by permitting usage of facilities only when they are not being used by men (often at 5:30 to 7:30 A.M.), and by allowing only a limited number of scholarships to be used for recruiting women athletes.[13]

According to women coaches and athletic directors at several universities, women's athletics are still discouraged in several ways. Men receive practice uniforms, women do not. Men typically are provided such athletic equipment as socks, athletic supporters, and garment bags, whereas women must provide their own materials. When playing out of state, men receive money for meals (women do not), sleep two to a room (women—four to a room), spend the pregame night away (women travel the same day as the game), and travel in buses that have a driver (women travel in vans driven by the women coaches*). Male coaches often have university courtesy cars (women coaches do not) and have larger offices and more secretarial help than female coaches. Women athletes must do their own pregame

---

*According to a male coach, male athletes travel in buses and women athletes in vans because "men are taller."

setups (line fields, haul benches, place cages on fields), but male athletes do not. If games are played during holidays, men athletes stay at motels, whereas women athletes stay at the student health center (where beds are available). Men's athletic programs receive up to 85 percent of the recruitment monies. Publicity for women's athletic programs is typically late and "thrifty," compared to the generous, slick, early brochures published for men's sports.

A common complaint is that women's power is titular, not real. That is, women may receive an impressive title in lieu of an increased salary, authority, or both. Title promotions give women the impression that they are supported and appreciated. Fancy-sounding titles can be counted—a nice bonus for an organization that wants to appear as though it is committed to affirmative action goals. Women are beginning to realize, however, that formal encouragement (a title change) can still result in informal exclusion from decision making. One interviewee, a young woman who was "promoted" into a entry-level management position in a manufacturing company, found her supervisor undercutting her power by using the excuse that "I'm trying to make you a good manager":

> He's had my desk moved so he can watch me from his office. He listens to my phone conversations, yells at me when other division managers are in the office and tells our secretaries—who are responsible to me, not him—to get his approval before they do the work I assign them. . . . Worst of all, he takes credit for my work . . . the reports come from him without any mention of my name. Sometimes, he just takes my name off the reports.

Supportive discouragement is especially common vis-a-vis nontraditional student populations. Because of falling enrollments, colleges and universities have been initially very felicitous of reentry women—developing special recruitment materials, offering scholarships, and expressing interest in the applicant during admissions interviews. Once these students enroll, however, they are often not taken seriously. Many reentry women face a number of obstacles (e.g., coordinating child care and family responsibilites; coping with divorce, self-esteem, economic problems) that are not being addressed by higher education institutions because the latter do not take these problems seriously.[14]

A female faculty member reported two types of exclusion regarding reentry women. First, reentry women are often discouraged from participating in academic and social functions:

> Faculty (even women faculty) often assume that responsibilities such as child care take precedence over informal learning. . . . Last semester, after one of the evening graduate classes, a faculty member suggested that the students join him for a beer at one of the local pubs to continue a lively class discussion. He looked at the [reentry] woman and said, "We'll miss you, but I realize you have to get back to the kids." She went home to the kids.

Or sex-stereotypical characteristics of reentry woman are reinforced while their professional development is ignored:

During an advising session last semester, [a reentry student] expressed surprise, as she was leaving my office, that I had talked to her only about her academic progress: "This is the first time I haven't answered a lot of questions about my kids or my divorce."

Such reinforcement of domestic roles and discouragement of student roles may result in even greater guilt for being in class rather than performing unfinished domestic duties at home.

Encouraged but manipulated/exploited. A fourth type of supportive discouragement involves encouraging women and then using, manipulating, or sabotaging them. For example, several women in diverse settings (higher education, industry) reported receiving support for developing grant proposals, new programs, or services that took a great deal of extra time, effort, energy, and intelligence. When these projects were funded, the women were either taken off the projects or the monies were transferred to other projects.

One of the most subtle and devastating forms of exclusion is the sexual exploitation of women. Typically, the general literature warns women (especially those in subordinate positions) to avoid sexual relationships with their supervisors and instructors.[15] It should be pointed out, however, that women in equal or superordinate positions can also be manipulated—whether unintentionally or intentionally—because they are never on an equal footing with men, regardless of position. Sexual relationships with members of the same organization undermine women's self-confidence, self-esteem, and career development for several reasons: When the relationship is over, men may use intimate information against women; women learn to expect that they will get rewards in the future because of sex rather than achievement; and women can never be sure whether their intelligence and accomplishments or sexual availability is being rewarded.

FRIENDLY HARASSMENT

Friendly harassment refers to sexually oriented behavior that, at face value, looks harmless, playful, and even friendly. However, if it creates discomfort, embarrassment, or humiliation, it is a form of subtle discrimination. The three most common forms of friendly harassment are flattery, hostile humor, and psychological intimidation.

Flattery. A popular children's parable across a number of cultures is the story of the fox and the crow. The crow sits high on a branch holding a cluster of juicy grapes. The fox, intent on getting the grapes, praises the crow's beautiful voice and begs her to sing a song. The flattered crow starts to sing, and the fox runs off with the grapes. (It is probably not coincidental that in all cultural variations of the story, the fox is male and the crow is female.)

Flattery is a long-recognized form of seduction, power, and control. During the sixteenth century, Niccolo Machiavelli cautioned the prince to guard, among other things, against flatterers "who abound in all courts." Using flattery to get one's way is usually associated with women. Girls learn early and quickly that flattery is an effective tool for eliciting affection, interest, and "love" from men. Similarly, housewives, who traditionally have had little power and are still responsible for keeping the male ego intact, rely on flattery to get husbands to do what they want them to do. Men also use flattery to influence, persuade, and seduce. Because, however, men often use flattery in occupational areas and women have been socialized to use flattery in social and domestic spheres, men's use of flattery has more powerful effects.

When women succumb to flattery in the work place, the economic costs can be high. For example, an insurance agent said that until she realized what was going on, years of flattery from male peers were instrumental in getting her to do their work:

> I was in an office with two guys whose productivity was lower than mine. They would often tell me how great my work was, how organized I was, and would ask my help in finishing their reports. I felt sorry for them, so, for a long time, I'd help them with their reports, follow up on clients, and do some of their paperwork. It was only after they were promoted and I wasn't that I realized I had been used.

Women are more vulnerable to flattery than men in work situations for two reasons. First, they have been socialized to be modest, dependent, helpful, accommodating, perfectionist, service-oriented, and to be liked and needed:

> Too many women tend to gear their behavior in the workplace to the approval or disapproval of others. They seem to have an excessive need to be liked, to be approved of and loved. . . . Conversely, if they are disapproved of, disliked, unloved, then they are in the same measure "worthless."[16]

Thus, the more approval women receive—through flattery, for example—the harder they work. The harder they work and the greater the verbal appreciation, the more likely they are to have a positive self-image. The more positive the self-image, the harder they work:

> My boss would come around, about once every two weeks, telling me what a great job I was doing. He would also mention that, unlike other divisions, he was making sure that my pay was the same as that of male programmers who started the same time I did. What I didn't realize, for almost seven years, was that I had been working overtime—without extra pay—and the other guys hadn't. As a matter of fact, some of them often left early. (Programmer in sales department in industry)

It is not unusual for women to be so elated by the promise (or actuality) of equal salaries that they do not look any further in comparing, for example, benefits, vacations, overtime, work loads, or pension plans with those of men in the same positions.

Women may be vulnerable to flattery because they accept traditional sex stereotypes and are naive about the politics of the work situation. Men often capitalize on these weaknesses. About a year ago, one of the authors gave a talk on subtle sex discrimination to a group of seniors in a private girls' school in Baltimore. Categorically, the girls (who are bright, consider themselves "liberated," and will probably attend prestigious colleges) denied the existence of subtle sex discrimination. We finally got into a discussion of interpersonal relations during dating:

INTERVIEWER: When you're out with a guy, does he talk about you, how you feel, what you want to do, and what you like?

[The students are looking around, giggling, and shifting in their seats.]

STUDENT 1: All we ever talk about is him—sports, school, and his trip to the Caribbean during the Christmas break.

STUDENT 2: No, he never asks anything about me or how I feel.

STUDENT 3: I smile and nod a lot, but I don't think there's anything wrong with that.

STUDENT 4: I sometimes get tired of talking about him, him, him . . . but if I don't, he won't like me.

INTERVIEWER: Don't you think your present relationship should include an equal give-and-take in terms of discussing your interests?

STUDENT 1: No, because the boys in college will be different.

STUDENT 2: I don't mind. I plan to be a doctor, and I know I'll be treated as an equal then.

Although these young women are somewhat aware of and annoyed by their role as flatterers and ego enhancers, they genuinely believe that "the world out there" is different for adults. In all likelihood, they will become comfortable with or accustomed to the role of nurturer, listener, flatterer, and helpmate, and will accept such behavior as normative.

Hostile humor. During the course of our interviews, one woman faculty member in a business school stated in exasperation, "You know, if women are expected to act like 'ladies,' why all the sex harassment and dirty jokes about women?" Humor and jokes serve a number of functions: They reinforce group solidarity; define the deviant/outsider group; provide a safety valve for discussing taboo topics; and result in tension release, hostility, and anger toward any group that is seen as marginal, despised, or threatening.[17]

A cursory examination of comics and cartoons in newspapers and such magazines as *The New Yorker* and *Playboy* reveals a changing orientation toward women. In the 1950s and 1960s women were depicted in stereotypical roles as dumb but manipulative housewives (*Dagwood*), sexpots (*L'il Abner*), or well-meaning widows

(*Mary Worth*), who helped men resolve their romantic and personal problems. By the mid-1970s and the 1980s, women's sexuality and independence became threatening. Thus, cartoons attacked lesbianism, expressed sympathy toward men's "emasculation," and portrayed women as victims of violence (rape, incest, and sadism).

In their research on the use of humor in advertising, Courtney and Whipple found that both men and women found it funnier when women, rather than men, were ridiculed; that women more than men enjoyed the self-disparagement of a woman; and that men enjoy sexist humor "where the status of men is not under threat."[18]

Our interviews suggest, moreover, that the manner of telling sexist jokes, rather than the content, has undergone subtle changes. Interviewees reported that the number of sexist jokes they hear is probably increasing. Instead of just plunging into a joke, however, the joke teller (almost always a male) will acknowledge his awareness of a possibly unenthusiastic reception by some of the listeners with such introductions as "Some of you libbers may not think this is funny, but . . . ." Thus, the audience is *told* that their being offended will be ignored. Also, by publicly acknowledging that the content of the joke may be offensive, the joke teller implies that we should all be "liberated" enough to accept the sexist content. Such implications are sophisticated and startle the listener into "liberated" silence.

Psychological intimidation. There are many types of harassment—ranging from the explosive physical violence discussed in Chapter Four to subtle psychological intimidation. One of the most common forms of psychological intimidation is sexual innuendo. Of the more than 300 men and women interviewed for this book, most reported at least one recent instance of having been harassed (or having harassed) through "intimidations about physical intimacy." Women faculty in a variety of disciplines report that male students regularly use sexual teasing and double entendre messages instead of getting to the problem at hand (for example, a late paper or a missed exam). Secretaries, women faculty, and women in the private sector said that their names are often used in tones that suggest endearment and intimacy. A director of a college public information office said that pregnant women, especially, are targets for sexual innuendos—they encounter a number of offensive statements about the baby's paternity, jokes about the ability of pregnant women to have sexual intercourse, etc.[19]

Another form of psychological intimidation that is especially subtle because its effects are not immediately visible is that of setting the stage for seduction. In the case of faculty, for example, male instructors lay the groundwork for future sexual overtures "through patterns of selective attention and reward": "Friendliness, extra help, flexibility in grading and extended deadlines were seen by respondents as means by which [male] instructors tried to accumulate credit for potential sexual exchanges. . . . [Some male instructors] falsely praised [women] students' work to render them more vulnerable to future sexual advances."[20] Because some companies and universities have begun to discourage overt and outright sexual harassment, women are more likely to find themselves inundated with kindness and attention—not out of respect or affection but to facilitate future seduction.

A recent form of subtle harassment is one of decreasing women's credibility and professional acceptance through inferences about lesbianism. Homosexual behavior is still feared and tabooed in our society. Because women are already in powerless positions, they are especially vulnerable to accusations of homosexual activity: "There is still a great deal of discrimination against women in academe, and it gives men a double reason to want to keep them out of departments if there are questions about whether a woman is a lesbian. . . ."[21] Inferences about lesbianism are an effective source of social control and maintain sex-inequality as the status quo. One university athletic director related that "a couple of women whom we had called to get them to help us lobby on Title IX had said flat out they had been told by people on their campuses, 'If you start lobbying on Title IX, we are going to make certain accusations about you.' "[22]

A fourth type of subtle harassment is fixation on gender, which deemphasizes or ignores women's accomplishments and achievements. For the most part, men are uncomfortable with women in equal status positions and do not know how to deal with them as people. Thus, to avoid displaying sexual interest, they overreact and treat women toughly. For example, one faculty member said she had recently been on a search committee where the two women candidates were treated "differently" from the four male candidates; the women were asked many factual questions about the university and were often interrupted during their responses. Male candidates, on the other hand, were allowed to ramble, to talk about nonacademic issues (sports, cars, real estate), to digress. They were encouraged to ask—rather than answer—questions and were rarely, if ever, interrupted. Because women are more likely to be grilled, they are more likely to make mistakes, to become tense or worn down earlier in the day, and to be perceived as not being "collegial" (an important trait in higher education) because there is minimal relaxed, informal interaction. (A male, by the way, was hired.)

Women in corporate sales and marketing departments are similarly "kept in their place" through condescending behavior that focuses on their gender rather than their professional roles. For example, one mid-level manager in marketing said that she was at an important meeting where she and a comparable-level male manager (from another department) disagreed on a critical issue. As the disagreement grew more heated, her male counterpart exploded, "Look here, little girl . . ." and plunged into a patronizing attack. She was so taken aback and embarrassed, she responded in a "typically female" way—she withdrew from the debate. After the meeting, one of her peers put his arm around her shoulders and said, "Don't worry, hon, [X] will cool off." In the first instance, the woman was clearly "put in her place" as a woman and a child (it is difficult to imagine a man dismissing a peer as "little boy" during a business meeting). In the second instance, and however well-intentioned, the behavior focused on the woman's sex rather than her professional role (how often does a man comfort another man with a little hug and refer to him as "hon"?).

In another situation, a woman faculty member in a business school provided the following example of her male colleagues' fixation on her sex rather than her professional role:

> I was in the hall reading the riot act to one of my students—a tall, big, basketball star—who had missed several exams. My chairman was walking by, came over, put his arm around my waist, smiled, and said to the student, "Isn't she cute? Don't you just L-O-V-E her?" They both laughed. It took a while to reestablish my professional credibility with this student.

A fifth type of subtle sex harassment is emotional preying. Many women are recent entrants to the work force. Their inexperience, self-doubt, low power, or problems experienced in dealing with two full-time jobs—one at home and one at work—may make them especially accessible to harassers who prey on emotionally vulnerable women:

> After the divorce, my relationship with my ex-husband got even worse. Most of the people in the office knew what was going on. . . . One day, one of the engineers asked me out to lunch to discuss a project we were working on. I was flattered because engineers usually look down on community planners. Pretty soon we were talking about my personal problems. [Sam] was very understanding, supportive . . . very sweet, and I really let my hair down. Within a few months, we were having an affair. When I started getting serious, he became really angry. He said he was happily married and had gone to bed with me to help me through some tough times! Like hell! I'm not the one who scheduled bogus golf games Saturday mornings. . . . We barely talk to each other now. . . . (Community planner in a highway administrative department)

Besides taking advantage of the situation, the harasser-as-scavenger may also create emotional needs and then swoop in to meet those needs. One of the most subtle ways to do this is through a role which Dziech and Weiner describe as "confidante":

> He may invite her confidences, but he also offers his own. In an attempt to impress or win sympathy from the student, he may relate or invent stories about his private and professional life. . . . The student often feels that he values and trusts her, so she becomes an involuntary confidante. . . . The relationship is moved into an intimate domain from which she may find it difficult to extricate herself.[23]

Although Dziech and Weiner's observations are based on an analysis of higher education, the confidante-harasser also exists in the business, industry, and government sectors.

Finally, our observations suggest that "friendly" harassment increases and becomes more subtle as the occupational level increases. We have noticed, for example, that harassment is considerably more subtle and less physical in managerial and technical positions than in sales and clerical positions. Although this hypothesis warrants a more systematic investigation, some studies have found a similar pattern:

Women working at the bottom of the economic scale are subject to the grosser expressions of sexual harassment. They often encounter cruel suggestive comments and crass physical assaults. Professional and managerial women . . . receive offers for after work drinks, expensive lunches and dinners, and business trips, with the implicit message that sexual favors are expected. *What this implies is that men up the ante for professional women.* [emphasis added].[24]

SUBJECTIVE OBJECTIFICATION

Subjective objectification refers to a form of subtle sex discrimination by which women are (1) treated as nonpersons or nonadults, (2) viewed as objects of an identifiable category, or (3) classified in terms of ascribed characteristics and subjective gender expectations rather than objective, achieved traits.

Nonpersons and/or nonadults. Women are often not seen as individuals who possess abilities, talents, and intelligence. Instead, they are seen as possessions and conduits for male accomplishments. A number of authors have documented women's treatment as property.[25] Even in the 1980s courts are slow in granting women protection from blatant and overt sexual assault by husbands and rapists, from discriminatory social security benefits, and from unequal insurance coverage. In terms of professional development, women are still expected to sacrifice their own interests for those of their husbands (or boyfriends) or to accept having their contributions ignored. In the arts and literature, for example, "women may not only be renamed as non-artists; their contributions of art may be absorbed into a man's and recategorized as his."[26]

Women are often seen and treated like children. As discussed earlier, women are often referred to as "baby," "little girl," or other similar terms that are used to address children. Like children, they are not expected to be able to handle responsibility or money or take part in important discussions and decisions (except, of course, in the jobs or roles that men don't want). Also, women and children are interrupted and excluded from important discussions and decisions. Women are often punished like children—their "allowances" may be taken away, they may be forbidden to associate with their friends, their physical mobility may be limited, they may be given curfews (for example, coming home from work in time to make dinner), or they may be threatened with physical punishment similar to that of children:

> When I was chair of our department, one of the senior male faculty was very unhappy about the woman faculty member we had just hired. Apparently, she challenged him, talked back to him, and contradicted him in public. As we talked, he got more and more angry about her behavior. Finally, he exploded, "What that young lady needs is a good spanking!" (Woman faculty member in political science)

As this interviewee pointed out, she had never heard a faculty member define a male's difference of opinion as unruly or rude behavior nor threaten to spank a male colleague.

Objects of a category. Besides being nonpersons, women are seen as "things" (objects) within a category (nonmen). Among other characteristics, being an object includes being perceived as nonindividualistic (that is, "women are all alike"), lacking independent social standing (that is, apart from men), seen as a "decoration" (to be adorned, collected, and displayed), and depersonalized because of a preoccupation with sexual acquisition (for example, "a piece of ass.")[27]

Frequently, women are reacted to in terms of their physical (that is, sexual) appearance rather than their ability or accomplishment. A (male) director of personnel in a bank told us that one of the recent interviewees for a job was a young woman who had been awarded her department's prestigious Accounting Award at graduation. When she was invited back for a second interview, a job offer seemed forthcoming. It wasn't. The personnel director told us that "she was an attractive, well-endowed young lady. After the first job interview, she was called back a second time because some of the men who had interviewed her told the rest of the guys to be sure to be there to see 'the biggest tits in Washington.'" She was paraded around and ridiculed behind her back. The fact that she was one of the top students in her graduating class was ignored!

Men also tend to give women's decorative role a higher priority than women's health or job requirements. In terms of the former:

> Some physicians don't take girls' athletic injuries seriously. For example, they put off surgery—admitting it's probably necessary—because, as one doctor said recently to one of my students, "You don't want an ugly scar on your knee, do you?" (Girls' high school athletic director)

A female tennis coach at a girls' high school said that her boyfriend, who picked her up after work, would complain continuously, "I don't understand why you always wear sweat suits to work. Don't you have any skirts?" Pointing out that sweat suits were her work uniform did not diminish the complaints. Another female coach, in women's college lacrosse, said that she can sustain friendly relationships with men only if she doesn't beat them in sports:

> As long as we play *other* teams in racquetball, the guys don't mind my being the only woman on the team and beating the other men. When I beat my teammates on a one-to-one basis, however, they don't talk to me for days. Sometimes I lose purposely because I don't want to ruin our club's morale; it's not okay to beat your own teammates when you're the only woman in the club.

One of the groups that is most likely to be treated as depersonalized decorations are secretaries. Because they represent the company's "pretty exterior," secretaries are typically expected to be young and attractive. Some employment agencies *still* require women applying for jobs as secretaries and receptionists to submit pictures of themselves with their employment applications. The formal job description may stipulate such job-related skills as typing, word-processing, filing, and familiarity with office equipment. Informally, however, these job applicants must also meet the employer's standards of beauty and be "decorative," or else they will not be hired. Many women spend up to 50 percent of their (low) salary on wardrobes and grooming products. And because there are few secretarial jobs that do not require such accoutrements, secretaries and receptionists find that they have little choice in the matter. In many jobs, of course, both men and women are expected to conform to dress codes. For men, however, expectations of being appropriately dressed can be met more easily because they get higher salaries. In an office environment (where men are paid more than women), a man earning $40,000 a year can live up to the company's dress code much more easily than the woman earning $12,000 a year.

Ascribed versus achieved traits. Not only are women categorized and treated as objects, but they are also evaluated in terms of their ascribed rather than achieved characteristics. Much of what women do (an achieved role) is undervalued or ignored because we see the work as reflecting innate sex characteristics (an ascribed role). What women do inside and outside the home is labeled as "women's work," and "women's work" is not seen as terribly important. Examples of how the achievements of women are undervalued follow.

1. The lifting of heavy objects occasionally by men is evaluated higher than women's repeated lifting of lighter loads for more exhausting periods.
2. Men are responsible for property, and women for persons. The latter are evaluated as less important and less skilled than the former.
3. Because decision making is seen as more important than doing the homework that leads to decisions, men in white-collar jobs get rewards and secretaries don't.
4. Because evaluation systems "reward brass and ignore tact," men's verbal aggressiveness is rewarded and women's interpersonal skills are ignored.
5. Men are rewarded and subsidized for on-the-job training, while women are expected to have the necessary training (e.g., "anyone can type").
6. Men and women both work in unpleasant and dangerous job situations. Because, however, men's dangers are more dramatic (for example, fumes and the heat of steel mills), they are noticed more than women's equally hazardous but less dramatic problems (for example, continuous clatter of office machines, unhealthy ventilation, radiation, poor furniture).[28]

What women do is devalued both because women's work is seen as a "natural" extension of their innate traits (in other words, "women don't mind doing boring work") and because women are still expected to live up to their "biological destiny." In a study of news stories examined over a year's period, Foreit et al. concluded that "personal appearance, age, marital status, spouse and children are more important to newspaper reporters when describing women rather than when describing men."[29]

Among other things, living up to their "biological destiny" (that is, bearing and rearing children and serving men) precludes women's interacting with men on equal terms in occupational areas. This exclusion becomes a self-fulfilling prophecy. For example, in a study of faculty perceptions of the leadership qualities of male and female physical education departments, Christensen et al. found that male department heads evaluated male faculty members higher than female faculty members. The authors attribute this finding, in large part, to the fact that male department heads were "more intimate and in greater harmony" with male faculty members than with female faculty members.[30] In other words, men evaluate each other's work more highly and positively because they work and play together. Women, on the other hand, are excluded from men's games, are expected to be at work while men play, and are expected to have professional interests that differ from those of men:

> When the Orioles season starts, male faculty *en masse* cancel classes, don't attend faculty senate meetings and important tenure and personnel committee meetings to go to the parade, the opening game, sit around in bars, etc. Everyone seems to accept this as normal; such macho behavior is even encouraged. If, however, one of the women faculty skips an occasional committee meeting to present a paper at a women's conference the [male] faculty and [male] administrators treat us like malingerers. (Woman faculty member at large state university)

Similarly, in a study of 1,500 subscribers to the *Harvard Business Review,* Rosen and Jerdee concluded that there are "two general patterns of sex discrimination" toward women managers: "(1) There is greater organizational concern for the careers of men than there is for those of women, and (2) there is a degree of skepticism about women's abilities to balance work and family demands."[31] In terms of the second finding, male managers castigated women's, but not men's, stereotypical attributes:

> It would seem to be the women who are expected to change to satisfy organizational expectations. For example, written comments from participating managers often suggested that women must become more assertive and independent before they can succeed. . . . *The managers do not see the organization as having any obligations to alter its attitudes toward women. Neither, apparently, are organizations about to change their expectations of men* [emphasis added].[32]

Thus, subjective objectification continues to treat women, as a group, as nonpersons who are seen as mindless children, sex objects, or household fixtures. A major problem is that almost equal numbers of men and women accept and encourage such definitions and subsequent reactions.

RADIANT DEVALUATION

Since the early 1970s women are less likely to be openly maligned or insulted. Instead, they are devalued more subtly but just as effectively. Often, the devaluation is done in glowing terms:

> Newly commissioned Ensign Kristine Holderied and her family met with
> President Reagan at the White House yesterday as he congratulated her for
> being the first woman to graduate at the top of a military academy class. . . .
> Holderied, 21, of Woodbine, spent several minutes with the president be-
> fore he escorted her to a briefing session being conducted for female editors
> in the Old Executive Office Building. . . .
> *After meeting Reagan, the U.S. Naval Academy graduate said the president*
> *"said it was fantastic, that it shows what a woman can do."*[33] [Emphasis
> added.]

A woman psychologist, who was one of the popular instructors in her college and
had a reputation for being a very good teacher, said she would get good teaching
evaluations from her (male) chair but that the positive evaluation would be couched
in sex-stereotypical rather than professional terms—she was described as being
"mama-ish," having an "attractive personality" and "charming" approach to
teaching.

Women can also be devalued by ignoring their presence or accomplishments.
In a study of 3,361 national survey questions used by polling organizations from
1936 to 1973, Hesse et al. found that most of the questions focused on men alone,
did not cast women in professional or powerful roles ("except for the time-worn
question about voting for a woman as president"), and reflected sex inequality in
wording:

> Overwhelming bias by stereotyped content, by omission, and by gender word-
> ing exists in the polling questions used for five decades. Men absolutely domi-
> nate in frequency of representation and in the roles portrayed. Nouns and
> pronouns fail to convey generic meaning, but serve to perpetuate differential
> male and female behaviors and relationships. The questions offer virtually no
> opportunity to express equitable attitudes toward men and women.[34]

Besides exclusion, women's achievements may be belittled by "damning with
faint praise." In a study of 243 letters of recommendation for a junior-level faculty
position in sociology, Guillemin et al. concluded that "blatant references to physical appearance" have disappeared and descriptions of women candidates in wife
and mother roles are "probably much less common." However, "the representation
of woman as future colleagues falters instead on the more abstract criteria of career
performance and potential." That is, there is little discussion of the woman's past
or potential contributions in such important areas as research, scholarly productivity, and teaching effectiveness.[35]

Also, women's work is often trivialized. Raising children is seen as easier and
less important than being a postal carrier; doing research on the military is evaluated as making a greater contribution (regardless of quality) than research on
women or women's issues; almost anything that an all-male department teaches (despite low enrollments) is seen as more critical than "that little writing workshop"
required of all students but taught predominantly by women in English departments. As seen in the recent discussions of comparable worth, there is a great deal

of resistance to the idea that women and men who obtain similar training—even though the jobs are different—should receive comparable pay.

Women (and women's work) are devalued and discredited not because women's jobs are different from those of men, but simply because the work is done by women. In the areas of speech and communication, for example, some studies have suggested that women may be taken less seriously than men because women communicate and express themselves in less powerful ways. For example, they use more tag questions ("It's a good movie, isn't it?"), unfinished sentences, and disclaimers ("I could be wrong, but . . ."); they ask questions rather than make statements and generally "support" rather than guide conversations.[36] A more recent study has shown that sex rather than communication patterns may be a more important predictor of perceived power and status. In a study of the usage of tag questions and disclaimers, Bradley found that men, but not women, were able to use tag questions and disclaimers "with virtual impunity"; they were not seen as less credible, weak, or nonassertive.[37]

LIBERATED SEXISM

Liberated sexism refers to the process that, at face value, appears to be actively and self-consciously treating women and men equally but that, in practice, increases men's freedom while placing greater burdens on women. Some of it is well intentioned and some manipulative.

Overloads. A funny thing happened to women on the way to the office during the last decade. Somewhere between wanting to be more than housewives (in the late 1960s) and entering the labor force for economic reasons (throughout the 1970s), many women found themselves, in the 1980s, with two jobs—one inside and one outside the home. Ironically, women working these "double days" are often defined as "liberated women."

Liberated from what?

As a number of studies have shown, a working wife's/mother's housework time decreases by about 10 to 15 hours a week not because the husband helps out but because the housework doesn't get done.[38] The woman uses shortcuts (frozen dinners, greater reliance on fast-food stores) or hires help to do work she used to do herself (child care, laundry, home improvements). Men's domestic activities increase between 10 and 60 minutes a week—and usually only in households with preschool children. Even when the husband/father occasionally volunteers (or is asked) to help, organizing his help may be as time-consuming as the woman's doing it herself:

> Yes, dad will take Mary to the dentist. But it was mom who 1) remembered that Mary needed to go to the dentist, 2) made the appointment, 3) wrote the note to get Mary excused from school and reminded her to take it to school, 4) saw that Mary brushed her teeth and wore one of her least disreputable pair of jeans, . . . 5) reminded dad to take Mary the morning of the appoint-

ment, 6) paid the bill when it came in the mail, and posted the next six month appointment on the family calendar afterwards.[39]

The woman is seen as "liberated" because she works outside the home. In reality, however, her work has freed her spouse from having total economic responsibility for the household without his sharing in the household and domestic responsibilities.

Another example of work overload is mentoring.* To provide women students with professional socialization, both men and women faculty and administrators have expected women—and *only women*—to take on the job of mentoring women:

> Every time a woman wants to do a thesis in our department, she's automatically assigned to me because it's assumed that I have both the time and interest to supervise every woman student. I've started refusing just because I don't have the time to do so, but I feel guilty about it even when I know that no one else in the department is chairing more than one or two thesis committees. (Woman faculty member in a management department)

> Male professors assume that female students will want to research "sissy" topics or will not be self-motivated (in other words, will be too dependent), so why pawn them off to the male faculty. . . . (Female sociologist)

The pressure for women to do a "double shift" (with no increase in pay, of course) increases women's work loads significantly without reciprocal work increases for men. "Women faculty frequently find themselves sought out by increasing numbers of women students and junior faculty, appointed to innumerable committees which need representation from women, and assigned heavier courseloads than men."[40] Although it can be argued that women's entry into the labor force has provided them with somewhat more options than they have had in the past, "liberation" should not be confused with exploitation.

Entry into nontraditional jobs. A highly publicized spectre of equality has focused on the entry of men and women into nontraditional jobs. There are, however, several variations by sex. First, women have more difficulty being accepted into traditionally male jobs (as carpenters, engineers, mechanics, firefighters) than men into traditionally female jobs (as nurses, flight attendants, elementary school teachers). As a male nurse put it: "I am singled out by the male doctors as the most competent nurse, and I'm always told what's happening with the patients even though I am not the nurse assigned to the patient."

In contrast, women nurses often complain that doctors treat them like domestic help rather than professionals. Thus, men in nontraditional jobs will be seen as better just because they are not women. The second difference is that men find

---

*Mentoring is used throughout the book to refer to superordinate-subordinate relationships in which the more powerful person (professor, employer) "grooms" and socializes the novice (student, employee) to become a successful, accepted participant in the organization/agency/institution/profession.

that "female" jobs are "handy stepping stones" to management slots.[41] This is rarely the case for women in either "men's" or "women's" jobs. Three years after a court-enforced affirmative action plan at AT&T, "affirmative action placed thousands more men in traditionally women's work than it placed women in traditionally men's work"–especially at nonmanagement levels, where women's positions were displaced by new technologies.[42] Thus, although women enter nontraditional jobs, they rarely receive the training necessary for job transfers to more competitive, upper-level positions.

Most of the training for careers and upward mobility is extremely one-sided. Women are expected to fit into the existing system; men are expected to maintain the status quo. Thus, there are dozens of articles teaching women how to act, talk, dress, and think like a man.[43] Once again, we are placing the burden for change on women and not men and reinforcing the sex-stereotypical expectation that women must meet men's approval but not vice versa.

Women's acceptance of the double standard. However unintentional, liberated sexism also comes from women, including feminists, who accept the double standard. After the 1984 election, Geraldine Ferraro did a 30-second television commercial for Diet Pepsi in which she emphasized her role as mother ("We can be whatever we want to be and being a mother is one of the choices I'm most proud of"). Both feminists and nonfeminists accused Ferraro of "selling out," being a political huckster, prostituting herself, and forsaking women's issues. Yet, when Lee Iacocca and Mikhail Baryshnikov did similar commercials, no one questioned their moral character or made gloomy predictions about their professional credibility. Tasteless behavior is not a crime. Why, then, single out women for punishment—especially when opinion polls suggest that the public has less respect for politicians than automobile moguls or internationally known ballet artists? There was a great deal of negative publicity about Ferraro's legitimately earning $500,000. In contrast, the public rarely hears any criticism of the men who were convicted and sent to prison after the Watergate burglary in the early 1970s and who have made considerably more than $500,000 describing their illegal activities.

Women sometimes encourage the double standard both at home and in the work place. Many mothers try to curb their daughters' but not their sons' sexual activities. If there is a premarital pregnancy, in most cases it is the girl, not the boy, who is blamed for engaging in sexual intercourse and for failing to use contraceptives and who is expected to assume social and economic responsibility for the baby. In many households, children's chores are still assigned in terms of gender rather than ability or interest or on a rotating basis. In our interviews, several secretaries said that they resent watering plants, making coffee, and taking personal phone calls for women bosses but not men bosses. They also said that they expect women bosses to be more friendly, to be more accepting of tardiness and absence, and to show a greater personal interest in the employees than men bosses. These and other double standards free men from work and responsibility, reinforce sex stereotypes, and dilute women's authority.

BENEVOLENT EXPLOITATION

Women are often exploited. Much of the exploitation is carried off so gracefully, however, it often goes unnoticed.

Dumping. One of the most common forms of exploitation is dumping—getting someone else (i.e., a woman) to do a job you don't want to do and then taking credit for the results:

> Whenever my supervisor gets a boring, tedious job he doesn't want to do, he assigns it to me. He praises my work and promises it will pay off in his next evaluation. Then, he writes the cover letter and takes full credit for the project. . . . I've never been given any credit for any of the projects—and some were praised very highly by our executives. But, I suppose it's paid off because my boss has never given me negative evaluations. (Female engineer in aerospace industry)

Another form of dumping—much more elusive—is to segregate top workers by sex and depend on the women to get the work done while the men merely critique the work and implement the results in highly visible and prestigious ways. An aide in a highly placed political office said that one of the reasons her boss was extremely successful politically was because he recognized that his female aides were better, harder working, more committed, and more responsible than the male aides. Thus, he surrounds himself with such women, gives them fancy titles, and gets 60 to 70 hours of work out of them at much lower salaries than those of men. When the projects are finished, he gives a lunch for all his aides and praises the women's work. Even as the dessert is served, new projects for the women are announced. The men, however, publicize the projects and get widespread recognition. As another ex-political aide put it: "It took me many years to realize that I had no power. If [politician X] left the office tomorrow, I'd be out of a job. The men, however, whose names were attached to my projects and who are influential businessmen, would be hired by [politician X's] successor." In this type of situation, women's contributions are exploited: They are not cumulative, not visible, and not influential in the public arena, and their accomplishments are, consequently, not transferable across jobs. Men, on the other hand, obtain cumulative, visible, transferable rewards for which they do very little work.

Sponsorship abuses. A very effective form of benevolent exploitation is to expect/teach women to be dutiful and loyal to men in leadership roles because such sponsorship will "eventually pay off." Women spend lifetimes being research assistants, invisible coauthors, and even authors—believing that their "sponsor" will one day recognize the contributions publicly. During their highly publicized divorce proceedings several years ago, Mrs. Spock charged that she should have been a coauthor of Dr. Spock's best-selling books on baby care. When an acknowledgment states something like "To my wife, who did most of the work on this book," it often should be taken literally. Unfortunately, women rarely receive any of the recognition, awards, and royalties for their work.

Showcasing. "Showcasing" refers to placing women in visible and seemingly powerful positions in which their talents, abilities, and intelligence can be pulled out, whenever necessary, for the public's consumption and the institution's credibility.

One form of showcasing is to make sure that the institution's token women are present (though not participating) in the institution's meetings with "the outside." Thus, in higher education, a woman faculty member is often expected to serve on national committees (recruitment; articulation with high schools, community colleges, and colleges), grant proposals (to show the involvement of women), search committees (just in case affirmative action officers are lurking around), and a variety of external "women's-type" activities such as panels, commissions, and advisory boards. There is no compensation for these additional duties. Moreover, the women are not rewarded in later personnel reviews because this is "women's work" and because "women's work" has low status.

If an occasional committee is an important one, the women chosen are typically nonfeminists who won't "embarrass" the institution/agency/organization by taking women's issues seriously. Instead, they are Queen Bees,* naive neophytes, women who are either not powerful or are insensitive to sex discrimination.

Another form of showcasing is giving women directorships in dead-end jobs which are considered a "natural" for women:

> There's probably less discrimination in personnel offices because the job needs a person with traditionally female skills—being nice to people, having verbal abilities, and not being a threat to anyone because a director of personnel is a dead-end job. (Director of personnel in higher education)

Most "people" and service-oriented jobs are critical for any society's survival. Since, however, capitalistic economic systems require productivity and profit, stereotypically male traits (such as competitiveness, egotism, conformity, toughness) will be rewarded more highly than stereotypically female traits (such as dependence, altruism, creativity, tact). Giving women occasional, seemingly important titles creates the impression that both sexes participate in highly valued economic activities.

Technologically based abuses. Americans place a high value on progress, product improvements, and technological advances. ("New," "improved," or "better than ever" detergents, toothpaste, and shampoos appear on the market

---

*"Queen Bees" refer to women who are convinced that they have been successful solely because of their efforts and abilities rather than recognizing that their success could not have become a reality without the sacrifices, pioneering efforts, and achievements of their female predecessors. Because of their adamant "I'm-terrific-because-I-pulled-myself-up-by-*my*-bootstraps" beliefs, Queen Bees typically either ignore or resist helping women become upwardly mobile. Thus, Queen Bees openly support men who reject sex equality and provide men (and other Queen Bees) with public rationalizations for keeping women in subordinate positions (in other words, as female drones).

annually, and many people go into debt purchasing such "necessities" as home computers, microwave ovens, electronic games, and VCRs. The profits generated by such "discoveries" are not translated into higher salaries for the many women who work in "high-tech" industries. In the case of new technologies, for example, employers often convince women that their newly developed skills are inadequate and should not be rewarded:

> While office technology creates opportunities for higher pay for some of us, for many others it is used as an excuse for keeping salary levels down. An employer may ignore the new skills you have learned in order to operate your machine and argue it's the machine itself that does all the work so that you are worthless.[44]

Employers/supervisors may discourage women from pursuing personal or professional development programs that might make them more dissatisfied with or question their current subordination:

> Under the negotiated rules, secretaries were entitled to take whatever courses they wanted at a state university, tuition reimbursed. We had . . . no application forms . . . although our immediate supervisors and the office supervisor knew and approved the tuition provision (after we educated them). The Queen Bee three places up on the hierarchy professed ignorance and had to be convinced anew when one of the secretaries wanted to take a history course . . . only in the last three years has anyone gone through the hassle and taken the courses. (Ex-secretary in higher education)

The implication here is that some groups of workers (especially office workers) are presumptuous in assuming that their professional development is significant enough to warrant the institution's attention or expenditures. Perhaps more importantly, college courses might lead to office workers wondering why they are performing high-tech jobs at low-tech salaries.

Another way of exploiting women is to put them through unnecessarily grim and arduous job interviews as a way of downplaying their expertise and ability (and, consequently, pay rates):

> Secretarial job interviews are brutal. You can have a recent certificate, be working on a job, and have excellent references—but you still must take a letter on unfamiliar subject matter and type it on whatever typewriter is available. I can only compare it to having an engineer take a final with an unfamiliar calculator or a carpenter do a demonstration with someone else's (often in poor condition) tools. (Ex-secretary in higher education)

Finally, "progress" has been a higher priority than the job hazards resulting from new technologies and automation. In most cases, the people using the new technologies are office workers—almost all of them women. The most commonly used new office equipment is the video-display terminal (VDT). There is evidence that long-term exposure to VDTs may be dangerous. Operators of VDTs experience eyestrain, neck and back pain, headaches, and blurred vision; the radiation and chemical fumes emitted by the terminals are believed to cause stress, cataracts, miscarriages, and birth defects.[45]

Yet, management has done little to improve work conditions even when many of the improvements are not costly. As one respondent put it, "Why save labor when it's cheap?"

Nudity in advertising. One of the most widespread forms of exploitation is to use female nudity to sell everything from toothpaste to tractors. Such advertising may not be seen as exploitation because women are expected to be "decorative." The implicit message to men and women is that the primary role of women is to provide pleasure, sex, or sexual promise:

A sexual relationship is . . . implied between the male product user and his female companion, such that the advertisement promises, in effect, that the product will increase his appeal to her. Not only will it give him a closer shave, it will also provide a sexually available woman.

Often the advertisements imply that the product's main purpose is to improve the user's appeal to men, as the panty-hose advertisement which claims "gentlemen prefer Hanes." The underlying advertising message for a product advertised in this manner is that the ultimate benefit of product usage is to give men pleasure.[46]

The consistent and continuous message that advertisements send—to both men and women—is that women's roles in society are limited to two—that of housewife or sex partner. Other roles are not taken or presented seriously. Thus, women may dominate advertising space, but they are not dominant.

CONSIDERATE DOMINATION

Just as women are presented and treated as nonentities and nonpersons, men are dominant and dominate. The dominance is rarely seen as a negative characteristic because it has been internalized and institutionalized and is often portrayed as amicable, loving, and concerned.

Internalized. Language teaches, shapes, and reinforces sex role expectations and relationships between women and men. Children learn at a very young age, through interaction with parents and other adults, that males are dominant. In a study of sex differences in parent-child conversations, Greif found that fathers demonstrate their high status and control through interruptions and simultaneous speech,* especially with daughters. Also, wives reinforce their husbands' dominance. According to Greif, "fathers are more likely to interrupt and engage in simultane-

---

*Simultaneous speech refers to the process in which two or more people start speaking at once. The less powerful person withdraws, allowing the more powerful person to continue.

ous speech with their preschool children, and . . . both mothers and fathers are more likely to interrupt and speak simultaneously with daughters than with sons."[47] The message is that what children have to say is not important. And, what girls have to say is the least important.

The message is learned well and dominates male-female interactions even when the woman has a higher status than the man. For example, in a study of first-year graduate students in a social work master's degree program, Brooks found that "although male students interrupted both male and female professors more often than did female students, they interrupted female professors significantly more often than male professors. . . ."[48]

Besides interruptions, men demonstrate their dominance in interpersonal relations in other ways that show that they control the situation. Even when a respected woman is speaking, men in less prestigious positions will often yawn, leave the room, engage in asides and side conversations, clean their fingernails, look at their watches, leave the room to make phone calls, read their mail, pass notes, flip through notes, stare out the window, or physically turn away from the woman speaking.

Institutionalized. Men's dominance is built into our language, laws, and customs in more formal ways. According to Schur, the "hyphenization" phenomenon—for example, woman-doctor, woman-executive, woman-athlete, woman-driver—suggests women's "occupational deviance":

> Since high status occupations and prized competencies tend to be stereotypically "male," the hyphenated designations of women imply a further "put-down." Because she is female, a woman is assumed not to have overall competence for the prized roles that a man would have. Hence, she should be described . . . only relative to the occupation's other female occupants, rather than in terms of universalistic (i.e., sex-neutral) criteria.[49]

Thus, when women move into professional or other roles reserved for men, their anomalous position must be "marked" by qualifiers (for example, female surgeon).

Female subordination is also reflected by comparing women to food since food is something we all enjoy: "We describe females as such delectable morsels as a 'dish,' a 'cookie,' a 'tart,' 'cheesecake,' 'sugar and spice,' a 'cute tomato,' 'honey,' a 'sharp cookie,' and 'sweetie pie.'"[50] Comparing women to "things" that provide pleasure is institutionalized; such comparisons are made across social classes, age groups, and institutional settings.

Legal and political systems have been especially instrumental in subordinating women's rights and making women subservient to men. Courts and legislatures have historically defined, labeled, and stereotyped women as infantile and incompetent, seductive and immoral, and nonpersons and nonentities. Thus, widowed women are still given male executors, women are penalized for such consenting crimes as prostitution, and women assume their dependence and identity through a male.

Amicable. A considerable amount of domination is accepted by women because they share intimate relationships with men who have convinced themselves and women that male domination is "for your own good" or the good of significant others. A female faculty member in an all-male department was refused a leave of absence to finish her dissertation because "you need all the teaching experience you can get," "the department is afraid to lose someone as good as you," and "a lot of students need you." She continued to get outstanding student evaluations, served on committees tirelessly, did not finish her dissertation, and was not reappointed a year later.

Women often will be pressured into fulfilling men's sexual needs (real or imagined) regardless of how tired, overworked, and stressed they feel:

> In terms of sex, I always feel "on call." I have only 1/18 of the day to myself and sometimes go to bed very late because I need a few hours to myself—to think, to establish physical and emotional space. . . . Yet, no matter how exhausted I am, I have sex with my husband whenever he wants to because he makes me feel guilty about not being nurturant sexually. . . . (Female politician in local government).

To maintain friendly relations and to fulfill expectations of nurturance (both because women love/like the man and fear his looking elsewhere for gratification), women serve a subordinate sexual role. Not only do they not reject sexual intercourse when they are not "in the mood," but they are also less likely to demand sex when *they* want it or seek sexual gratification in extramarital relationships. Women are still expected to be more accepting, understanding, and forgiving than men about marital infidelity.

Male domination is generally accepted because occasional male behavior that appears nondominating reinforces women's hope that men really do care about women:

> The building I'm in is the only one that's not air-conditioned on the campus. Every other employee there is a female (grants director, dean of students, child care services). One of my male colleagues recently offered me a desk in his air-conditioned building. I thought the offer was wonderful until I realized that his attitude was one of "everything *you* do can be packed in a briefcase and moved within the hour." I really resented the implication. (Director of public information at a university)

The speaker's initial and immediate reaction was gratitude—"Isn't he thoughtful!"—until she realized that the desk was an easy "gift" to give (no one else needed it) and that the message behind the offer was less than respectful of her as a colleague. In most cases, women rarely question the tiny perks they receive. Instead, the grateful acceptance of minor gratuities blunts major, long-term dissatisfactions.

COLLEGIAL EXCLUSION

> It is sometimes impossible for any woman, no matter how high her qualifications, to be hired at certain schools. A Harvard department head stated that he has "men on the staff who will vote against a woman for a job just because she is a woman. They just don't want women around."[51]

Men are currently somewhat less likely to make such blatantly sexist statements. Instead, they make them in more subtle ways—for example, through physical and social exclusion.

Physical exclusion. A very subtle form of physical exclusion is isolation. Isolation during important meetings, get-togethers, lunches, and conferences makes women feel like outsiders:

> I've attended several dean's conferences where about six out of the seventy participants are women. Women are usually ignored—during panels and informal discussions—because men think they have nothing to learn from women. (Woman vice-president at a university)

Or, women may be ignored during critical decision-making periods even though they provide the background work and research that determine how decisions will be made:

> Several times, my male colleagues used my records of my patients to do research. It's never occurred to them to ask me to participate on these projects or to ask my opinion about diagnoses. I know I'm doing a good job, but I feel very isolated professionally. (Female physician at a major medical school)

Another form of physical exclusion is to keep women out of male clubs and training programs. In a study of women employed in traditionally male craft jobs (which were opened up to women because of court-ordered affirmative action programs), one of women's most common complaints was that men excluded them from critical on-the-job training.[52] Although some all-male clubs have started admitting women because of public pressure, a number of exclusionary clubs still exist:

> Businessmen and lawyers still meet with no embarrassment in places that exclude women and will continue to do so until some legal provisions bar this behavior. And women who are denied access as members will miss out on the talk, the social learning, and the contacts made in the relaxed and pleasant settings that clubs provide.[53]

Women are physically excluded from committee meetings and informal get-togethers (where much of the business is done) that are scheduled at times that men know women will be unavailable because of personal or professional commitments:

> I pick up my kids from school every Wednesday at 3:30. All of my colleagues know this. And I know the two or three hours each week when they're not available for meetings. There have been a number of times when one of them scheduled a last-minute meeting that they knew I couldn't attend because of the late notice. (Woman politician on county council)

A similar pattern exists in higher education. Qualified, intelligent women are more likely than less-qualified men to be appointed to silly, noncredible committees for long terms. When they are finally up for tenure or promotion review, a common reason for not granting women tenure is that they have not participated in "important" committees.

Such exclusionary behaviors are just as effective during discussions of salary increases:

> Last year, I found out, by accident, that my salary was about $5,000 lower than that of my male colleagues with comparable experience, seniority, clerkships, where we got our law degrees, and publications. When I asked the dean why my salary was so much lower, he said it was because I had never chaired any committees. Well, he's *never* appointed women faculty to chair committees, even after we often volunteered to do so. (Female law school faculty member)

Physical exclusion not only affects involvement in the community but also results in the woman's being a "marginal" person in terms of her own and others' perceptions. She fails to make contacts, to become visible and active in the employment environment, and to establish the credibility necessary for promotions, salary increases, and working relationships with colleagues.

Another intriguing example of physical exclusion comes from the literature on the utilization of physical space. According to Henley, women's environment is largely man-made, man-controlled, and designed to make men (not women) comfortable and secure.[54] Women are expected to take up as little physical space as possible (for example, secretarial pools), to have limited spatial mobility, and to create living spaces that nurture men and children but ignore women (for example, dens, family rooms, "master" bedrooms, small and unworkable kitchens, children's playrooms). Also, women's time is constricted and not valued. It is assumed that women's time is unimportant and can be extended at the last minute (for example, waiting for hours at a pediatrician's office, putting in a "few hours" after work without compensation).

Regardless of job responsibilities, men typically assume that the women's time and space are not important:

> I was an account executive and my ex-husband was in sales. He made less than I did but always acted as though my role as wife was more important than my job. This went on for years and I accepted it. The straw that broke the camel's back was the time that he called me at work one morning and said he had invited thirty-five people to a sit-down dinner that evening. When I said that I had to work, he got annoyed: "Well, just take the day off; this is important to me." (Low-level manager in banking industry)

Women's typical reaction reinforces men's attitude that women's time and space are not important. Thus, women change their schedules at the last minute to accommodate men, anticipate men's (and children's) every possible need, and sacrifice their own time and space to those they serve.

Social/professional exclusion. Interaction between present or prospective colleagues/peers also varies by sex. In a study of 459 graduate students at the University of Illinois (at Urbana), Berg and Ferber found that "one of the most significant differences between men and women graduate students . . . was in their interaction with men and women faculty."[55] Especially in the male-dominated fields of physical and biological sciences, 78 percent of the male students and 54 percent of the female students said they had come to know one or more male faculty members "quite well." Because male faculty are more likely to have mentoring resources and provide them largely to male students, women students are at a disadvantage.

Also, women are ignored or sanctioned if they do not meet expectations regarding women's appropriate behavior or attire:

> Men—in comparable positions—can wear anything they want and people listen. But when I stand up to speak, people's attention is focused more on my outfit or figure rather than my verbal contributions. I must be color-coordinated or they won't listen. (Registered nurse teaching specialized courses at a hospital)

Women are excluded because they are in nontraditional positions, roles, or jobs. For example, a female member of the Maryland legislature said that her colleagues do not take women seriously because women are assumed to be "too principled and not political enough." On the other hand, women are ignored if they are tough, aggressive, and political because such behavior is "unfeminine." The only women on the board of trustees of an electric cooperative in a New England community wrote the following about her board's trip to inspect a hydroelectric site:

> When a team of engineers presented a study [on electricity produced by methane], they avoided eye contact with me and spoke directly to the men on the board. It was so obvious that they were presenting their findings "over my head," that I decided to take action in order to demonstrate I had an understanding of the project. I asked a technical question regarding "pelletizing" the dry end product for fuel. It made some difference, but I can see that I have to be ever alert to dealing with subtle discrimination constantly and that I am not being paranoid.

In this situation and others, women are assumed incapable of understanding technical matters, and they will be ignored.

In a recent case of women's exclusion by law firms, Elizabeth Hishon charged that she had been passed over for a partnership, after several years of grueling work in a real estate firm, because she had been evaluated not on the quality of her work but on such intangibles as her "office camaraderie." The Supreme Court ruled that federal anti-discrimination laws apply to partnerships, and Hishon won the right to sue the company for sex discrimination. Although the most prestigious law firms are willing to hire women in 22 to 35 percent of their apprenticeships, female partners rarely exceed a 2 or 3 percent rate.[56] Thus, women are still excluded from the more lucrative, prestigious, and important professional positions.

On a more macabre note, even when women are seemingly accepted as equals during their lifetime, they are relegated to the ranks of "just women" after their death. When NBC's Jessica Savitch died during an automobile accident in 1983, a number of newspapers eulogized and highlighted her personal characteristics rather than her professional accomplishments. An editorial in Baltimore's *Evening Sun* focused on her marriages, miscarriage, looks, and competition from younger (female, of course) anchors: "She was so exquisitely beautiful that she could have been Miss America . . . despite demonstrable talent in her work, there were still whispers that she was 'a bit of fluff,' 'NBC's Playboy bunny.' "[57] When male anchors die, on the other hand, we rarely hear about their affairs, toupees, impotence, biceps, illegitimate children, or other nonprofessional activities and characteristics.

It should be emphasized that the subtle sex processes discussed in this chapter are not exhaustive. There are a variety of other processes that are more ingenuous, sophisticated, and rarely suspected both because they are not immediately visible and because we have been socialized to practice and accept subtle sex discrimination.

The next chapter will examine mechanisms that are even more difficult to uncover and document. This obstacle, however, should not preclude our awareness of the existence and mechanisms of covert sex discrimination.

NOTES

1. Laurel Richardson, "No, Thank You! A Discourse on Etiquette," in *Feminist Frontiers: Rethinking Sex, Gender and Society,* ed. Laurel Richardson and Verta Taylor (Reading, Mass.: Addison-Wesley Publishing Co., 1983), p. 6.
2. Ethel Strainchamps, (ed.), *Rooms with No View: A Woman's Guide to the Man's World of the Media* (New York: Harper & Row, 1974), p. 146.
3. See, for example, Nijole Benokraitis and Joe R. Feagin, *Affirmative Action and Equal Opportunity: Action, Inaction, Reaction* (Boulder, Colo.: Westview Press, 1978); Karen deCrow, *Sexist Justice* (New York: Vintage Books, 1975); and Carol A. Whitehurst, *Women in America: The Oppressed Majority* (Santa Monica, Calif.: Goodyear Publishing Co., 1977).
4. Susan Fraker, "Why Top Jobs Elude Female Executives," *Fortune,* April 16, 1984, p. 46.
5. Nancy M. Henley, *Body Politics: Power, Sex, and Nonverbal Communications* Englewood Cliffs, N.J.: Prentice-Hall, 1977), p. 64.
6. Jonah R. Churgin, *The New Woman and the Old Academe: Sexism and Higher Education* (New York: Libra, 1979), pp. 53–55.
7. Ibid.
8. Nijole V. Benokraitis, "Employment Patterns of Displaced Homemakers: An Exploratory Study" (report submitted to Administration on Aging, March 1981).
9. There is no standard, uniform definition of reentry women in the literature. Throughout this book, a reentry woman is defined as any women thirty years of age or older who has interrupted her education after high school for five or more years and is entering or reentering college for the purpose of completing a baccalaureate degree.
10. Joanna Russ, *How to Suppress Woman's Writing* (Austin, Texas: University of Texas Press, 1983) p. 13.
11. Christine L. Ogan, "On Their Way to the Top? Men and Women Middle-Level Newspaper Managers," *Newspaper Research Journal* 1 (May 1980), pp. 54–55.

12. Eugenia P. Gerdes and Douglas M. Garber, "Sex Bias in Hiring: Effects of Job Demands and Applicant Competence," *Sex Roles* 9 (1983), p. 314.

13. Thomas Boslooper and Marcia Hayes, *The Femininity Game* (New York: Stein and Day, 1973).

14. See, for example, Rees Hughes, "The Non-Traditional Student in Higher Education: A Synthesis of the Literature," *NASPA Journal* (1981), pp. 51–64; Melanie Rawlins, "Life Made Easier for the Over-Thirty Undergrads," *Journal of College Student Personnel* (1980), pp. 65–73; Kathie Smallwood, "What Do Adult College Students Really Need?" *Journal of College Student Personnel* (1980), pp. 65–73; and Loribeth Weinstein, *Field Evaluation Report, Recruitment and Admission: Opening the Door for Re-entry Women* (Washington, D.C.: Project on the Status and Education of Women, 1980).

15. See, for example, Betty Lehan Harragan, *Games Mother Never Taught You: Corporate Gamesmanship for Women* (New York: Warner Books, 1977); Lin Farley, *Sexual Shakedown: The Sexual Harassment of Women on the Job* (New York: Warner Books, 1980); and Michael Korda, *Male Chauvinism and How It Works* (New York: Random House, 1973).

16. Janice LaRouche and Regina Ryan, *Strategies for Women at Work* (New York: Avon Books, 1984), p. 14.

17. See, for example, Stephanie Sanford and Donna Eder, "Adolescent Humor during Peer Interaction" (paper presented at the American Sociological Association meetings, San Francisco, 1982); A. J. Chapman and H. C. Foot, (eds.), *It's a Funny Thing, Humour* (Oxford: Pergamon Press, 1977).

18. Alice E. Courtney and Thomas W. Whipple, *Sex Stereotyping in Advertising* (Lexington, Mass.: Lexington Books, 1983), pp. 127–130.

19. See, also, examples in Beryl A. Radin, "Leadership Training for Women in State and Local Government," *Public Personnel Management* 9 (March-April, 1980), pp. 56–57.

20. Donna J. Benson and Gregg E. Thomson, "Sexual Harassment on a University Campus: The Confluence of Authority Relations, Sexual Interest and Gender Stratification," *Social Problems* 29 (February 1982), p. 243.

21. Cited in Cheryl M. Fields, "Allegations of Lesbianism Being Used to Intimidate, Female Academics Say," *Chronicle of Higher Education* 27 (October 26, 1983), pp. 1, 22–23.

22. Ibid., p. 22. Also, Title IX of the 1972 education amendments bars sex discrimination in federally assisted educational programs and activities.

23. Billie W. Dziech and Linda Weiner, *The Lecherous Professor: Sexual Harassment on Campus* (Boston: Beacon Press, 1984), pp. 122–123.

24. Constance Backhouse and Leah Cohen, *Sexual Harassment on the Job* (Englewood Cliffs, N.J.: Prentice-Hall, 1981), p. 33.

25. See, for example, Sheila M. Rothman, *Women's Proper Place* (New York: Basic Books, 1978); Mary P. Ryan, *Womanhood in America* (New York: Franklin Watts, 1983); and Amy Swerdlow and Hanna Lessinger, eds., *Class, Race, and Sex: The Dynamics of Control* (Boston: G. K. Hall & Company, 1983).

26. Russ, *How to Suppress Women's Writing*, p. 50.

27. See Edwin M. Schur, *Labeling Women Deviant: Gender, Stigma, and Social Control* (New York: Random House, 1984), pp. 33ff., for general and specific discussions of objectification from which some of the characteristics were drawn.

28. These characteristics of "hidden employment biases" summarize and extend Clarice Stasz, *The American Nightmare* (New York: Schocken Books, 1983), pp. 189–190.

29. Karen G. Foreit et al., "Sex Bias in the Newspaper Treatment of Male-Centered and Female-Centered News Stories," *Sex Roles* 6 (1980), pp. 479–480.
30. Charlene E. Christensen, Keith Milner, and James E. Christensen, "An Analysis of Faculty Perceptions of Leadership Qualities of Male and Female Physical Education Departments," *Research Quarterly* 49 (October 1978), pp. 269–277.
31. Benson Rosen and Thomas H. Jerdee, "Sex Stereotyping in the Executive Suite," *Harvard Business Review* 52 (March-April 1974), p. 58.
32. Ibid.
33. "Ensign Meets President," *Evening Sun,* Baltimore, May 25, 1984, E-3.
34. Sharlene J. Hesse, Ina B. Burstein, and Geri E. Atkins, "Sex Role Bias in Public Opinion Questionnaires," *Social Policy* 10 (November-December 1979), p. 56.
35. Jeanne Guillemin, Lynda L. Holmstrom, and Michele Garvin, "Judging Competence: Letters of Recommendation for Men and Women Faculties," *School Review* (February 1979), p. 169.
36. See, for example, Pamela M. Fishman, "Interaction: The Work Women Do," *Social Problems* 25 (April 1978), pp. 397–406; Robin Lakoff, *Language and Woman's Place* (New York: Harper & Row, 1975).
37. Patricia H. Bradley, "The Folk Linguistics of Women's Speech: An Empirical Examination," *Communication Monographs* 48 (March 1982), pp. 73–90.
38. See, for example, S. Robinson, cited by M. A. Ferber and B. Birnbaum, "The Impact of Mother's Work on the Family as an Economic System," in *Families That Work: Children in a Changing World,* ed. S. B. Kamerman and C. D. Hayes (Washington, D.C.: National Academy Press, 1982), pp. 97–98; S. Yoger, "Do Professional Women Have Egalitarian Marital Relationships?" *Journal of Marriage and the Family* 43 (December 1981), pp. 867–81; and J. B. Bryson and R. Bryson, eds., *Dual-Career Couples* (New York: Human Sciences Press, 1978).
39. Jean Curtis, cited in J. Gappa, D. St. John-Parson, and J. O'Barr, "The Dual Careers of Faculty and Family: Can Both Prosper?" (paper presented at the American Association for Higher Education meetings, Washington, D.C., 1982).
40. Roberta M. Hall and Bernice R. Sandler, "Academic Mentoring for Women Students and Faculty: A New Look at an Old Way to Get Ahead" (Washington, D.C.: Project on the Status and Education of Women, 1983), p. 4.
41. *U.S. News and World Report,* August 10, 1981, pp. 55.
42. Sally L. Hacker, "Sex Stratification, Technology and Organizational Change: A Longitudinal Case Study of AT&T," *Social Problems* 26 (June 1979), p. 545.
43. See, for example, Joan Harley and Lois A. Koff, "Prepare Women for Tomorrow's Managerial Challenge," *The Personnel Administrator* 25 (April 1980), pp. 41–42; Christine D. Hay, "Women in Management: The Obstacles and Opportunities They Face," *Personnel Administrator* 25 (April 1980), pp. 31–39; Ellyn Mirides and Andre Cote, "Women in Management: Strategies for Removing the Barriers," *Personnel Administrator* 25 (April 1980), pp. 25–28, 48; and Rose K. Reha, "Preparing Women for Management Roles," *Business Horizons* (April 1979), pp. 68–71.
44. Ellen Cassedy and Karen Nussbaum, *9 to 5: The Working Woman's Guide to Office Survival* (New York: Penguin Books, 1983), pp. 93–94.
45. Ibid., pp. 77–78.
46. Courtney and Whipple, *Sex Stereotyping,* pp. 103–4.
47. Esther B. Greif, "Sex Differences in Parent-Child Conversations," *Women's Studies International Quarterly* 3 (1980), p. 257.
48. Virginia R. Brooks, "Sex Differences in Student Dominance Behavior in Female and Male Professors' Classrooms," *Sex Roles* 8 (1982), p. 688.
49. Schur, *Labeling Women Deviant,* p. 25.

50. A. P. Nilsen, H. Bosmajian, H. C. Gershumy, and Julia P. Stanley, *Sexism and Language* (Urbana, Ill.: National Council of Teachers of English, 1977), p. 32.
51. Example cited in Janice Pottker, "Overt and Covert Forms of Discrimination Against Academic Women," in *Sex Bias in the Schools: The Research Evidence,* ed. Janice Pottker and Andrew Fishel (Cranbury, N.J.: Associated University Presses, 1977), p. 386.
52. Brigid O'Farrell and Sharon L. Harlan, "Craftworkers and Clerks: The Effect of Male Co-Worker Hostility on Women's Satisfaction with Non-Traditional Jobs," *Social Problems* 29 (February 1982), pp. 252–265.
53. Cynthia F. Epstein, *Women in Law* (New York: Basic Books, 1981), p. 286.
54. Henley, 1977. See, also, Gerda R. Wekerle, Rebecca Peterson, and David Moreley, eds., *New Space for Women* (Boulder, Colo.: Westview Press, 1980).
55. Helen M. Berg and Marianne A. Ferber, "Men and Women Graduate Students: Who Succeeds and Why?" *Journal of Higher Education* 6 (November-December 1983), pp. 629–648.
56. "With Justice for Some," *Newsweek,* June 4, 1984, pp. 85–86.
57. "A Fallen Star," *Evening Sun,* Baltimore, October 28, 1983, p. D3.

6

How Covert Sex Discrimination Works

Covert sex discrimination refers to unequal and harmful treatment of women that is hidden, clandestine, and maliciously motivated. Unlike overt and subtle sex discrimination, covert sex discrimination is very difficult to document and prove because records are not kept or are inaccessible, the victim may not even be aware of being a "target," or the victim may be ignorant of how to secure, track, and record evidence of covert discrimination.

Six types of covert sex discrimination are discussed in this chapter—tokenism, containment, manipulation, sabotage, revenge, and co-optation. Tokenism and containment typically prevent large numbers of women from entering high-paying, high-status, powerful positions. Manipulation, sabotage, and revenge are more likely to discourage moving up the ladder. In the corporate world, for example, tokenism and containment ensure that a limited number of women will be hired as supervisors or managers; manipulation, revenge, and sabotage will prevent their moving into higher positions as vice-presidents, presidents, or chairmen of the board. Similarly, in higher education, token women might be hired, especially in male-dominated departments, at the lower levels—that is, as lecturers, instructors, and assistant professors. Whether tokens or not, they will be contained at these lower-level positions with little likelihood of promotion to associate professor or professor. Tokenism and containment are horizontal employment barriers, whereas manipulation, revenge, and sabotage limit vertical mobility.

Because it enlists and rewards women's support for sex inequality, co-optation provides a double dosage of discrimination. That is, women who are co-opted by the system often play an active role in tokenism, containment, manipulation, revenge, and sabotage. In this sense, women may be complicit in maintaining horizontal and vertical discrimination.

TOKENISM

Despite its widespread usage since the 1970s, the term "tokenism" is rarely defined. For our purposes, tokenism refers to the unwritten and usually unspoken policy or practice of hiring, promoting, or otherwise including a minuscule number of individuals from underrepresented groups—women, minorities, the handicapped, the elderly. Through tokenism, organizations maintain the semblance of equality because no group is totally excluded. Placing a few tokens in strategically visible places precludes the necessity of practicing "real" equality—that is, hiring and promoting individuals regardless of their sex.

General characteristics. Across almost all occupational areas and often regardless of age, degree of experience, religion, color, level of education, intelligence, and ability, female tokens are marginal/alienated members of the work group, highly visible, and excluded from entering upwardly mobile opportunities. They experience continuous stress because they are always on display and rarely recognize tokenistic maneuvers.

There is a close relationship between tokenism and powerlessness. For example, Rich characterizes female tokenism as a "false power which masculine society offers to a few women who 'think like men.'"[1] And, according to Laws, "tokenism is likely to be found wherever a dominant group is under pressure to share privilege, power, or other desirable commodities with a group which is excluded."[2] Tokenism is a conscious, calculated effort to avoid charges of discrimination and possible subsequent investigations that might uncover widespread and effective exclusionary policies and practices.

How tokenism works. There are three types of commonly practiced tokenism that limit women's equal participation in the labor force. A popular form is based on *numerical exclusion,* which uses quotas to maintain a predominantly male work force:

> As soon as they come into my office, a lot of recruiters tell me exactly how many women they plan to hire and in which departments. They say things like, "This year we need two women in accounting, one in marketing, and one in data processing." Some [of the recruiters] have fairly detailed data showing exactly how many women they should be hiring for their company.

(What if the most qualified candidates are all women?)

Most recruiters automatically assume that women are *not* the most qualified—they got high grades because they slept around, they're not serious about long-term job commitments, they don't understand the business world and so on. . . . They interview the [women] students we schedule, but rarely hire more than the one or two they're told to hire. (College job placement director)

Because male quotas are high—95 to 99 percent—it is not difficult to fill the low percentage of slots allocated to token women.

Pragmatic tokenism hires and retains women as long as it is cost effective to do so. As long as there is a large pool of talented women who are happy to get any job, have high productivity rates, do not protest about serving as window dressing, and do not demand genuine progress, tokenism runs smoothly. If tokens push for real improvement—especially in salaries—they are often fired. Turnover is inexpensive because there is a plentiful supply of replacements, even at higher levels: ". . . levels of management, as business sees it, that's not a problem. There are already more candidates for management than business could ever use. And the benefits of a cheap labor force far outweigh the dubious value of having a larger pool of managerial talent."[3] This "revolving door" brand of tokenism is profitable for companies because it ensures a continuous flow of hardworking and competent employees at low costs.

In contrast to pragmatic tokenism, *symbolic tokenism* is less transparent because the tokens appear to be treated "just like anyone else"—their salaries are competitive, and some receive training for higher level jobs or hold responsible positions. Despite such embellishments, these women are tokens. They are placed in specially reserved, highly visible niches to symbolize the institution's "commitment to equal opportunity." Because they are always on display, symbolic tokens enjoy some of the accoutrements that accompany all attractive showcases, for example, titles, offices, and expense accounts. Since they are being paid for their visibility and not their credibility, however, they are marginal members of the organization—isolated, excluded from powerful peer networks, and "placed in [sex-stereotypical] role traps that limit effectiveness."[4]

Playing tokenism games with nontokens. Even in those situations where women are not tokens, accusations of tokenism are effective strategies for keeping women "in their place." Such accusations create suspicion; raise doubts about women's intelligence, abilities, and achievements; and decrease competition because women might not enter or might withdraw from the economic race. For example, women who are told that they are being hired to "meet a quota" will sometimes refuse the interview or the job offer:

I have a 3.9 [on a 4.0 scale] and I'm in the top 5 percent of my graduating class. When I went to the interviews at school, the recruiters from two of the biggest firms said they were interested in me because they had to hire women. . . . The more I thought about it later, the angrier I got. Doesn't my 3.9 mean anything? I'm not working for a company which tells me, to my face, that my years of hard work don't mean anything. (Undergraduate accounting major)

Bright and hardworking women may be especially offended by tokenism (when they see it) and turn down attractive offers. On the one hand, they are probably wise not to enter a company or agency that openly treats women as tokens. On the other hand, such refusals reinforce and encourage companies to use tokenism as a successful ploy in discouraging women's entry into jobs.

CONTAINMENT

"Containment" refers to the unwritten and usually unspoken policy or practice of restricting women's entry into designated jobs and positions so as not to threaten or displace the composition of dominant—that is, white male—group members. While tokenism establishes the limits on how many women will be allowed entry into (especially nonfemale) jobs, containment specifies where the entry will take place. Thus, tokenism ensures *quantitative* exclusion, whereas containment ensures *qualitative* exclusion.

Before discussing how containment works, several points should be noted. First, although tokenism and containment are discussed separately here for analytical purposes, the two processes are actually highly interdependent. Although a sequential order is implied, tokenism and containment probably operate simultaneously in most situations. When they are not occurring simultaneously, the order is not significant because both processes are interactive.

Containment relies on first establishing and then maintaining "appropriate" male-female domains in all areas. Containment procedures are learned early, are deeply internalized, and are cumulative.

Establishing male-female domains. In American institutions—the family, economy, polity, religion, education, and military—gender is generally one of the most important predictors of behavior across almost all stages of the life cycle. Because the importance and impact of early gender socialization have been well researched and well documented across numerous disciplines,[5] we will not review these well-known findings here. Suffice it to say that most of us spend the first twenty years of our lives learning and internalizing norms and values that will later make containment in employment perfectly natural, normal, acceptable, and even comfortable.

Using the term in a broader context, women's (and men's) behavior is limited, that is, "contained," from the time they are born. Both sexes learn that girls and boys (and, later, men and women) speak, think, act, dress, smell, feel, play, work, pray, fight, drink, eat, smoke, sit, stand, bend, walk, drive, shop, sleep, make love, write, urinate, belch, and argue *differently*. In these and other activities, men are or should be independent, in control, knowledgeable, and in command; women are or should be dependent, submissive, uninformed, and controlled. What is important is not that men and women are taught to be different, but that women's "different" is seen as *inferior* to men's "different."

Maintaining male-female domains. Upon entering adulthood, some individuals have the opportunity and resources to dig their way out of the avalanche of sexist rhetoric and behavior in which they grew up. Many do not. They do not, in large part, because containment procedures, especially in employment, effectively maintain male-female domains through such activities as mentoring, stalling, demotions/promotions, and exclusion from important decision-making functions.

Mentoring. There is a great deal of consensus that women do not achieve as much as they might in education and employment because they lack mentorship.[6] During a recent national conference on higher education, women faculty and administrators said that one of the barriers for women is a lack of mentorship:

> The hardest thing in academe is that we have all had some degree of success, but we had nobody then and nobody now to help us along.
>
> I have a goal of being a dean, maybe even a college president someday. . . . But how do I go about doing that? I don't know how to get that without mentors.[7]

There is an ever-growing literature applauding and encouraging mentorship between male sponsors and female recipients.[8] Needless to say, women have much to gain from mentors.

Because mentorship processes differ by sex, male mentorship can feed containment. Male mentors often use female mentees to do their "dirty work"—typing, making computer runs, writing first drafts, interviewing, handling correspondence with coauthors or prospective publishers—and do not recognize or reward the mentee's productivity formally, publicly, or monetarily. Thus, the women are "contained" in such positions as research assistant and clerk. Male mentors also promote containment by encouraging mentees to pursue sex-stereotypical specialization or jobs:

> It is true that women traditionally have not become surgeons and have instead pursued specialties such as pediatrics or psychiatry; however, a number of the respondents argued that this was not a "free will choice" but rather was the "line of least resistance. . . ." Several [medical student] women noted that they had been "turfed" to specialties, such as pediatrics, because women were seen by the decision makers as "better in some situations than others."[9]

Male mentors often use female mentees to enhance their own professional status.[10] By being associated with a female mentee, even a chauvinistic male sponsor can curry favor with both liberal men and feminist women. Moreover, since the mentor is not a radical, he is also "safe" within his conservative male circle of colleagues. The male mentor can keep the mentee's work within "acceptable" boundaries that will not jeopardize his professional image among his peers (for example, the mentee does research on women without challenging male dominance). Because the mentee has few options, she will tone down, as directed, her research/writing to appease the male circle of elites and her sponsor's subsequent credibility in that circle. However, because the mentee is doing feminist research, the sponsor will also be applauded in more liberal quarters. Other payoffs are more direct. In business and industry, female mentees who turn out well-written reports, write successful money-making proposals, and generate innovative marketing strategies will create or enhance the mentor's reputation for being intelligent and very productive. In academia, hard-working women can double or triple the mentor's publication rate. Because the mentee is "only an assistant," the male mentor can reap immediate as well as long-term professional and economic benefits.

Stalling. Another effective containment procedure is stalling. When women try to move beyond their token positions (especially in male-dominated areas), supervisors and peers discourage such ambitions through a variety of delaying techniques:

> I worked in the shipping and receiving department but wanted to drive the trucks for more money. My supervisor claimed that he couldn't spare me, that the trucks were difficult to drive (even though I had driven eighteen-wheelers in the past) and that driving a truck would cause trouble with the rest of the women in the department. (Female employee in a parcel service company)

Women's applications for promotion are often "misplaced" or are sent to the "wrong department." After completing the necessary training or educational requirements, women are told that there is a "hiring freeze" even though men are hired. Or, women may give up after waiting, sometimes for several months, because "the committee hasn't met," a key decision maker is "in Europe," or "we can't make a decision until the department has been reorganized."

Demotions/promotions. Another method for maintaining boundaries between men's and women's jobs is to hire women at relatively high levels and later move them into lower-paying or less responsible positions:

> When I was hired, I needed job training to meet the specialized computer needs of the department. Several months went by—no training. I learned some things on my own through trial-and-error, but the progress was slow and I made mistakes. Every time I reminded my boss about the training, he'd say, "In a couple of weeks," but nothing happened. Eight months into the job I was told that my position was being terminated but that I could move into similar positions in other departments. The other positions turned out to be word-processing jobs—at lower levels and lower salaries. After I left, I heard that [Company X] hired a guy in my job and started training him the first day. (Data processor at a large department store)

Thus, an initially promising job can deteriorate, quietly and almost imperceptibly, into a demotion.

Promotions are also used to maintain established male-female employment domains. A female chancellor at a large state university noted that the departments that deal with money and budgets (comptrollers, fund-raising, grants) are led by men; women are promoted as "assistant to" but not "director of" such departments. In legal firms, similarly, women attorneys are "promoted," regardless of specialization, to female-dominated areas:

> My specialty is labor law. The only promotion offers I've gotten were in domestic and family law. The promotions would have meant more money initially, but not in the long run. Divorces, child custody, and all of that are important, but our company sees it as a service, a throwaway. (Female attorney in a large legal firm)

When the draft ended in the early 1970s, the military recruited women to meet projected manpower shortages. The typical route to high ranks in the military is through combat. Because women are not allowed to serve in combat, promotion opportunities are limited to command of support units and other peripheral positions. In the Navy, for example, the 175 women surface-warfare officers who are preparing for sea duty can serve on only 33 of the Navy's 527 ships, and those 33 operate only on the fringes of the fleet—as repair vessels, research ships, tenders (small ships that service larger ships), and the like. As one female officer stated, "To spend twenty years to get to be a captain of a tender isn't enough incentive."[11]

Thus, promotions can maintain containment by ensuring sex segregation—especially at supervisory and managerial levels.

Exclusion from decision-making groups. Even if an individual has been hired into or promoted to an objectively powerful position, another method of maintaining male-female authority is to exclude women from important decision-making processes.

One form of exclusion is not to elect or appoint women to decision-making bodies. In a study of university governance, for example, Muller found that although men and women were equally interested in governance and were equally willing to serve on committees, men were "far more likely to be involved" because women were not asked to serve on committees or were not nominated to represent their peers.[12]

Another common exclusionary device is to set up "separate but equal" male-female programs. The women's programs are headed by women, are visible, and sometimes get public attention. However, because the women are not involved in budgetary decisions or because the women's program is subsumed under men's programs, the equality is only cosmetic. In the area of athletics, for example, regardless of level (high school, college) or locus of control (county recreation departments, state government, education boards), the allocation of resources of girls' and women's athletic budgets are male controlled and male dominated.[13]

Finally, screening by gatekeepers also creates and maintains containment. Gatekeepers are individuals who examine an applicant's credentials and decide who is qualified or unqualified for employment consideration. They may act independently (as a personnel director) or within a larger collectivity (as a union or referral agency). According to Harragan, "employment agencies and executive-search agencies serve as the screening agent to eliminate women from companies which cannot be caught doing it themselves. This goes on in a very underhanded, covert way, so ambitious women have to play a most sophisticated form of corporate politics when dealing with placement firms."[14] Although Harragan does not describe the "sophisticated . . . politics" directly, she implies the problems through a discussion of such circumvention techniques as dealing with headhunters, what to omit from resumes, and how to deal with past and prospective employers.[15]

It should be remembered that containment procedures are interlocking and cumulative:

$$\text{gatekeeping} \longleftrightarrow \text{stalling}$$
$$\downarrow$$
$$\text{exclusion from decision making} \longleftrightarrow \text{promotions}$$
$$\uparrow$$
$$\text{mentoring}$$

For example, in higher education, a faculty search committee may be the gatekeeper. The committee often rejects applicants who are not like them using a variety of formal (Ph.D. degree, publications, teaching experience) and informal (sex, physical appearance, personality) criteria. As discussed in Chapter Five, either the committee or the dean (or both) can use stalling techniques to discourage qualified candidates. Even if a woman is hired, her exclusion from important decision-making bodies (as personnel and budget) will negatively affect both her own chances for promotion ("She has never served on important committees") and those of other women (by not being an associate or full professor, she cannot participate in groups that determine the criteria for promotions). Without tenure and a higher rank, her influence on mentees can be very restricted in terms of time, status, and academic freedom. On the other hand, available mentors will supervise mentees in ways, as discussed above, that justify and maintain the status quo.

Whether it is a university search committee or a job interviewer in business or industry, the gatekeepers are typically men who are uncomfortable in dealing with women. According to a consultant for several Fortune 500 companies, the biggest hurdle women face is fitting in with male managers: "At senior management levels, competence is assumed. . . . What you're looking for is someone who fits, someone who gets along, someone you trust. . . . How does a group of men feel that a woman is going to fit in? I think it's very hard."[16] Similarly, in a study of 173 male and female managers at two companies, Harlan and Weiss found that women managers felt that male managers excluded women from informal mentoring situations:

> Sometimes I see store managers that invite the guys for coffee in the morning because they feel comfortable and they can talk sports with the guys or whatever it might be. But they leave out their women department managers. And

when you do that, the guys are getting more information than the girls are to work with because while you're sitting there having coffee, you might be talking about the Red Sox, but most of the time you're talking about what we're going to do with the department here or whatever we're going to do with this . . . or business in general.[17]

Because women are excluded from informal get-togethers by gatekeepers, they can be contained more easily within entry-level positions.

As noted earlier, tokenism and containment determine *how many* women will enter certain occupational positions and *where* they will be located. Whereas tokenism and containment limit women's entry, manipulation, sabotage, and revenge discourage their occupational *progression* and actively encourage job *exits*.

MANIPULATION

There are a number of effective manipulative strategies that discourage women's economic progress. Questioning or casting aspersions on a woman's qualifications or ability will threaten, weaken, or subvert a woman's power, credibility, and usefulness. If, especially, the woman is seen as a "troublemaker," male superiors "may insinuate that the misbehaving woman is basically incompetent, which may lead other women to fear being associated with her cause."[18]

I've been working for this operation for six years. Our supervisor makes a point of reminding me and the other women of our routes and transfers almost every week even though the written schedules are posted on the bulletin board. He treats us as though we can't remember what we're supposed to be doing. (MTA bus driver)

If a woman holds a formal position of power and authority, men (and women) subordinates can manipulate the female superior into not recognizing and not using her power by bypassing her in the organizational structure. Bayes and Newton provide an example of this in their analysis of a mental health organization where, in one department, male staff members were subordinates and a woman was the superior:

When senior male staff spoke to her [Dr. A., the female superior] about their work, it was in the spirit of obtaining her consultation to them, thereby obfuscating their subordinacy. They struggled to be independent of her, to distance themselves from her authority. They had difficulties in accepting criticism from Dr. A. and would go to great lengths to defend their work. For her part, Dr. A. found herself being excessively cautious in offering a negative assessment of male staff members' work.[19]

Another manipulative strategy is to give women undesirable jobs under the guise of "equal treatment":

Some of us [women] have more seniority than men but our schedules are changed more often, we get the undesirable routes, and the buses we're assigned are in the worst possible working order. When we go to the union meetings to complain, there is always a male driver who complains that women are "too soft for the job" and reminds us that we can't expect any "special treatment." (MTA bus driver)

Such "hazing" is not uncommon in some jobs and is a way of "testing" new employees—regardless of sex. We have found in our research, however, that women undergo such treatment for a much longer period than men and that such "testing" is a justification for assigning women, under the equal opportunity cloak, to unpopular, dirty, and sometimes dangerous jobs (for example, bus drivers, construction workers, police officers).

SABOTAGE

Through sabotage, employers and employees purposely and consciously undermine or undercut a woman's position. Although sabotage can be contrived and carried out by individuals, it usually involves covert agreements between two or more persons. Because sabotage is difficult to prove, it is also easy to deny. In almost all cases, it comes down to "my word against yours" because saboteurs do not leave a "paper trail."

Sabotage strategies vary by degree of sophistication, which depends on whether the woman is in a traditionally female job, a traditionally male job, or a job in which boundaries are, in principle, nonexistent because they are, in practice, not job related.

Traditionally female jobs. In traditionally female jobs (domestic, service, clerical), male sabotage is normative, because men at a comparable job level have higher status (owing to higher wages) or because men have supervisory positions. In terms of the latter, for example, there is a substantial literature documenting male supervisors' sexual harassment of women subordinates because, among other things, men expect women to service all their (real or imagined) needs at all levels. Thus, office workers are the most common targets of sabotage if they don't "put out."

In comparable job levels, men can use sabotage because their job functions are less vulnerable to inspection and represent higher control than those of women:

I was hassled by the bartender and the male kitchen staff. When you're a waitress, you have to keep in the good books of the guys backing you up. If the bartender takes a dislike to you, he can slow down on your orders to the point where you get no tips at all. The kitchen staff can sabotage you in other ways. The food can be cold, it can arrive late, and orders can be all mixed up.[20]

In traditionally female jobs, male sabotage is blatant, unmasked, raw, and unsophisticated. It is used openly to control and take advantage of women's inferior job status.

Traditionally male jobs. In traditionally male-dominated jobs, sabotage strategies are more sophisticated. In contrast to the "good ole boys" mentality, which literally and proudly espouses a "women-are-good-for-only-one-thing" rhetoric, traditionally male job occupants react to women negatively because women are seen as potentially threatening the "old gang" cohesion, camaraderie, and esprit de corps. Such fears may be justifiable since there has been historical proof that women can do many "men's jobs" (as witnessed during World War II) and because, more recently, "quota hiring" has shown that many "men's jobs" can be done more than adequately by women.

Because the traditionally male jobs in such occupations as law enforcement, construction, and manufacturing are considerably higher paying than traditionally female jobs and because women are vulnerable to layoffs owing to political machinations and inflation, women's entry and success in traditionally male jobs are especially problematic: The economic competition becomes stiffer, and social relationships are potentially jeopardized. Women serving in such "combat" jobs as law enforcement and fire fighting are treated suspiciously by co-workers' wives, are excluded from lunches and social gatherings by peers, and are continuously treated like women rather than co-workers by the men, who scurry to hide girlie magazines and "watch their language."[21]

In an effort to preserve long-accepted strongholds over men's jobs, men use a variety of sabotage techniques to discourage women's participation and success in traditionally male jobs:

> I've been in this job nine years and I still have problems with the guys. About a year ago, whenever I returned from my route, I'd find a bunch of mail that I hadn't picked up. The district manager said I wasn't doing my job and gave me an undesirable [high crime] route. I found out later that the district manager gave my route to a new guy who was a friend of the family. (Black female mail carrier)

> My co-workers would watch me talking to customers. When I went in to get the paperwork, they'd ridicule me to the customers. "She hasn't been here that long," "Women don't know much about cars." Then, they'd go over the same questions with the customers and get the sale. (Automobile salesperson)

> Every time there's a promotion (for corporal), I put my name in. I always get rejected even though I have seniority, have put in the same number of years on the street as the guys, and have the same firing range results as the men. When there's a temporary opening, a sergeant from another precinct is pulled into the temporary spot even when I request the assignment. . . . I think my supervisor is trying to mess up my work record purposely—I'm the last one to find out about special events and new cases, and I have been late for important meetings because I was told about them five or ten minutes before they start. (Female police sergeant)

Ever since I became a meter reader, the guys have always teased me that I'd be attacked by dogs, raped, kidnapped, or not return. . . . That's scary, but I tried to ignore it. . . . What gets me is that sometimes I get to the customer's house and none of the keys I picked up fit. I have to go back to the company to get the right keys. I don't know who's doing it, but someone doesn't want me in this job. (Seven-year meter reader for a gas and electric company)

In contrast to women in female-dominated jobs, women in male-dominated jobs find that they are "set up" to fail but are not told, openly, that this is due to their gender.

Sex-neutral jobs.   The most sophisticated sabotage strategies occur in professional, technical, and administrative (and sometimes sales) jobs where sex is totally irrelevant to job performance. Because these occupations do not require physical strength but require professional or academic credentials (Ph.D., J.D., M.A., M.S.) and longer and more specialized training, there is presumably a greater objective reliance on sex-neutral qualifications. That is, being a chemistry professor requires neither such "female" traits as a "cute" figure and pleasant personality (often required in female-dominated jobs) nor the muscles to lift 1,000-pound test tubes (often required in male-dominated jobs). One would expect, then, that sex-neutral jobs would be the least discriminatory. Such expectations have not proven to be true.

Quite to the contrary, sex-neutral jobs are often the most discriminatory because they are the most threatening to males dominating the higher echelons of the economy. The sabotage techniques are so subtle and covert that women see the sabotage long after it is too late to do anything about the discrimination:

One mid-level manager [at a nationally known company] said she had gotten excellent ratings from her supervisors throughout her first year of employment. In the meantime, the company psychologist had called her in about once a month and inquired "how things were going." She was pleased by the company's interest in its employees. At the end of the year, one of her male peers (whose evaluations were known to be very mediocre) got the promotion and she didn't. When she pursued the reasons for her non-promotion, she was finally told, by one of the company's vice presidents, that "anyone who has to see the company psychologist once a month is clearly not management material." She had no way of proving she had been sabotaged.[22]

In other examples, a female insurance agent is directed by the manager to nonelitist client accounts (in contrast to her male counterparts) and then not promoted because her clients take out only "policies for the poor"; an urban renewal administrative assistant who is more qualified than her supervisor (and is frank about wanting his job) finds the information in her folders scrambled over a period of months and is told that her "administrative chaos" will lead to a demotion; and a faculty member in an all-male political science department is thanked for her committee and advising work but dismissed because of insufficient publications, while her male counterpart, who has several publications (because he has been protected from committee or advising work), is promoted.

Besides these and other adroit sabotage maneuvers, some strategies are less subtle but equally effective: "Not to be overlooked in the list of possible institutional responses [to sex equality] are outright lying, distortions of the truth, omission of information, and misleading statements. . . ."[23]

REVENGE

Revenge, especially when it is done creatively, is effective in limiting women's upward mobility. Revenge punishes vocal women who complain about sex inequality and discourages open criticism from observers. A study of women in the newsroom showed that women who sued their employers found themselves writing more obituaries, working more graveyard shifts, and passed over in promotions. Even when out-of-court settlements have included promises to remedy discriminatory practices, management has pursued such vengeful activities as moving women laterally but listing the moves as promotions in the house letter and giving inflated experience ratings to new male employees so that men's starting salaries were higher than those of women with equal experience.[24]

Women who sympathize or appear to sympathize with the complainant(s) or their colleagues may also become targets of revenge:

> After [Company X] settled out-of-court, there was a great deal of resentment. Even the women who benefited from the settlement were hostile toward them [the women who had filed the class action suit]. To ease some of the tension, I got permission and some money to organize a workshop to discuss future opportunities. I was very careful. . . . I hired some men as speakers, provided a light lunch, and sent out attractive, carefully worded but upbeat invitations. The turnout was modest, but not a single man showed up —not even the guys in management who had approved the workshop and paid for it! About three months later, my position was abolished. They changed the title and hired a man. (Assistant director of personnel and labor relations in manufacturing)

Besides being punished for her seemingly sympathetic stance toward the women who sued the company, in this case the respondent may also have been sabotaged. By supporting the workshop on paper, management had proof that the company was not bitter about the settlement and was showing an interest in improving the work climate for women. Yet the "troublemaker" was fired. After she lost the job, some of her co-workers said, privately, that the workshop had been described as "creating even more conflict," "divisive," and "anti-management." As in other forms of covert discrimination, there was no "hard evidence."

Men, and especially non-minority men, who endorse women's rights may be seen as "biting the hand that feeds them" and "betraying the system" and may be punished accordingly. Some reprisals are economic: salaries may be frozen, prestigious jobs taken away, and fringe benefits decreased.[25] Other reprisals, equally effective, include social ostracism, name-calling and jokes about being "a sissy" or being "gay," and polite exclusion from "the boys'" basketball games during lunch or drinks after work. Most men are very aware of such reprisals and avoid incurring the wrath of their male peers. They are especially careful about their relationships with feminists:

> Of the [43] male faculty, I'm pretty good friends with two of the men. We read each other's work, go out to lunch once in a while, drop by each other's office and call each other almost on a daily basis. But, you know, if they're going to lunch with a couple of the other guys and I bump into them, they *never* ask me to join them. They're cool and businesslike and act as though they barely know me. Even worse, when they're in my office, they criticize sexist remarks that they laughed at during a committee meeting two hours earlier. . . . [Pause] . . . Maybe you should be doing research on unpaid whores. . . . (Woman faculty member in a computer science department)

This woman's feeling that some of her best male friends are "pimps" is not unique. A number of the women we spoke to reported being treated very differently by their male "friends" in public and private situations. Some of the women understand and even accept such contradictory behavior because, ironically, they don't want the men to be hurt by reprisals. According to a woman hospital administrator:

> One of the doctors is also a family friend. His wife is a nurse. When we get together socially, we spend hours discussing the crap that nurses get from doctors. He's more radical than his wife and keeps encouraging me to fight for nurses' rights at the hospital. Not too long ago, I sent around a proposal to modernize the nurses' stations and to increase the salaries of the nurses who teach specialized courses at the hospital. I heard that [Doctor X] jumped all over the proposal and made some snide remarks about hospital administrators.
>
> (Have you ever talked to him about the ridicule?)
>
> Oh, no. I was very hurt. . . . My feelings toward him have changed. . . . But why bring it up? He's not going to change the other doctors' attitudes anyway. Why should I ask him to jeopardize the respect he gets from the other doctors?

Both at home and especially in the workplace, promoting women's equality or associating with women who are fighting for women's rights often results in social and economic reprisals for both men and women. Revenge is a clandestine but very effective way of keeping the status quo.

CO-OPTATION

Co-optation refers to the process of bringing selected women into the system and then using these women to control the entry and promotion of other women—through subtle and covert sex discrimination mechanisms.

Co-optation can be a source of upward mobility. Because mobility is severely limited (there are always more applicants than available positions), the co-opted typically attribute their progress to their own intelligence, success, and hard work. That is, they identify themselves with a handful of "deserving elite": "The token woman is encouraged to see herself as different from most other women; as exceptionally talented and deserving; and to separate herself from the wider female condition; and she is perceived by 'ordinary' women as separate also. . . ."[26]

By improving the position of a few women, co-optation reinforces the subordinate position of the majority of women. Scattering a few women throughout seemingly powerful positions gives the appearance that the institution recognizes talent and is "sex blind" and egalitarian; it also implies that there are few women in top levels because most women are unqualified or not competitive enough. Co-optation encourages blaming the self rather than the social structure. Thus, the status quo is maintained.

If, moreover, the co-opted are also gatekeepers, the responsibility for sex equality shifts from the dominant group to the co-opted. Thus, the dominant group can be "innocent bystanders" while the (few) women maintain group solidarity against "outsiders" (that is, other women).[27]

Finally, co-optation provides false role models to other women. Women who are newcomers to the job market, are unaware of covert sex discrimination, or are in isolated positions may assume, mistakenly, that the co-opted *really* did "make it" on their abilities, are powerful, and are worthy of imitation, respect, and admiration.

THE (IN)SIGNIFICANCE OF MERIT

Merit is commonly evoked to justify or rationalize the unequal distribution of rewards and resources. Merit is "determined" through formal and informal procedures that are typically undefined, uncodified, and vary across individual situations, agencies, organizations, and states.

Formal procedures. The civil service was established in the 1920s to replace upper-class favoritism and patronage by politicians with more "objective" selection procedures based on merit.[28] Although neither the civil service nor other groups have ever defined merit nor established criteria for measuring merit, there are a variety of formal methods for determining merit—seniority, credentials, IQ tests, exams, grade point averages, and numerous licensing procedures.

Regardless of the method used, the results of trying to determine merit have not been scientific, objective, or "fair" for several reasons. First, what do we mean by merit? Do we mean those individuals who are deserving of rewards because they are hardworking, intelligent, self-sacrificing, able, or talented? One of these characteristics? Two? All? Second, there is often no relationship between merit, ability, and rewards.

Material rewards *do* seem to be necessary, not to attract people to do "important" jobs, but to get them to do dull and uninteresting ones that make very little use of their abilities. Not that all the so-called important jobs always require much ability, either. A great many highly paid executive and professional jobs are not particularly difficult, and the conditions of work connected with them often demand little effort or product.[29]

Third, although merit remains undefined, the measures used to gauge merit—such as IQ tests—are seriously flawed and may be measuring social class and environment rather than ability or intelligence.[30] Fourth, because exclusion is based on ascribed rather than achieved characteristics, large groups of the population, because of their age, sex, or race, will be eliminated from competition at birth, without any evaluation of their accomplishments. Finally, even when formal measuring instruments are developed, they are not applied uniformly because of waivers (for example, veterans preference), temporary appointments, or special titles.[31]

Informal procedures. Merit decisions based on informal procedures are even more subjective, personal, intuitive, and capricious.[32] Informal procedures include word-of-mouth recommendations, referral through friendship or work networks, reference letters, class-based affiliations (such as belonging to the same social clubs), alumni donations, nepotism, custom, and tradition:

> Traditionally, medical schools have given favored treatment to people of privilege. [In 1973] . . . the Chicago Medical School admitted favoring 77 out of 91 applicants on whose behalf pledges of financial support were made. In 1976, the dean at Davis verified news reports that he had a few "special interest" slots which allowed him to place children of wealthy, powerful, or famous parents. A dean at a Pennsylvania school, Hahneman, said that half of all applications included letters from politicians and that such pressures sometimes swayed committees.[33]

Basically, informal merit procedures are based on selecting people with whom the incumbents can identify, feel comfortable, and interact easily within and outside the work environment—in other words, "someone like me." Thus, women will be seen as outsiders, intruders, and interlopers and will be avoided accordingly. Because informal merit criteria and selection are unwritten, however, they are extremely effective mechanisms of covert discrimination.

Both formal and informal merit criteria and selection procedures often ignore a great deal of talent, ability, creativity, and promise:

> The stupidity problem—the plain fact that so many of our leading men are, at best, only marginally more competent than the average person, and, at worst, downright incompetent—is the direct result of our misplaced faith in tests, in the "proving ground of education," and in other formal and informal methods of picking out the "best men."[34]

We typically assume that merit is an important and fair method of differentiating between the "winners" and the "losers." We assume that the most powerful, the rich, and those in leadership positions *must* be meritorious or else they would not be rich, powerful, and in leadership positions. We continue to place our blind faith in merit as an important ideological guidepost even though merit remains undefined and unmeasured. Finally, we continue to assume that merit is working even though we continuously see evidence to the contrary. Most of us fail to consider the possibility that evaluations based on merit use merit as a weapon to reduce competition and resources rather than as a valid measure for rewarding hard work and talent regardless of one's sex.

By categorically excluding women (as well as minorities, the elderly, and other groups), our merit systems have largely ignored the abilities and intelligence of some of the "best and the brightest." The consequences of ignoring women through overt, subtle, and covert discrimination are discussed in the next two chapters.

NOTES

1. Adrienne Rich, "Privilege, Power, and Tokenism," *Ms* (September 1979), pp. 42–44.
2. Judith Long Laws, "The Psychology of Tokenism: An Analysis," *Sex Roles* 1 (January 1975), p. 51.
3. Janice LaRouche and Regina Ryan, *Strategies for Women at Work* (New York: Avon Books, 1984), p. 113.
4. Rosabeth Moss Kanter, *Men and Women of the Corporation* (New York: Basic Books, 1977), pp. 248–249.
5. See, for example, Margaret L. Anderson, *Thinking about Women* (New York: Macmillan Publishing Co., 1983); James A. Doyle, *The Male Experience* (Dubuque, Iowa: Wm. C. Brown Company Publishers, 1983); Marie Richmond-Abbott, *The American Woman: Her Past, Her Present, Her Future* (New York: Holt, Rinehart and Winston, 1979); E. Friedl, *Women and Men* (New York: Holt, Rinehart and Winston, 1975); Rhoda K. Unger, *Female and Male: Psychological Perspectives* (New York: Harper & Row, 1979).
6. See, for example, Elizabeth M. Almquist and Shirley S. Angrist, "Role Model Influences on College Women's Career Aspiration," *Merrill-Palmer Quarterly* 17 (1971), pp. 263–279; Lucia A. Gilbert, Jude M. Gallessich, and Sheri L. Evans, "Sex of Faculty Role Models and Students' Self-Perceptions of Competency," *Sex Roles* 9 (no. 5, 1983), pp. 597–607; Peter V. Marsden, "Restricted Access in Networks and Models of Power," *American Journal of Sociology* 88 (1983), pp. 686–716.
7. Liz McMillen, "Despite New Laws and Colleges' Policies, Women Say Sexism Lingers on Campus," *Chronicle of Higher Education,* February 6, 1985, p. 28.
8. See, for example, Breda M. Bova and Rebecca R. Phillips, "The Mentoring Relationship as an Educational Experience," ERIC Documents, ED 224944 (1976); E. Collins and P. Scott, "Everyone Who Makes It Has a Mentor," *Harvard Business Review* 56 (July-August 1978), pp. 89–101; Roberta M. Hall and Bernice R. Sandler, "Academic Mentoring for Women Students and Faculty: A New Look at an Old Way to Get Ahead" (Washington, D.C.: Project on the Status and Education of Women, 1983); Elizabeth J. McNeer, "Two Opportunities for Mentoring: A Study of Women's Career Development in Higher Education Administration," *Journal of NAWDAC* 47 (Fall 1983), pp. 8–14.

9. Diana Kendall and Joe R. Feagin, "Blatant and Subtle Patterns of Discrimination: Minority Women in Medical Schools," *Journal of Intergroup Relations* 9 (Summer 1983), pp. 16-17.
10. This paragraph relies heavily on Laws, "The Psychology of Tokenism."
11. Francine Schwadel, "Women Move Up in the Military, But Many Jobs Remain Off Limits," *Wall Street Journal,* March 14, 1985, p. 33.
12. Julia K. Muller, "Interest and Involvement of Women in University Governance," *Journal of NAWDAC* 42 (1978), pp. 10-15.
13. See Patricia Huckle, "Back to the Starting Line," *American Behavioral Scientist* 121 (January-February 1978), pp. 379-392.
14. Betty Lehan Harragan, *Games Mother Never Taught You: Corporate Gamesmanship for Women* (New York: Warner Books, 1977), p. 158.
15. Ibid., pp. 158-164.
16. Susan Fraker, "Why Top Jobs Elude Female Executives," *Fortune,* April 16, 1984, p. 46.
17. Anne Harlan and Carol Weiss, "Moving Up: Women in Managerial Careers" (Wellesley, Mass.: Wellesley College Center for Research on Women, 1981), p. 53.
18. Virginia E. Pendergrass, Ellen Kimmel, Joan Joestring, Joyce Peterson, and Edilee Bush, "Sex Discrimination in Counseling," *American Psychologist* 31 (January 1976), p. 38.
19. Marjorie Bayes and Peter M. Newton, "Women in Authority: A Sociopsychological Analysis," *Journal of Applied Behavioral Science* 14 (November 1978), p. 15.
20. Constance Backhouse and Leah Cohen, *Sexual Harassment on the Job* (Englewood Cliffs, N.J.: Prentice-Hall, 1981), p. 9.
21. See, for example, Karen Stabiner, "The Storm over Women Fire-Fighters," *New York Times Magazine,* September 26, 1982, p. 100.
22. Nijole Benokraitis, "Sex Discrimination in the 80s," *Maryland Women* (Baltimore, Md.: Maryland Commission for Women, 1983), p. 4.
23. Pendergrass et al., p. 30.
24. Terri Schultz-Brooks, "Getting There: Women in the Newsroom," *Columbia Journalism Review* (March-April 1984), pp. 27, 29.
25. Ibid., pp. 28-29.
26. Rich, "Privilege, Power, and Tokenism," p. 44.
27. Laws, "The Psychology of Tokenism," p. 59.
28. See V. Subramanian, "Representative Bureaucracy: A Reassessment," *American Political Science Review* 61 (December 1967), pp. 1010-1019.
29. William Ryan, *Equality* (New York: Vintage Books, 1981), p. 84.
30. See Leon J. Kamin, *The Science and Politics of I.Q.* (Potomac, Md.: Lawrence Erlbaum Associates, 1974).
31. See Samuel Krislov, *Representative Bureaucracy* (Englewood Cliffs, N.J.: Prentice-Hall, 1974).
32. See Marx W. Wartofsky, Ivan Berg, Jr., Mary F. Berry, Butler A. Jones, Beatrice G. Konheim, Margaret L. Rumbarber, and William W. Van Alstyne, "Affirmative Action in Higher Education: A Report by the Council Commission on Discrimination," *AAUP Bulletin* 59 (Summer 1973), pp. 178-183.
33. Clarice Stasz, *The American Nightmare: Why Inequality Persists* (New York: Schocken Books, 1981), p. 113.
34. Ryan, *Equality,* p. 82.

7

Minority Women

INTRODUCTION

On May 29, 1984, one of America's most talented journalists, Leanita McLain, committed suicide at the age of thirty-two. Even at this young age, she had already won numerous major journalism awards. She was the first black person to serve on the *Chicago Tribune*'s editorial board in its 137-year history. *Glamour* magazine had acclaimed her as one of the most outstanding working women in the United States two months prior to her death. Why did such a brilliant and talented woman commit suicide? A complete answer would doubtless be complex, including McLain's troubled private life as well as her workday life. But one key factor looms large in her despair: the problem of coping with a culturally different, often discriminatory white world. The writer Bebe Moore Campbell has assessed the culture shock faced by black women like McLain who must live in the white world: "Black women consciously choose their speech, their laughter, their walk, their mode of dress and car. They trim and straighten their hair. . . . They learn to wear a mask."[1] They often face sex discrimination from male peers and superiors. They suffer from white prejudices and subtle suggestions that they are in their high position only because of affirmative action, not because of their talent. And they suffer greatly from moving away from their backgrounds, their cultural ties to friends and relatives who remain in the ghetto. They feel, as Leanita McLain herself wrote, very guilty: "I am uncomfortably middle class."

Historical background. The women's movement in the nineteenth century was led mostly by white women, but it had its roots in the freedom struggle of black slaves. White feminists such as Elizabeth Cady Stanton were sensitized to sexual oppression by their involvement in the antislavery movement. They were abolitionists before they were feminists. But by the 1860s sex discrimination had become a major concern, so much so that vigorous arguments raged between male and female abolitionists, with most male abolitionists arguing that "this is the black man's hour." To this argument, Stanton replied that women, black and white, could not wait:

> Some say, "Be still, wait, this is the negro's hour." But I believe this is the hour for everybody to do the best thing for reconstruction. A vote based on intelligence and education for black and white, man and woman—that is what we need. . . .
> You say, "this is the negro's hour." I will not insist that here are women of that race, but ask, is there not a danger that he, once entrenched in his inalienable rights, may be an added power to hold us at bay? Why should the African prove more just and generous than his Saxon compeers? Again, if the two millions of Southern black women are not to be secured in their rights of person, property, wages, and children, then their emancipation is but another form of slavery.[2]

Stanton was one of the first to emphasize the importance of black women being secured in their rights of person and property. She was also emphasizing that women, black and white, were as much in need of liberation as black male slaves. At least since the middle of the nineteenth century the causes of black and female liberation have been linked; a major reason for this is that black women are in both groups.

In the twentieth century race and sex discrimination have been closely linked as well. The Equal Rights Amendment (ERA) for women, not yet a part of the U.S. Constitution, is patterned closely after a nineteenth-century amendment to the Constitution, the 14th Amendment, which guarantees equal rights for blacks, particularly black men. Moreover, the most important of all anti-bias legislation passed since 1900, the 1964 Civil Rights Act, was first phrased only to prohibit employment discrimination on the basis of race, religion, and national origin. A conservative member of the U.S. House, Howard Smith, introduced an amendment to include sex in the prohibition, hoping to kill the entire bill by including a provision male liberals could not accept. However, after a vigorous struggle, Smith's amendment was passed. Women activists were struggling at the time to get sex discrimination included in the amendment. Their pressure helped offset the efforts of conservatives who thought that including women would sabotage the legislation.

This congressional history illustrates that the world faced by minority women is not just a man's world, but a white man's world. The world of employment is dominated by white, usually Anglo, male employers and managers. The world of education is dominated by white male administrators and teachers. The world of politics is dominated by white male presidents, legislators, judges, and local officials. Just because there are a few white, black, and brown women scattered about, often as tokens, does not mean that the employment, educational, and political worlds are desegregated. Naomi Sims, a black businessperson, has recently noted that

> This is a white man's world, and the fact that there are a few black women legislators, judges, college presidents, and self-made millionaires does not prove that most of use are on the move. The majority have to fight pitched battles every step of the way up—first to get a decent education, then to get a job, and after that we must struggle to get income parity and promotional opportunities.[3]

FIGHTING PITCHED BATTLES:
BLACK WOMEN AND UNEMPLOYMENT

A job as freedom? Black women have been holding down steady jobs outside the home for more than three centuries: first as slaves, then as poor farmers, and, in the twentieth century, as maids, restaurant and laundry workers, and, more recently, clerical workers. Black women have had to work for their own survival and the survival of their families. The proportion of black women in the labor force has long been higher than that for white women. In 1960 only 37 percent of white women were in the labor force, compared to 83 percent of black women. By the mid-1980s the white figure had grown to just over half, still much lower than the three quarters of black women who were working outside the home. Black women have struggled in jobs outside the home, often serving as the chief breadwinners because of racial discrimination against black males, discrimination resulting in low wages and high unemployment. Because of this long history of required work, black women today come to the work place with a different view from that of white males and many white females. Black women do not typically define themselves solely in terms of their work, their occupations. They are used to thinking in terms of home and family. Yet they must compete in a job world where many white males define themselves primarily in terms of their occupations. If the job requires a neglect-the-family attitude for success, such as a sales job requiring travel, this attitude may have a particularly severe impact on black women who are used to putting their families first. This is also a problem for many white women. Immigrant women have worked, in large numbers, outside the home since the turn of the century, because often their husbands could find jobs only as laborers or as transient, migrant workers—jobs that have been extremely low-paying (often below the minimum wage), have not been unionized, and have rarely provided severance pay or health and medical benefits. More recently, working- and middle-class white women have entered the work force to help the family to keep up with inflation.

The double day is so pervasive because most white working women still accept sole responsibility for domestic and child-care responsibilities and work in low-paying jobs that supplement, rather than maintain, the family income. Such problems are magnified for many minority women who have to work to keep their families alive.[4]

The fact that black women have had to work has led some to suggest that black women are already "free." In one sense this view may be true. Black women have not had the excessively sheltered or protected lives led by many white women. The need for freedom from the "housewife prison," a view articulated by predominantly white women's liberation groups, has not been a need for black women, who have long had the "freedom" (necessity!) to work outside the home. On the one hand, this necessity to work has allowed black women to develop great strength of personality and an extraordinary ability to survive. Housework has never been the only concern for black women, as it has been for many white wives in middle- and upper-income families. Most black women have worked extremely hard inside and outside the home, a double struggle that has made them more self-reliant.[5] On the other hand, black women have been subordinated and exploited in their jobs outside the home. The freedom to develop personally was sharply limited in the cold reality of daily work.[6]

Anthropologist John Gwaltney interviewed a black woman from Tennessee who told him her father used to say that the "only two people who were really free was [sic] the white man and the black woman." Yet this woman went on to say that her father was wrong. Life had taught her that neither black men nor black women were truly free. By the time of the interview she had worked for sixty-four years "busting the white man's suds and mopping the white man's floors and minding the white man's kids." From her point of view the only people who are free in this world are "the people that can tell other people what to do and how they have to do it." Exploited labor outside the home does not make one free, just a different type of servant.[7]

THE EFFECTS OF SEX AND RACE DISCRIMINATION

What type of work have black women done? What sort of incomes do they have? Do they face high unemployment?

Black women, as Cheryl Gilkes has pointed out, started out with a 100 percent labor force participation rate. Whether girls or women, they worked in the field, factories, and homes of the white male governing class. Most female slaves worked in the fields.[8]

After slavery, most black women remained in the fields of the South, as farm workers, sharecroppers, and tenant farmers. Many also served as domestic workers, a group that grew in numbers as blacks left the fields for towns and cities. In 1890 there were 2.7 million black girls and women over ten years of age; out of this number more than one million were wage workers. Virtually all worked as sharecroppers or agricultural workers, as private maids (domestic service), or as laundry workers. As they moved north, blacks moved into domestic service; in 1899 fully 60 percent of the black workers in the state of Pennsylvania were domestic workers.[9] In 1919, 77 percent of black women employed outside the home still worked as farm laborers or private household workers (maids). Two decades later, only 12 percent were farm workers, but fully 60 percent were still private household workers, mostly in the cities.[10] In 1960 about 38 percent were private household workers; by 1984 the percentage had dropped to only 6 percent, as black women finally moved into new job categories, particularly those occupied by white women.

Employment Today

Today a large proportion of black women are employed in white-collar jobs, particularly clerical jobs such as typists. The occupational breakdown in Table 7.1 shows that black women are much more similar in their job distribution to white women than to white or black men. Although white women hold a higher percentage of managerial and professional jobs than black women (23 versus 16 percent), the proportions of white and black women in clerical jobs are similar. Black women are much more likely than white women to hold low-paid maid and other service jobs. It is also clear in Table 7.1 that white men predominate in the better-paying categories such as managerial and precision craft jobs. The differences between men and women workers are even greater than these data suggest, since within these categories women hold the lower-level, lower-paying positions. In recent years much has been made of the educated black women who have moved up into better-paying professional and managerial jobs. According to U.S. Bureau of the Census data,

TABLE 7.1. Occupational Distribution by Race and Sex, September 1984 (Percentage*)

OCCUPATION	WHITE MEN	BLACK MEN	WHITE WOMEN	BLACK WOMEN
Managerial workers	14	6	9	5
Professional workers	12	6	14	11
Technical workers	3	2	3	3
Sales workers	12	5	14	8
Clerical and support workers	6	9	30	25
Precision craft workers	21	16	2	3
Machine operators, assemblers	8	11	7	12
Transportation workers	7	11	1	1
Handlers and laborers	6	11	2	2
Private household workers	0	0	2	6
Protective service workers	2	4	1	1
Other service workers	6	14	15	23
Farmers, farm workers	6	4	1	1

Source: U.S. Department of Labor, Bureau of Labor Statistics, *Employment and Earnings,* October 1984 (Washington, D.C.: Government Printing Office, 1984), table A-23.
*Columns do not add up to 100 percent because of rounding.

about one-fifth of employed black women fall into the professional/technical/ managerial category. Yet this official tabulation is misleading because many of the jobs placed there are low-paying and not what the public would think of as professional or managerial; that is, the category includes dieticians in elementary school cafeterias, café and bar managers, and practical nurses. Very few are lawyers, doctors, corporate managers, or architects. Higginbotham has pointed out that most black women professionals, such as teachers and nurses, have worked in segregated settings. Even today, black professionals are "found in agencies and hospitals located in Black communities and serving Blacks, Latinos and other people of color." They are "colonized professionals" dependent on public sector agencies—many of which have seen major governmental cutbacks in the 1980s. Three quarters of black women work outside this white-collar category and for the most part earn relatively low wages.[11]

Domestic household workers are said to be an "obsolete" job category rapidly disappearing from U.S. society. Yet, as Judith Rollins has emphasized, the number of women in this category is the same as it was a hundred years ago. There is some evidence that it may be a growing category. Today a disproportionate amount of this "dirty" work is being done by minority women. And it is very low-wage work, because many employers ignore the law passed in 1974 that requires a minimum wage for private household workers. In 1982 domestic workers averaged only $2,433 a year; those who worked full-time, year-round, averaged only $5,883. Employers also ignore the legal requirement (since 1951) to pay social security for domestics. In addition, few domestics receive the fringe benefits common to other workers.

One of the most significant aspects of this work is that it is done for other women. White middle- and upper-income women, Rollins notes, use the physical labor of these women to free themselves for more enjoyable and prestigious activities and thus "to enhance their sense of self worth and provide ideological justification for the hierarchical social structure which affords them privilege."[12] These predominantly nonwhite domestics are exploited not only in material terms, in getting the most work for the lowest wage, but also in psychological terms. In her research report Rollins cites the emphasis on deference and the treatment of domestics as "children" or "inferiors." From her own experience as a domestic and from interviews with domestics and their employers, Rollins concludes that white women as employers feed off "the low paid labor and the personhood of the domestic" in ways that make the employer's life-style better.[13]

The exploitation of both white and nonwhite domestic women workers reflects the larger issue of male domination of economic systems. For many people, the work place provides a sense of identity, self-esteem, and self-worth. Because the work world is expected to fulfill men's and not women's social and emotional needs, women are often exploited. As we discussed earlier, "Queen Bees" are manipulated by male gatekeepers to discourage women's advancement. In the case of domestics, white women employers are often "middlemen." Their husbands control the money and decide how much domestic work is worth. Since household work is not seen as "real work" by men and many women ("I don't work; I'm a housewife"), women employers are unlikely or powerless to argue for higher wages for domestics.

Another important related factor is social class. Because men control money, the more money a man has the more able he is to marry ("buy") an attractive, young woman who will enhance his social and business image. One of the earmarks of being successful or wealthy is having domestic help. This is especially prestigious if the domestic help is a "live-in" rather than "just a cleaning lady." The former symbolizes "real" affluence. Both white and nonwhite middle and upper classes may have domestic help to show that the husband is successful. If the wife has exchanged her good looks for his money, she will be grateful to have the time to attend beauty spas, exercise classes, and recreational activities that will prolong her youthful appearance. It is unlikely that she will be aware of such social issues as the economic exploitation of domestic help or will challenge *his* decisions about how *he* spends *his* money.

Unemployment. The impact of cutbacks in the public and private sectors can be seen in official unemployment statistics. The unemployment rate for black women has been much higher than that for white women, as can be seen in the data in Table 7.2. For black female teenagers the 1982 figure was 47 percent, compared to only 22 percent for white females. The black female unemployment rate has been double that of the white female and male rates for many years. In addition, the underemployment rate, which includes those with very low wages and those who work part-time but want full-time work, together with those so discouraged they have given up looking for work, is very high for black women—at least 30 to 35 percent of all black women workers.[14]

TABLE 7.2. Unemployment Rate for White and Black Women (Percentage)

YEAR	WHITE WOMEN	BLACK WOMEN
1972	5.9	11.8
1977	7.3	14.9
1982	9.4	17.6

Earnings. Black and Hispanic women have also suffered from low incomes, as can be seen in Table 7.3.[15] In every year the typical earnings for white men exceeded the earnings of black, white, and Hispanic women. White men earn much more per week in wages and salaries than any of the women. In terms of earnings from full-time work, minority women are closer to white women than to minority men. This is because minority women mostly hold "women's jobs" and because women's wages in general are lower than those of men.

TABLE 7.3.   Median Weekly Earnings for Full-time Wage and Salary Workers

YEAR	WHITE MEN	BLACK MEN	WHITE WOMEN	BLACK WOMEN	HISPANIC WOMEN
1970	$157	$113	$ 95	$ 81	n.a.
1975	225	173	138	130	n.a.
1980	329	247	206	189	177
1982	382	281	244	223	207

In 1983 the median annual incomes for full-time, year-round workers were as follows:

White men	$23,114
Black men	16,410
White women	14,677
Black women	13,000
Hispanic women	11,870

We again see that white men earn far more than all other groups and that minority women's incomes are closer to those of white women than to those of black men. Black women raising children on their own are particularly likely to be poor because of the cumulative impact of sex discrimination in employment and wages, as well as higher unemployment and underemployment rates. In 1983 more than half (57 percent) of all black people in families headed by a female fell below the government poverty level, compared to less than a third of comparable whites.[16] Besides low earnings, minority women have minimal employment benefits. In a 1982 study of black employed women, Woody and Malson found that only slightly more than one-fourth of black women earners were covered by pension plans, and only about one-third had access to group health coverage in the work place.[17]

Education. Black women as a group are not in lower-paying jobs because they are poorly educated. Data (1982) on the years of school completed for people over twenty-five years of age show the following:

White men	12.7
White women	12.5
Black men	12.2
Black women	12.1
Hispanic women	10.7

With the exception of Hispanic women, the differences in education by race and gender are generally modest. White men as a group have a slight educational advantage over white and black women. Yet the job and income differences between white men and white and black women are much greater than the education differences.[18] The comparable educational levels between men and women show that black and Hispanic women are not less qualified than their male counterparts and should be employed at higher occupational levels than at present. The data show that these women merit egalitarian consideration. As the previous discussion on merit pointed out, however, women are not recognized or rewarded, because there is little relationship between individual achievement and ideologies based on merit.

The consequences of lower incomes. Because black women live in families with significantly lower incomes than those of white families, they often find themselves without some of life's necessities, including nutritionally adequate food. In 1980 the critical infant mortality rate (infant deaths per 1,000 live births) and the maternal mortality rate (maternal deaths per 1,000 live births) differed significantly by race: The infant mortality rate was 11.0 for whites and 21.4 for blacks; the maternal mortality rate was 6.7 for whites and 21.5 for blacks. Black infants under one year of age die at about twice the rate of white infants, largely because of poverty related causes: the low and moderate incomes of black mothers, inferior food and nutrition, poor housing, and inadequate medical care (particularly during difficult deliveries). Black mothers, for similar reasons, die at three times the rate of white women. It is clear that childbirth is more dangerous for black women than for white women.[19]

Matriarchs with higher incomes? Much social science and popular writing about black women has portrayed them as domineering matriarchs with greater income and power than black men; this matriarchy is allegedly responsible for a broad range of social problems in black ghettos. Yet the data on black husband-wife families show otherwise. Because of sex discrimination in jobs and wages, black women make even less money than their husbands. In low-income black families, for example, 85 percent of the husbands make more than their wives. Decision-making patterns in husband-wife families are typically egalitarian. Hill's review of the relevant data shows that black women tend to have more power than white women in family settings, but that in most black families decision making is shared or balanced. Since black men are actively involved in family decisions, the stereotype of black men as "castrated" by black women is inaccurate.[20]

SEX DISCRIMINATION IN THE WORK PLACE

Minority women face the double jeopardy of sex and race discrimination on the job. For minority women, sex discrimination takes the numerous forms we have noted in previous chapters. The literature on minority women that we have reviewed gives special attention to sexual harassment in the work place. A survey by the Working Women United Institute found that, in general, women in blue-collar jobs encounter sexual harassment more often than women in clerical and professional jobs. But it is black women, in blue-collar and white-collar categories, who seem to experience the most sexual harassment. Indeed, studies of sexual harassment have found that black women are twice as likely to be victims of sexual harassment as white women.[21] Reviewing the evidence on racism and sexism, MacKinnon has suggested that "black women's reports of sexual harassment by white male superiors reflect a sense of male impunity that resounds of slavery and colonization."[22] During slavery, thousands of black women slaves, from ten to sixty years of age, were raped by white men, including owners and overseers, who considered them to be personal property. Even after emancipation, white men in the South could rape black women with impunity. Black officials serving during Reconstruction worked hard to protect their wives and daughters from white men. After Reconstruction, the new powerlessness of blacks meant a return to sexual exploitation by white males on a large scale.

Evidence for MacKinnon's point can be found in a number of major court cases filed by black women. In the 1977 court case *Miller* v. *Bank of America* a black women, Margaret Miller, presented evidence that a white male superior had promised her a promotion if she would be sexually "cooperative" with him.[23] In building her case, Miller suggested that her employer, the Bank of America, allowed men in practice and in policy to sexually harass women employees. Bank officials, however, argued that cases such as these were personal examples of sexual harassment for which the bank itself should not be blamed.

In another important case, *Barnes* v. *Train,* a black woman in the federal Environmental Protection Agency charged that her white male boss had conducted a "campaign to extract sexual favors," including sexual remarks and numerous sexual propositions, and that after she refused, her superior removed her job duties and eventually got rid of her position. Barnes was unsuccessful in appealing her case to the Civil Service Commission and lost her suit in federal district court on the grounds that an isolated supervisor's actions were not covered by Title VII of the Civil Rights Act which banned sex discrimination in employment. However, a federal appeals court overruled the district court judge, determining that Barnes was indeed the victim of illegal sex discrimination:

> But for her womanhood, from aught that appears, her participation in sexual activity would never have been solicited. To say, then, that she was victimized in her employment simply because she declined the invitation is to ignore the asserted fact that she was invited only because she was a woman subordinate to the inviter in the hierarchy of agency personnel. Put another way, she became the target of her superior's sexual desires because she was a woman, and was asked to bow to his demands as the price for holding her job.[24]

White men are the major agents of sexual harassment of black women employees, because white men are more likely than other men to have the power to retaliate against women who reject sexual advances. Yet there are cases where minority men have harassed minority women, particularly in government employment settings. An example of this has been documented in *Williams* v. *Saxbe (Bell).* Williams, a black woman, reported that her black male supervisor in the federal Department of Justice had "engaged in a continuing pattern and practice of harassment and humiliation of her."[25] She argued that after she rejected his advances, she had been isolated by her black male superior and given unwarranted reprimands. Her recommendations, as a professional, were ignored by her superior. The federal district court ruled in her favor and asserted that retaliatory actions by male superiors for rejection of sexual propositions by women employees constitute sex discrimination under the law.

In a major Michigan court case a recently separated black woman, Maxine Munford, found herself at a new job because of her need to support two children. Hired as an assistant collections manager, Ms. Munford soon found herself to be a sexual target of her white boss. On her first day she was propositioned by her boss, who asked if "she would make love to a white man." After refusing many suggestions that she have sexual intercourse with him, she was fired. Her protests about the unjust firing were rejected by her boss's superiors, and she filed suit against the company on the grounds of sex discrimination. Holding that this type of harassment is sex discrimination, the federal court ruled that an employer has a duty "to investigate complaints of sexual harassment and deal appropriately with the offending personnel."[26]

Discrimination of this type has persisted into the mid-1980s. A black female television producer in Los Angeles recently described an incident she had in a hallway after a conversation with a top white male executive: "As I turned to leave, he swatted me on the behind with a rolled-up newspaper. I was in a state of shock."[27] This behavior is widespread. John L. Jones, an affirmative action executive at Xerox Corporation, recently pointed out that sexism is a major problem for black women in white-collar work.[28] This sexism does not affect only women in white-collar jobs. Sexual harassment is also faced by the million women, mostly minority, who work as maids and servants. In her study of domestics in Boston, for example, Rollins found a number of examples of sexual harassment. All the domestics she interviewed said they preferred working for a woman rather than a man, with the clear implication being the high risk of sexual harassment from a man.[29]

EDUCATION: ANOTHER ARENA FOR DISCRIMINATION

One study of high school seniors, male and female, black and white, found that the educational aspirations of black females were higher than those of white females and only a little lower than those of white males.[30] Yet when they move into educational settings, minority women face some real barriers to the achievement of their aspirations.

The impact of white male cultural dominance can be seen in our educational institutions, which are in the business of molding new students to fit established ways of doing things. In an analysis of minority women in medical schools, Diana Kendall has highlighted the cumulative impact of sex and race discrimination. Most dominant group members in medical school faculties and student bodies remain convinced that every medical school student and graduate should adapt to the white male mold. In Kendall's research, one Mexican American respondent defined the requirements of that mold:

> Not only do we have to fit the "Anglo mold," which sees medicine as curative rather than preventive, and which is impersonal and disease-oriented, we also have to fit the "male mold," which is aggressive, competitive, authoritative, a "take charge attitude," and a "little boys don't cry" bit. Furthermore, we have to try to think like they do culturally if we want good evaluations because you have to be aggressive in patient management, but not too aggressive; you have to ask questions and get involved with the patient, but not emotionally involved. The whole thing is like walking a picket fence.[31]

The fence that minority women students walk can be seen in the grades and evaluations given to these students during their clinical years in medical school. An example of how the white male mold shapes student evaluations is seen in these statements of two different doctors evaluating the same Puerto Rican woman medical student. The first evaluation is from an affluent, white male medical professor at a hospital:

> This student consistently had difficulty in relating to . . . house staff and some patients. Her behavior, at times, was inappropriate and it was our feeling that she failed to appreciate her limitations as a student. She seemed to resent and have difficulty coping with authoritarian [sic] figures. Her manner, at times, was quite overbearing, demanding, and quite frankly, inappropriate. Unfortunately, her personality problems tend to overshadow her work as a student. . . . Although intellectually we feel she could make a physician, unless she is able to correct her personality deficiencies, her future as a physician remains questionable.[32]

The Puerto Rican student must change herself to fit the mold. In sharp contrast to his comments are the statements of other physicians with whom this same student had worked in neighborhood clinics in the city. Typical of these comments are the following:

> She is clearly a bright, energetic and capable person and has demonstrated both independence and initiative in a situation where there is little supervision available. . . . Her relationship with other people was good, she was cooperative and flexible in situations requiring teamwork, and she accepted direction and criticism willingly.
>
> She demonstrates a broad intelligence, a refreshing individuality, integrity, and most of all, courage in opposing pretense and rigidity.
>
> _____, of all students, is very intent on the patient's welfare. She is not interested in power, in prestige, in making money. . . . She has the potential for being an unusual and outstanding doctor, the potential for being a doctor in settings that most students couldn't handle. Most of them are going to practice in white suburbia.[33]

The first doctor's evaluation compared this Puerto Rican woman to the white-male subcultural mold and concluded that she had "personality deficiencies." The second doctor compared her to the sort of doctor needed for a more diverse set of minority patients and concluded that she was excellent, the type of doctor that was needed in these settings. This minority student's career was nearly terminated by her white male professors because of her inability and unwillingness to fit the prescribed mold.

Black female students may also find a subtle type of categorizing in professional schools. One black female student stated that the way she was regarded at a teaching hospital—physicians sometimes mistook her for a nurse or cleaning lady—was devastating to her self-concept and therefore extremely stressful:

> I spend half my time on rotations explaining to everybody who I am. Some of the attending physicians and residents think I'm a nurse; others think I'm a ward clerk. Worse yet . . . some of the patients think I'm there to clean up their room. I have to keep telling people I'm a medical student even though that's what my name tag says. White male students don't have this problem because they start to dress, walk and talk like doctors and everybody says, "Oh yes, there's Dr. Smith," even when they aren't really doctors yet. They still call me by my first name.[34]

Even if this student's claim that half her time was spent explaining her status as other than a cleaning lady or nurse was overstated, it nonetheless points up a major problem that many minority women face. This problem can consume such large amounts of physical and mental energy that a minority student may not do as well in her medical (or other) studies as comparable white males, who do not have to spend additional energy defending themselves from subtle and covert sexist and racist attacks.

Jokes and other comments made about minority women patients have been reported by students as having an impact on them personally. Black women students have expressed frustration about the "off-the-wall" comments made about the "sexual promiscuity," "frequent reproductive habits," and "welfare" status of many black patients, as evidenced by this statement by a fourth-year black woman student in a medical school:

> A lot of the residents say really crude things right in front of black women patients . . . just as if they weren't present . . . about their size or about their reproductive habits. In one case we had a black woman who had complications after giving birth to her fourth or fifth child, and the residents and an attending physician kept talking right in front of her about how she needed to "learn how to hold her legs together."[35]

Another black woman student complained to a dean about an obstetrics professor who kept talking about "illegitimate black babies" and "illegitimate black mothers" without reference to white illegitimacy; the student was told to drop the matter because the professor held a "powerful position on the clinical committee."

Yet another problem facing black and other minority women students in educational settings is the absence of role models. There are few minority women teachers, particularly in college settings. One second-year black woman student reported that at her school, "the only black female role models are down scrubbing the floor or working in food service."[36]

THE PROBLEM OF VIOLENCE

Black women, like white women, are the victims of sex-related violence, of wife beating and rape. Rape is often discussed by the average white American in racial terms, as though all rape is the responsibility of black males. But white male sexual attacks on black women are a problem that has long been neglected.

Until recently, U.S. laws on rape were rarely enforced, except in the case of black men, many of whom were fraudulently accused of raping white women. Although most rapes occur between members of the same race, in cross-race rapes, the rape of black women by white males has been far more commonplace than the white fantasy about black men raping white women suggests. We previously noted the long history of white males, particularly in the South, being able to assault black women, sexually and otherwise, with no fear of being punished. This pattern, while on the wane, is still a serious problem for black women in some parts of the United States.[37] Black women have been raped by police and prison officials. In 1975, Joanne Little, a prisoner in a North Carolina jail, was accused of killing a white guard; on the stand she said the white guard had threatened her with an ice pick and raped her. Black organizations supported her. She was acquitted.[38] However, much rape of black and other nonwhite women simply goes unreported. We have previously noted the sexual vulnerability of black domestics to the husbands of their female employers and of black women elsewhere to sexual harassment. At its most extreme, harassment means forced sexual intercourse—rape.

In addition to attacks from white males, black women also face rape from black males in their home communities. Violent discrimination along sexual lines can occur at work or at home. Gwaltney, an anthropologist, found that many of the black women he interviewed were concerned about robbery and assaults from young black men in their communities.[39]

THE RELATIVE WEIGHT OF RACE AND SEX

We have already seen how both race and sex factors are important in the double-jeopardy oppression faced by minority women. In some cases their sex is the most important factor in the discrimination they face. In other cases race is the most important factor. And in many cases these factors play a joint role in the difficulties encountered.

In her examination of the occupations held by black and Hispanic women,

Almquist found that minority status was more important than sexual status in determining the *amount* of education that minority women get. Because they are often segregated residentially and because of their subordinate racial position, minority women tend to get less education than whites. But Almquist also found that sexual status was more important than racial status in determining the *type* of education that minority women get. Minority women are channeled into female jobs in the work place. Almquist compared minority men, minority women, and white women across the 350 specific job categories in the U.S. work force and found that minority women were much more similar in job distribution to white women than to minority men. In regard to occupation, "the net impact of being a woman is stronger than the net impact of being a minority group member."[40]

WOMEN'S LIBERATION MOVEMENTS: PRIMARILY FOR WHITES?

One might expect that black women, given their longtime presence outside the home, would be the leaders in the women's liberation movement. Yet they have not been active in that movement in large numbers. Naomi Sims has dramatized the caught-between dilemma of black women who try to move into mainstream jobs and culture. She asks whether black women should ally themselves with the oppressed group of black men or with the also oppressed group of white women:

> Can we trust either, as a group? Are we ever able to get ahead *because* we are Black or women, or only *despite* those attributes? Is our struggle one for racial parity. . . . Could it be that what we really want, deep down, is participation in the American Dream of a comfortable bourgeois existence, with the mortgage paid and the kids in college?[41]

How feminist are black women in their views of the world? A research study of opinion poll surveys examined the question of whether black women are more feminist than white women in their support of women in politics or of women working outside the home. This study found only small differences between the two groups, with substantial majorities of both black and white groups taking a feminist position. The study did find that black men were a bit less supportive than white women or black women, as well as less supportive than white men. Black men were more supportive of traditional sex roles for women than white men, although they were *more* liberal than white men on other social issues. In addition, other surveys of sex-role attitudes have found that black working women are more likely than white women to identify with such traditionally "masculine" job qualities as being career oriented, independent, and self-assured. These studies have found that black women emphasize "feminine" qualities, such as the importance of the nurturing role of the mother in the families. In this way they are androgynous, sharing both "masculine and feminine" qualities.[42] The attitudinal studies suggest that black women strongly hold to feminist attitudes about women in the work place, in careers, and in politics, Yet they also are strongly supportive of their homes and their children. This unique combination of views helps explain some of the differences of opinion among black women about the women's liberation movement.

In the early 1970s, Joyce Ladner wrote that the "problems to which members of Women's Liberation groups are addressing themselves are far less relevant to Black women."[43] Ladner argues that the enemies of black women are not black men, but rather the oppressive race discrimination that attacks black women, men, and children. Ladner argues that black men need support, not a movement of equalization between the sexes. Many minority men have echoed the sentiment that "women's lib" was irrelevant to minority women. Minority men, and even some white men, have tried to discredit the feminist movement in the eyes of minority women. A variety of myths have been created to support the view that feminism is not relevant: that the black woman is already liberated, that racism is the primary oppression black women confront, and that women's movement issues are too narrow.

But since the mid-1970s, black feminists have challenged these myths. In the 1980s the challenge has become very articulate and aggressive. For example, Barbara Smith, writing in 1976, pointed to the irony in the anti-feminist position among blacks:

> Feminism is potentially the most threatening of movements to Black and other Third World people because it makes it absolutely essential that we examine the way we live, how we treat each other, and what we believe. It calls into question the most basic assumption about our existence and this is the idea that biological, i.e. sexual identity, determines all, that it is the rationale for power relationships as well as for all other levels of human identity and action. An irony is that among Third World people biological determinism is rejected and fought against when it is applied to race, but generally unquestioned when it applies to sex.[44]

Black feminist politics has grown out of the black civil rights movements of the last few decades. A recognition that progressive and civil rights movements are often male dominated and sexist in operation has led some black women to organize to fight racism and sexism. Thus one issue black feminists have emphasized is racism in the (white) women's movement: "As black feminists we are made constantly and painfully aware of how little effort white women have made to understand and combat their racism."[45] But, as Barbara Smith has pointed out, sex discrimination cuts across racial groups. Sex discrimination does exist in black communities. Smith suggests that a "Black feminist perspective has no use for ranking oppressions, but instead demonstrates the simultaneity of oppressions as they affect Third World women's lives."[46]

Smith also points out that the women's liberation movement not only includes narrow and reformist perspectives but also more radical and critical views as well, with the latter being advocated by some white women as well as by nonwhite women.

Black feminist organizations have not received much publicity from the mainstream media, but they have expanded and prospered since the mid-1970s. In 1977 the Combahee River Collective, a black feminist group formed in Boston in 1974, issued a political manifesto that said that "we are actively committed to struggling against racial, sexual, heterosexual, and class oppression."[47] Black feminists have helped to set up a Third World women's clinic in Berkeley, California, and a women's Self-Help Collective in Washington, D.C. They have played a role in establishing battered women's centers in several cities. In 1980 they held the First National Conference on Third World Women and Violence in Washington, D.C. In addition, they have established journals and newsletters to link minority women together across the nation.

The black feminist movement has great potential for alleviating the feeling among many black women that they are the "mules of the world," to use Zora Neale Hurston's phrase. Barbara Smith suggests that the black feminist movement "clarifies the nature of the Black women's experience, makes possible positive support from other Black women, and encourages political actions that will change the very system that has put us down."[48] A major impulse from the black and Third World feminist movements has been that of seeing that oppressive experiences in employment, education, housing, and the legal system cannot be neatly distinguished into racism and sexism, for both types of oppression are reflected in everyday lives.

NOTES

1. Bebe Moore Campbell, "To Be Black, Gifted, and Alone," *Savvy* 5 (December 1984), p. 69.
2. Theodore Stanton and Harriet Stanton Blatch, eds., *Elizabeth Cady Stanton* (New York: Arno Press, 1969), vol. 2, pp. 109–110.
3. Naomi Sims, *All About Success for the Black Woman* (Garden City, N.Y.: Doubleday, 1982), p. 169.
4. Ibid., pp. 12–14.
5. Angela Davis, *Women, Race and Class* (New York: Random House, 1981), pp. 231–233.
6. Joyce Ladner, *Tomorrow's Tomorrow: The Black Woman* (New York: Doubleday Anchor Books, 1971), pp. 274–277.
7. John L. Gwaltney, *Drylongso* (New York: Random House Vintage Books, 1980), pp. 143–144.
8. Cheryl T. Gilkes, "From Slavery to Social Welfare," in *Class, Race, and Sex: The Dynamics of Control,* ed. A. Swerdlow and H. Lessinger (Boston: G. K. Hall, 1983).
9. Davis, *Women, Race and Class,* pp. 87–89.
10. Elizabeth Higginbotham, "Work and Survival for Black Women," in *Class, Race, and Sex: The Dynamics of Control,* ed. A. Swerdlow and H. Lessinger (Boston: G. K. Hall, 1983).
11. Ibid., p. 13.
12. Judith Rollins, "Employing a Domestic: A Case of Female Parisitism" (paper

presented at the annual meetings of the American Sociological Association, August 1984), p. 4.

13. Ibid., p. 14.
14. U.S. Bureau of the Census, *Statistical Abstract of the United States, 1984* (Washington, D.C.: Government Printing Office, 1984), p. 422.
15. Ibid., p. 434.
16. U.S. Bureau of the Census, *Money Income and Poverty Status of Families and Persons in the U.S.: 1983, Current Population Reports,* series P-60, no. 145 (Washington, D.C.: Government Printing Office, 1984), pp. 12–13.
17. Bette Woody and Michelene Malson, "In Crisis: Low Income Black Employed Women in the U.S. Workplace" (Wellesley, Mass.: Wellesley College Center for Research on Women, Working Paper No. 131, 1984).
18. U.S. Bureau of the Census, *Statistical Abstract of the U.S., 1984,* p. 144.
19. Ibid., p. 77.
20. Robert B. Hill, *The Strengths of Black Families* (New York: Emerson Hall Publishers, 1972), pp. 19–20; Robert Staples, *Black Masculinity* (San Francisco: Black Scholar Press, 1982), p. 9.
21. Sims, *All About Success for the Black Woman,* p. 179.
22. Catherine A. MacKinnon, *Sexual Harassment of Working Women* (New Haven: Yale University Press, 1979), p. 30.
23. Miller v. Bank of America, 418 F. Supp. 233,236 (N.D. Cal. 1977).
24. Barnes v. Costle, 561 F.2d 983 (D.C. Cir. 1977), at 992, n. 68. We are drawing here on the summary of the case in MacKinnon, *Sexual Harassment of Working Women,* p. 68.
25. Williams v. Saxbe, 413 F. Supp. 654, 655 (D.C., 1976).
26. Cited in MacKinnon, *Sexual Harassment of Working Women,* pp. 30, 74.
27. Campbell, "To Be Black, Gifted, and Alone," p. 73.
28. Ibid., p. 72.
29. Rollins, "Employing a Domestic," p. 16.
30. Walter R. Allen, "Family Roles, Occupational Statuses, and Achievement Orientations among Black Women in the U.S.," *Signs* 4 (Summer 1979), pp. 683–686.
31. Diana Kendall and Joe R. Feagin, "Blatant and Subtle Patterns of Discrimination: Minority Women in Medical Schools," *Journal of Intergroup Relations* 9 (Summer 1983), pp. 21–22.
32. Ibid., p. 22.
33. Ibid., pp. 22–23.
34. Ibid., p. 24.
35. Ibid., p. 24.
36. Ibid., p. 27.
37. Herbert G. Gutman, *The Black Family in Slavery and Freedom* (New York: Random House, 1976), pp. 387–390.
38. Davis, *Women, Race and Class,* p. 174.
39. Gwaltney, *Drylongso,* passim.
40. Elizabeth McTaggart Almquist, "Race and Ethnicity in the Lives of Minority Women," in *Women: A Feminist Perspective,* ed. Jo Freeman (3rd ed., Palo Alto: Mayfield, 1984), pp. 445–447.
41. Sims, *All About Success for the Black Woman,* p. 169.
42. Edward Ransford and Jon Miller, "Race, Sex and Feminist Outlooks," *American Sociological Review* 48 (February 1983), pp. 51–52; Marjorie R. Hershey, "Racial Difference in Sex-Role Identities and Sex Stereotyping," *Social Science Quarterly* 58 (March 1978), pp. 583–596.

43. Joyce Ladner, *Tomorrow's Tomorrow*, p. 277.
44. Barbara Smith, "Notes for Yet Another Paper on Black Feminism," in *Conditions: Five, The Black Women's Issue*, vol. 2, no. 2 (Autumn 1979), p. 124.
45. Combahee River Collective, "A Black Feminist Statement," in *Capitalist Patriarchy and the Case for Socialist Feminism*, ed. Zillah Eisenstein (New York: Monthly Review Press, 1979), p. 371.
46. Barbara Smith, *Home Girls* (New York: Kitchen Table—Women of Color Press, 1983), p. xxviii.
47. Ibid., p. 362.
48. Ibid., p. xxv.

8

The Consequences of Sex Inequality

INTRODUCTION

Women's increased participation in the labor force has produced benefits for both men and women. Many women enjoy the creative outlet, adult interaction, challenge, economic rewards, and self-confidence that a job outside the home may bring. Men also have experienced more options when their wives are working outside the home. For example, men feel less stress if the family's economic welfare is not solely their responsibility. They can take more risks, leave dissatisfactory situations, and look for better jobs if their wives' income provides "unemployment insurance." A working wife may be more sympathetic toward and supportive of a husband who is unhappy with his job if she also is dealing with problems at work. In addition, her greater independence can enhance the husband's autonomy and bring about a more egalitarian adult relationship. Some of the women in our study reported that after they started to work outside the home, they became less dependent on their husbands to provide "stimulating conversations" at home, started reading newspapers more regularly (to keep up with friends at work), and were more accepting of their husbands' time away from home.

> Our relationship improved after I started working. We talked about more things, he opens up more about problems at work, and he treats me like an

adult, not just a wife. . . . He's even asked for my opinion when he gets into a disagreement on politics with his buddies. (Real estate agent)

My husband is in sales and he spends about 60 percent of his time on the road. We used to fight about it all the time—especially after the youngest started school. I resented being alone, going to parties alone or not going because I felt uncomfortable among all the couples. After I started working, I made new friends and got involved in new activities. [Laugh.] My husband sometimes complains that I'm hard to keep up with, but I think he enjoys not getting pressure from me about traveling. (Saleswoman in department store)

Some of the men and women we interviewed felt that children of working mothers become more self-sufficient, more participatory in family responsibilities, more mature, less pampered, less self-centered, and more realistic about prospective adult work roles. Only future studies can determine whether such beliefs are rationalizations or accurate portrayals. Until then, at least some adults report having positive experiences with children growing up in households where the mother is employed outside the home.

Even some of the battles surrounding sex inequality in the work force have had positive effects. Many men and women have developed clearer expectations about their own goals, a more sophisticated perspective about institutional constraints, a greater sense of economic stability, and less fear about changing sex roles. Encountering sex inequality has resulted in the reappraisal by some men and women of historically rigid and exploitative gender roles, and the development of relationships that are based on intellectual rather than primarily sexual interests.

Despite these positive effects, sex inequality has widespread negative consequences on individuals, organizations, and society as a whole. In the real world, these effects overlap and are cumulative. For analytical purposes they will be discussed separately.

NEGATIVE EFFECTS ON INDIVIDUALS

Sex inequality has detrimental psychological, emotional, and career consequences for both men and women as individuals. These negative effects cross age, race, religious, and occupational boundaries.

Emotional and psychological effects. Because we place a high value on individual responsibility and success, women who encounter sex discrimination blame themselves rather than discriminatory practices and institutional structures. One consequence is that they become defensive, question their own abilities and talents, and withdraw from potentially rewarding situations:

I was our unit's representative on an important company-wide committee to develop better communications between the marketing, sales, manufacturing and R&D divisions. But nine times out of ten, my comments were ignored, attacked, or ridiculed, even though a number of my suggestions were implemented later under someone else's name. I decided I don't communicate well and resigned from the committee. (Mid-level manager in manufacturing)

Unlike men, women are taught and expected to be passive, to accept being ignored or ridiculed, and to take the blame when things go wrong. Thus, the effects of sex inequality are emotionally more harmful to women than to men.

During our many years of teaching, we have seen many women students accept poor grades on exams and papers almost automatically, with such docile and self-deprecating statements as "I guess *I* just didn't work hard enough," "*I'm* probably just not college material," and "My parents said *I* wasn't ready for college." Most male students, on the other hand, argue immediately that their low performance is not their fault: "I don't think *you* understood what I was trying to say in this paper," "I've heard that *you're* a really tough grader," "*You* didn't lecture clearly." Even though women often have more role conflicts than men, women are considerably more likely than men to blame themselves rather than others. Unlike women, men are more apt to blame the situation, someone else, or such social structures as the company and "the bureaucracy." In this sense, women are much less resilient in dealing with situations that may be unjust or unfair.

A major reason many women do not express or perhaps even feel hostility and aggression is that they have been conditioned culturally to play primarily supportive roles:

> Women tend to view their relationships with others as ends in themselves. . . . It has been customarily accepted that women in the working world are more aware of, and concerned about, the human interrelationships in a working group; possibly because of their "family orientation" and "caring" [socialization]. . . . Women are inclined to suppress their own achievement and leadership roles by slipping into supportive roles. . . .[1]

Playing primarily supportive roles creates self-image problems. That is, women often display such "traits due to victimization" as withdrawal, defensiveness, passivity, in-group hostility, and identification with the oppressors, as well as seriously impaired self-esteem.[2]

Men are also victimized. Men may be discriminated against, typically by other men, because of race, religion, handicaps, or height. However, unlike women, men are not categorically and automatically devalued because of their gender. Most men have the opportunity to prove their intelligence or mediocrity, hide some handicaps (such as religion, sexual preference, or record of mental illness), or overcompensate for such handicaps as race and height. At least initially, they will not be ignored because of their sex.

In contrast to men, women face many situational and emotional inconsistencies. Whether at home, at work, or in leisure situations, men are expected to be tough, aggressive, cool, and strong. Many of these expectations are detrimental to men's psyches and emotional growth.[3] Nonetheless, the expectations are unchanging and consistent. Women, on the other hand, must cope with changing, and often contradictory, expectations. They are expected to run their households but are labeled "castrating bitches" when they run offices. Our society rewards women for attracting men in social situations but condemns them for men's sexual advances (albeit unsolicited) in the work place. Similarly, women are socialized to be nurturant in social relationships but are criticized as not having "leadership potential" when they play nurturing roles at work.

Effects on careers. On the individual level, sex inequality has detrimental effects on women's, but not men's, careers and jobs. One of the most glaring differences is in the area of salaries and promotions. As we discussed earlier in Chapters Four and Seven, women continue to receive lower incomes than their male counterparts across *all* occupations, including those that are female dominated (sales, clerical, and service jobs). Women also continue to receive lower salaries within traditionally female-dominated areas. For example, a 1983–84 survey of faculty salaries shows that women earn about 10 percent less than men in such fields as home economics, health, and nursing.[4] Women's economic discrimination has been documented through a variety of sources—court cases, scholarly research, documentaries, and the mass media. Women have won some court cases. During the last two years, women faculty at Cornell University, the University of New Hampshire, and the Anne Arundel Community College have been awarded salary increases, across-the-board raises, and monies for professional development.[5] Also, in several recent cases the courts have reversed the negative decisions of male-dominated tenure committees.[6] Most women, however, do not challenge inequitable entry, salary, and promotion rates and procedures. Thus, most discriminatory practices continue uninterrupted.

Another way in which sex inequality affects women is by discouraging women's pursuit of male-dominated careers:

> I've always been a top student and came to [University X] on a math scholarship. During my first semester, my calculus professor really came on to me. He made advances and started sending me unsigned love letters. I rejected both and my grades started dropping. I can't talk to the other faculty because one of my friends is getting even more attention from the chair of the department. The only thing I can probably do is change majors or change schools. (Freshman at a top state university)

As this example illustrates, women in male-dominated disciplines have few options when they encounter sex inequality. Women students are especially vulnerable. They feel great disillusionment with and betrayal by the noble ideals verbalized by educational systems, are afraid to approach faculty because this might increase the discrimination, may stay away from critical courses to avoid sexual harassment, or may switch majors to female-dominated disciplines where they believe sex inequality is less widespread (or at least less blatant). Men who enter traditionally female-dominated careers are usually *not* similarly discouraged by women:

> I've had no problems at all. As a matter of fact, I'm surprised that I get so much help because most of the nurses realize that we [male nurses] will be promoted to administrative positions in no time at all. No one seems to be resentful. . . . I'm not sure I'd feel the same way. (Male nurse)

Other sources also show that men in traditionally female-dominated jobs receive help and support and only minimal, if any, hazing from female employees.[7]

Most of the women who work in the heavy industries (such as steel, mining, or automobile manufacturing) have spent many years in rigorous apprenticeship programs where they have acquired skills, performed dangerous work, and proved to their male colleagues that they can handle the job. When there is a recession, seniority rules ("Last hired, first fired") force many women who have been successful in relatively well-paying blue-collar jobs into low-paying female job ghettos. Unlike their male counterparts, "instead of bumping down the economic ladder a rung or two to semi-skilled industrial jobs, the women are usually forced to revert to low-wage, 'pink-collar,' sales and service jobs."[8] Many of these low-wage jobs are more exhausting and stressful than blue-collar jobs. For example, a displaced coal miner who sews collars onto waitress uniforms is described as follows:

> All day long she tries to block out the clatter from the more than 300 sewing machines crammed into her work room. And because she is paid "piece work"—55 cents a dozen for some collars, 39 cents a dozen for others—there is constant pressure to work quickly. "Even if you're working on the 55-cents-a-dozen collars, you've got to sew 70 dozen just to make $40," she says. "You can't stop for a minute."[9]

A third way in which sex inequality affects women's careers is in the area of stress. A number of studies have suggested correlations between high-pressure jobs and stress, hypertension, heart attacks, ulcers, and other physical maladies. Even well-paid and powerful executives may be suffering from less job-related stress than clerical workers. Secretaries often experience more stress than their supervisors because secretaries typically have jobs that are low in status but high in responsibility; have unsupportive or absent bosses; act as scapegoats, shields, or emotional sponges for dissatisfied consumers; and must live up to job expectations that are outside of the formal job description. In a study of 419 clerical workers at a major eastern university, Balshem found that receptionists working in clinics run by physicians who were also medical school professors experienced high stress because the receptionists absorbed much of the hostility aimed at the physicians:

> Although the doctor's lateness is, of course, not her fault, her position as the doctor's subordinate makes her a convenient target for the frustration of the patients. Excusing herself would be, she feels, moronic; she absorbs the sense that it is her responsibility to maintain at least a semblance of order in the clinic, but it is a strain for her to do so. Most likely, the doctor will never feel any of this hostility from his patients; it is all absorbed by his secretary.[10]

Women in responsible positions, moreover, are more likely than their male counterparts to encounter stress that is due to their sex rather than their occupational responsibilities:

> Built into the role of women managers there is conflict between the behavior women expect of themselves as women and as managers. A woman is constantly forced to consider how she can effectively retain her image of herself as a woman while reconciling the demands of that role with the demands of her managerial career.[11]

Unlike men, women find themselves playing roles that are both contradictory and mutually exclusive in the work place—that of "reconciler" and "leader." Such pressures produce anxiety and strain that men do not face.

Women may experience job-related stress resulting from sexual harassment:

> The tension, fear, and anger build up inside sexual harassment victims who have nowhere to turn for relief. Most victims experience psychological depression and despair. Many suffer physical ailments such as stomachaches, headaches, nausea, involuntary muscle spasms, insomnia, hypertension, and other medical illness caused by continual, unrelenting anxiety and frustration.[12]

Although a few men have reported sexual harassment from women, these cases are anomalous rather than typical.[13] For the offenders, sexual harassment releases, rather than creates, stress and tension. ("I was just having a little fun." "Fooling around at the office improves my performance.")

Finally, sex inequality limits women's job progression—even at high occupational levels. In a recent national survey of 722 female executives, almost half reported being socially excluded from the "male club" by being shut out of male activities, not being invited to business-related functions, and being left out of important informal discussions:

> The [male executives] don't invite you out to lunch or discuss business in the hallway. . . . You're not invited to many functions . . . not to the golf course or for the drink after work, where a lot of business gets transacted. . . . I'm not one of the boys. I can't hook into the informal chain of communications.[14]

Such exclusion makes women peripheral members of the organization and the work group and limits their participation in social networks that promote upward mobility.

NEGATIVE EFFECTS ON ORGANIZATIONS

Sex inequality at organizational levels has produced negative effects, which include suppressed talent, lowered productivity, and reduced creativity. Any organization (private or public, profit or nonprofit, large or small) whose hiring procedures are based on excluding or not promoting women will automatically exclude a pool of individuals who may be very talented and creative and who can enrich the organization's goals of higher productivity, better service, and better quality control.

Suppressing talent.   Despite historically rooted sex discrimination, a number of ground-breaking scientific discoveries, technological advances, and intellectual and humanitarian contributions have come from women (to name just a few—Madame Curie, Anne Lindbergh, Jane Addams, Florence Nightingale, Pearl S. Buck, and Margaret Mead).

Most of us would be appalled if some of the institutions that have used (although often exploited) women's talents decided to exclude women. Imagine, for example, the opera without Leontyne Price or Beverly Sills; the cinema without Mary Pickford, Bette Davis, or Meryl Streep; the 1984 Olympics without Mary Lou Retton or Joan Benoit; or the literary world without the Brontë sisters, Jane Austen, or Agatha Christie.

Yet, we continue to accept women's exclusion from a number of professional areas. In 1984, for example, the chairman of the gynecology department of Stanford University's medical school wrote a memorandum describing a female physician's pregnancy as a "disservice to herself and her colleagues." He objected to the woman's decision to have a baby before she completed the school's three-year obstetrics-gynecology residency program. That decision, he said, raised the spectre of women "as unreliable colleagues," and he questioned whether other women should be admitted to the residency program.[15] (The memorandum led to protests and the chairman's resignation.)

What was unusual about this case was not the chairman's discriminatory stance toward women, but that this stance was made public. In most cases women are simply not hired, not promoted, or discouraged in more subtle and covert ways, and the public never hears the issues. Occasionally, a judge says publicly that a woman "contributed" to rape because she was out alone at night, wore "suggestive" clothing, was picked up at a bar, or had had previous sexual intercourse.[16] In most cases, the judges simply let the rapist off without expressing chauvinistic statements that might be challenged. Whether it is a case of female physicians or rape victims, many women are still judged in terms of sex stereotypes rather than their present or potential talents and contributions. Children—especially girls, who comprise more than 90 percent of all sexual assaults on children—may be further victimized by male judges who have very sex-stereotypical views:

> Most revealing to me is the judge who ruled that a 5 year old female was a "temptress" in provoking a sexual encounter with a 20 year old male. . . . Wisconsin judge William Reinecke put the offender on probation and had him serve 90 days on a work-release program.[17]

Lowered productivity.   A related negative effect of sex inequality on organizations is lowered productivity. If women feel that their work is discounted, not recognized, and not rewarded because of their sex, the overachievement that typifies many women can be replaced with apathy, disillusionment, or lower commitment to the job:

> I used to really hustle in my job. For years, I'd work nights and weekends preparing really classy presentations, did a lot of homework before I saw a customer, and sent personal thank-you notes for meeting with me even if I didn't make a sale. Year after year, my sales records were higher than anyone else's in our division. After I was passed over for a promotion the second time, I realized I was breaking my back for nothing. I keep slightly ahead of most of the other people, so they wouldn't have an excuse for firing me, but I'm not a company man anymore. [Company X] can shove it. (Pharmaceuticals saleswoman)

Some of the lowered productivity is due to a conscious decision not to be abused, used, or exploited because the output is not rewarded. In many cases, however, reduced productivity is unconscious or unintentional. Because it takes women much longer than men to be promoted (and recognized in other ways), women's output and productivity may plateau as a result of long-term stress, fatigue, overwork, and a lack of monetary recognition. A number of women we talked to said that rewards were so slow in coming it was difficult to be motivated to work toward the next rung on the ladder:

> I had to have 50 percent more publications, do twice the committee work, and teach at least twice as many of the large, introductory classes as the men in my department before I was promoted [to associate professor]. I'm tired. . . . I'm especially tired of jumping hoops that men don't have to jump . . . and I know I've been jumping hoops because I now serve on personnel committees and see the standards applied differently to men and women. . . . Even with the $4000–$5000 salary difference, I'm not sure it's worth the effort to go for full [professor]. (Forty-three-year-old faculty member in a political science department at a large state university)

This woman, like many others, initially accepted the reality of doing twice as much as men do to get promoted, to be seen as "credible," and to be taken seriously. After a while, however, a number of these women begin to turn their time, talents, and abilities toward more rewarding projects outside the organization.

Perhaps one of the greatest depressors of productivity is having to fight sex discrimination:

> I'm forty-five years old. I started with this company right after high school. For years, my boss was promoted and took me with him. Last year, he decided he wanted a younger secretary even though my work has always received very high ratings, I'm efficient and attractive (according to my friends). I initiated grievance procedures. Because of my company's policies, I'm in my present position until the [grievance] committee makes a decision. . . . I still do the work, but it's been minimal. . . . I've spent a lot of my time either gathering evidence, worrying, or being angry about all of this. (Executive secretary in utilities company)

In all of the above cases, women's productivity decreases, and the organization loses.

Reduced creativity. Both psychological and physical oppression produce timidity, insecurity, and a lack of self-confidence. All of these reactions discourage the creative thinking and risk taking that accompany discovery and innovation. It is neither accidental nor coincidental that many of the most important scientific breakthroughs and artistic contributions have come from work environments that foster autonomy, promote independence, and tolerate personal and professional "deviance" (for example, universities and research and development divisions in industry).

Treating women as though their gender is more important than their abilities and intelligence can be especially detrimental in discouraging women's creative participation in an organization. Women's "psychological oppression" can include "the feeling of being caged, being kept on a leash, being limited and stunted." Women may see themselves as "limited beings, incapable of many activities, particularly societally important activities involving power, decision-making, and leadership." What may result is "a woman's conviction that there are many things which she cannot and/or should not attempt to do, simply because she is incapable, by virtue of being a woman."[18]

Because of sex-segregated occupations, women are not involved in jobs and activities that encourage creativity. Also, they have not demanded creative job assignments or greater control (over jobs) that could increase creativity. It has been only in the last few years, for example, that office workers—one of the groups with the most restrictive and routinized work environments—have begun to show an interest in unionization. Part of the motivation to unionize is economic. Some workers, however, are rebelling against work situations that discourage creativity—creativity that could otherwise produce positive results for the company:

> I spend most of my time typing statements. . . . After about the third notice, I have to send out threatening letters. It occurred to me that we might collect more if someone from the office called the guilty party before the threats went out . . . you know, to find out what the situation is and whether we could set up a partial payment program. When I suggested this to my boss, he blew up. He said I was paid to type, not think. (Secretary at a collection agency)

Employers continue to be very resistant to unionization efforts, especially among office workers. In 1971 the prestigious *Harvard Business Review* recommended that companies "avoid unionization of their clerical work force by ignoring the problem and doing business as usual."[19] A recently published "survival manual" for office workers suggests that management's attitudes toward the unionization of clerical workers has not changed significantly during the last decade. Office workers are warned that the employer might give the organizers a raise or promotion without making other changes, the employer might stall by asking for a consultant's report that might take several years to prepare, or the employer might fire employees for organizing.[20] Resisting unionization can save a company money in the short term. If, however, it also discourages creative participation, it will lose money in the long run.

Discouraging women's participation in interesting jobs is dysfunctional for an organization because it stifles talent and forestalls implementing beneficial changes. Locking women into uninteresting and noncreative jobs can also be detrimental to an organization because it limits competition to a very small group of individuals. This lack of competition reinforces male dominance:

> After bullying for so long, are males more apt to move over quietly and welcome females into the sandbox . . . ? Hardly! Being a bully . . . has its rewards. The bully has the entire sandbox to himself, every now and then he can experience the exhilaration of pushing another person around, of showing off to all the bystanders just how strong and powerful he really is. For males, being a bully is fun.[21]

Most importantly, being a bully means that men don't have to compete with 51 percent of the population. Thus, mediocrity may also be reinforced.

NEGATIVE EFFECTS ON SOCIETY

Sex inequality also has widespread adverse effects at the societal level. Four areas that reflect women's subordination due to sex inequality include volunteerism, "double days," divorce/childlessness, and health.

Volunteerism. In 1981, Betty Friedan, Bella Abzug, and President Reagan all called (independently) for a return to volunteerism to restore services that were cut by the Reagan administration. Despite its philosophical merits, volunteerism supports and reinforces sex inequality in a number of ways.[22]

First, volunteer work is different for men and women. For men it usually means serving in prestigious policymaking or advisory capacities, with the encouragement of the employer to take time off from work to serve as the company's "goodwill ambassador" to the community. For women, volunteerism means providing direct services at their own expense (transportation, lunch). Second, because women volunteers work almost exclusively at the lowest levels of the volunteer hierarchy, they obtain little valuable work experience or training. Popular mythologies to the contrary, displaced homemakers have been continuously frustrated to find that their resumés, which have meticulously translated fifteen to twenty-five years of volunteer activities into marketable skills, elicit such negative responses from prospective employers as "But have you ever *really* worked?"[23] Third, because gender determines one's role in volunteerism, women volunteers are highly underutilized and underrated in terms of their intelligence, abilities, and credentials. It is not at all unusual, for example, for a female Ph.D. to be asked to spend fifteen hours a week laminating alphabet cards while the local hardware salesman is appointed to the Board of Education. Fourth, women volunteers are used to exploit women working in low-paying, low-status, vulnerable jobs. For example, when Proposition 13 was passed in California, women volunteers supplanted the low-level women on the library staff who were terminated because of budget cuts. Fifth, volunteerism victimizes women by placing unrealistic demands on their time, energy, and resources. Since the early 1970s, women's socioeconomic positions have changed dramatically: More than 50 percent of all women who work (for pay) do so to support themselves or their families; almost 60 percent of all working women are mothers who are balancing (often very precariously) child-care, home, and job responsibilities; the highest percentage of moonlighters is women between thirty-five and forty-four years of age who are moonlighting not to earn "pin money" but to meet regular expenses and to pay off debts.[24] Because women—and not men—are expected to be giving, nurturant, and altruistic, they are pressured to volunteer and suffer the negative consequences of being superwomen. If they do not volunteer, they feel guilty about not fulfilling traditionally female expectations of "providing service to the community" regardless of cost. In either case, women lose. So do their families.

Double days.   As increasing numbers of women entered the labor force, there was an implicit expectation that sex roles and family structures would change to accommodate working women. However, instead of men sharing in domestic responsibilities, women have worked "double days"—a full day in paid employment and a full day in unpaid domestic work:

> I teach classes until about 1:00 P.M. every day. I usually have several hours of committee meetings, administrative work, or student appointments until about 4:00 P.M. The kids get out of school at 3:15. Even if I have to miss important meetings, I make sure I pick them up by 4:15 to avoid paying for the next hour. [This respondent pays $5.00 an hour for each child for the after-school program.] After we get home, I supervise their homework and music lessons, make dinner and clean up, drive them to Brownie meetings, religious classes, or the library. There's also the Little League, ballet classes. . . . I do part of the laundry while they're getting ready for bed. My husband comes home at about 8:00, eats dinner, reads the paper, watches the late news, and goes to bed. The house is fairly quiet at about 11:30 P.M. From then until about 3:00 A.M., I prepare for classes, grade exams, and try to do research. (Community college professor)

As the above quotation illustrates, many working wives have accepted the "fact" that combining paid and unpaid work is entirely their responsibility, even when their husbands are present. Many working women have never even entertained the notion that domestic chores should be a responsibility shared equally by *both* working adults. Quite to the contrary, "the woman's job commitment has been viewed as secondary to her domestic responsibilities."[25] In contrast to their spouses, working women rarely have time for leisure, recreation, relaxation, or socializing with friends:

> My husband and some of our friends are constantly pressuring me to have some couples over for a party or a dinner. Since I have to do all the work— prepare the food, clean the house, buy the booze—partying is a chore. I spend weekends doing the laundry, mending, shopping, and servicing appliances that keep breaking down. . . . Even going out is tiring business because it means I have to do all the housework on Sunday. (Manager in a public relations firm)

Double days are especially difficult for women who have children. Although women with children elicit somewhat more domestic help from their spouses than childless wives, the difference is negligible.[26] Studies of working mothers show that fathers in dual-earner families perform very few child-care and domestic tasks.[27] For example, diary data collected for two samples—one in 1967-68 and the other in 1977—found that the average number of hours spent on household work was about the same for fathers in dual-earner families and fathers whose wives did not work outside the home. In homes where the children were between two and seventeen years of age, fathers in both types of households reported spending 1.5 hours a day on household tasks in 1967–68; in 1977, fathers in dual-earner families reported spending 0.5-1 hours more per day on such tasks than fathers in single-earner families. In homes where children were one year old or younger, both sets of fathers had the same level of participation—three hours a day.[28]

The major difference was among mothers. Employed mothers spent two or three hours less a day on household chores than unemployed mothers. For example, in 1967–68, employed mothers whose youngest child was one year of age spent six hours a day on household tasks; unemployed mothers spent nine. In 1977 the rates were eight and nine hours, respectively.[29] Similarly, several recent studies of professional families show that fathers have considerably lower housework and child-care participation rates than mothers. Even when both spouses have full-time jobs, the mother spends at least twice as many hours as the father in child care and domestic tasks.[30]

Women working double days are also extremely vulnerable to role overloading. That is, women who work in and outside the home are expected to handle children's illnesses (and thus miss work), family get-togethers and festivities (anniversaries, holiday dinners, and birthday celebrations), and to care for both her and her husband's aging parents:

> My husband's mother has Alzheimer's disease. My husband has three sisters, but none work outside the home. My husband and his sisters decided my mother-in-law should move in with us because, with my working, we have a higher income than my in-laws. Our income isn't much higher than theirs, but it is slightly higher. . . . I guess, too, that since I've always worked full-time and managed a home, everyone figures I can manage. Since I'm a nurse, I didn't feel I could refuse.

Although there is increased social acceptance of women who work outside the home, responsibility for the home still rests almost exclusively with women. Thus, they bear dual burdens—both domestic and economic.

Some writers are suggesting that working women are dealing effectively with double days by refusing to do housework:

> Cleanliness is no longer next to godliness. Gone are the days when house-keepers dusted . . . their lightbulbs to perfection and waxed their floors to re-flection. "There's a whole new generation of women out there who wouldn't be caught dead on their hands and knees scrubbing a floor. . . ."[31]

Such statements are misleading. First, although the article from which this extract was taken states that "many consumers" (including secretaries, nurses, and students) are hiring cleaning maids, all of the examples in the article describe professional women or women who run their own businesses. As discussed earlier, empirical data show that even these women still scrub their own toilets, kitchen sinks, and floors. Second, such facile generalizations ignore the impact of sex socialization and ethnic and social class differences. Middle and working classes either cannot afford housecleaning services or have a real antipathy toward both letting strangers into their homes or into their "dirty" homes. For example, an East European bankteller in her early forties never got around to hiring much-needed household help because she never had time to "straighten things and clean the house" before the cleaning woman came! In many working-class families, the woman is "allowed" to work outside the home only if she keeps the house spic and span and is an outstanding homemaker:

> We need my income to survive, so I work. But my husband gets a lot of rib-bing by his pals if I'm not around to make hamburgers and serve the beer when they play cards or watch football games. On top of that, the house better look good because the house always looked good when his mother worked. And she worked in a factory all her life. My mother worked in a local sweatshop. To the day she died, everything was always clean—plants, tops of refrigerators, chair rims, windowsills, pantry shelves. . . . My house isn't as clean as hers, but I sometimes clean house until midnight or later. (Garment worker)

Divorce/childlessness.   Unlike men—who enjoy the benefits of having both a job and a family—many women are finding that they cannot have both and must choose between the two if they are to be effective in either endeavor. Thus, an increasing number of women—especially those with high educational levels—are postponing marriage, remaining single, not having children, or getting divorced because it is difficult being a double-day wife. A recent Gallup study found that about 25 percent of the 2,037 women executives interviewed felt that their success in a job has been achieved at the expense of their families: "Says a 36-year-old executive in a service industry, 'My time away, because of work, compared with the time my

husband spent at work, resulted in our growing apart and eventually going our separate ways. . . .' "[32]

Our interviews show similar results. Although women's working was not the cause of divorce, double-day stress exacerbated existing problems that sometimes led to a divorce:

> There's always been tension about things like my entertaining his friends (which I didn't like), my husband not spending enough time with the kids and decorating the house according to his taste and not mine. After I went to work, these problems got worse. I became more insistent about his helping around the house. He got angry because I had even less time and energy for entertaining. . . . When I started buying things I wanted for the house that he didn't like out of my own paycheck, he really exploded. (Administrative assistant in a public relations agency)

Although we didn't collect systematic data on the question, there seems to be a relationship, as might be expected, between problematic marriages ending in divorce and the woman's working at higher occupational levels. That is, when the woman develops enough economic autonomy to leave a problem-ridden marriage, she does.

For the most part, divorce decreases, rather than increases, women's domestic responsibilities. Many divorced women said that they no longer had to attend to their ex-husband's work-related functions, spend time entertaining and socializing with in-laws, or engage in time-consuming activities that met the husband's needs (taking clothes to the laundry, preparing elaborate meals, shopping for his clothes). Also, divorced women reported having considerably more time to pursue their own interests and spend more time with their own friends.

Divorce increases women's responsibilities in those jobs traditionally performed around the house by men—for example, yard work, car maintenance, fixing small appliances, and home improvements. Many women said, however, that they learned these skills when it was necessary to "survive or fall apart," resolved part of the problem by moving into smaller, maintenance-free housing, or "exchanged" services with friends and neighbors:

> One of my neighbors helps me with minor car repair, advises me on things like buying painting equipment, and helps me do things like clean out the gutters. In return, my daughter or I babysit for them once or twice a month. . . . So far, it's worked out pretty well for both sides. (Executive secretary in legal firm)

A number of our female respondents said that divorce was advantageous in terms of decreasing double-day responsibilities. However, remarriage rates are high nationally. So are the rates of second and third divorces.[33] Such seeming contradictions can be explained in two ways. First, because marriage is romanticized and is still seen as the only "legitimate" expression for sexual intercourse, both sexes continue to seek stability and legitimacy through marriage. Also, serial monogamy (marrying several people one at a time) suggests that marriage is disappointing, restrictive, dissatisfying, and dysfunctional. This may be especially true for working wives and working mothers whose "romantic bubble" bursts when they have to perform the conflicting roles of wife, mother, lover, companion, nurse, employee, volunteer, and cook.

Health. Data have shown that married women have higher rates of mental disorder than married men.[34] Also, women have higher rates of first admissions to private psychiatric hospitals, psychiatric care in general hospitals, and psychiatric outpatient care.[35] Furthermore, married women are more likely than any other group to experience depression, have psychosomatic ailments, and worry about death.[36] In an analysis of research results on gender-related health problems, Doyle suggests that emotional disorders—such as depression, severe anxieties, and eating disorders—are found more commonly among women than men because women are more likely to turn conflict and tension inward and punish themselves while men are more likely to turn conflict outward toward others and engage in antisocial physical behavior.[37] Studies of the prevalence of depressive symptoms show that employed husbands consistently fare better than employed wives.[38] As one author notes, "In spite of the folk jokes and legends about marriage being a trap for men set by women, marriage seems to have relatively fewer negative effects on men."[39]

SOCIAL POLICY AND THE NEGATIVE CONSEQUENCES ON SEX EQUALITY

Regardless of whether they are a cause or an effect, social policies have created, supported, and reinforced sex inequality. Currently, social policies have widespread negative consequences on women's work and family life. Some of the major policies harmful to working women are in the areas of family and child care, welfare, social security, and employment.

Family and child care. Almost 60 percent of all working women have a paid maternity leave of only a few days; only about 40 percent have the equivalent of a paid, six-week disability leave. Those who must take an unpaid leave of absence have no guarantee that they can return to their job.[40] Day care remains a utopic goal rather than a reality. Although an estimated several million children need care, facilities are currently available for only about 900,000 children.[41] As witnessed by a recent rash of child abuse cases, services for child care are inadequate and even harmful.

Although women have the burden of responsibility for child care, they have little control over reproduction and child-care policies. For example, although birth control is a personal matter, it is "controlled by decisions of the state, the social organization of scientific and medical institutions, and the normative system of public values and attitudes."[42] Recently, moreover, anti-abortion movements have been trying to limit women's access to abortion counseling and services. It should be noted that these groups are also fighting the expanded welfare services that would be necessary to care for the millions of unwanted or abused children resulting, in part, from unwanted pregnancies.

Welfare and social security. Of the almost 35 million Americans living in poverty, almost 60 percent are women. All but 22.3 percent are women and children under eighteen years of age.[43] Thus, poverty is a woman's problem. Since, moreover, many of these women have to turn to welfare, welfare is also a woman's problem. That is, housewives are unprotected in their later years, divorced women often lose their former husband's retirement benefits, and widows have limited access to their late husbands' retirement or health benefits. Also, because women constitute the vast majority of part-time and temporary workers, they are not eligible for disability, health, or retirement programs.

Our belief in the myth that men will take care of women and children economically has increased the numbers of women in poverty. For example, an estimated 4 to 7 million predominantly middle-class displaced homemakers have found themselves in poverty since the term "displaced homemaker" was coined in the mid-1970s. Also, failure to award and enforce alimony and child-care payments in divorce cases has resulted in women's increasing the poverty and welfare rolls.

According to Pearce, welfare policies have locked women into poverty by forcing women to take jobs that are insufficient for their families' needs, have trained women for poverty-level, traditionally female, low-paying jobs, and have made no provisions for child care in such training programs as WIN (Work Incentive Program) and CETA (Comprehensive Employment and Training Act).[44]

Employment. Long before they reach the legal working age, schoolgirls— especially those in lower income families—get "very traditional, sex-stereotyped messages [which], in fact, encourage teenage pregnancies. . . . Teachers and administrators are well-meaning; they want to help students. . . . But most of them don't realize that when they give the message to young girls that the only role, or their major role, is to be a wife and mother, they are encouraging teen-age pregnancy."[45]

Even when not handicapped by teen-age pregnancies that discourage them from receiving the training necessary to enter the labor force, women encounter a plethora of employment policies and structures that encourage and reinforce sex inequality in the work place.

As discussed earlier in Chapters One and Two, affirmative action legislation is being rapidly diluted under the Reagan administration. Even before these reactionary efforts began, most of the employment legislation safeguarding and promoting women's employment rights was ineffective because enforcement was largely only symbolic. Affirmative action agencies have always been plagued by such problems as vague and ambiguous guidelines, inadequate funding, small staffs, inadequate staff training, and, perhaps most importantly, a lack of enforcement. Although a few court-ordered remedies have imposed quotas for the hiring of minorities, and a handful of women have obtained satisfactory out-of-court settlements, a vast majority of discrimination complaints are not investigated, are investigated inadequately, or are not enforced after discrimination has been documented.[46] However, because the anti-affirmative action rhetoric is emotional and receives a great deal of media attention, most of us assume that work conditions for women have *really* improved during the last decade or so. It is simplistic to assume that the barrage of anti-equality rhetoric is a barometer of genuine social change. Quite the contrary, the opponents of sex equality are engaging in verbiage and activities to forestall, delay, and sabotage any changes that might threaten the status quo, which supports (white) men.

In summary, this chapter has discussed some of the negative effects of sex inequality at individual, organizational, and societal levels. These negative effects have an immediate impact on women, but they also affect men and children. In the end, sex inequality affects all of us. The next chapter proposes some remedies for these problems.

NOTES

1. Christine D. Hay, "Women in Management: The Obstacles and Opportunities They Face," *The Personnel Administrator,* April 1980, p. 33.
2. Edwin M. Schur, *Labeling Women Deviant: Gender, Stigma, and Social Control* (New York: Random House, 1984), p. 39.
3. See, for example, Robert A. Lewis, ed., *Men in Difficult Times* (Englewood Cliffs, N.J.: Prentice-Hall, 1981).
4. Jean Evangelauf, "Women Trail Men in Faculty Salaries Survey Finds," *Chronicle of Higher Education,* March 28, 1984, pp. 1, 26.
5. "4-Year-Old Sex Bias Suit Is Settled at Cornell," "U of New Hampshire Boosts Female Professors' Salaries," *Chronicle of Higher Education,* October 17, 1984, pp. 2–3.
6. See, for example, Nina McCain, "Sociologist in Sex-Bias Case Offered Tenure at Harvard," and Austin C. Wehrwein, "Court Reverses Librarian's Tenure Award at U of Minnesota," *Chronicle of Higher Education,* January 16, 1985, p. 3.
7. See "As Men Move in on Women's Jobs," *U.S. News and World Report,* August 16, 1981, pp. 55–57.
8. Carol Hymowitz, "Layoffs Force Blue-Collar Women Back into Low-Paying-Job Ghetto," *Wall Street Journal,* March 6, 1985, p. 37.
9. Ibid.
10. Martha Balshem, "Job Stress and Health among Women Clerical Workers: A Case Study (Preliminary Results)" (paper presented at the American Anthropological Association meetings in Denver, Colorado, November, 1984), p. 5.
11. Harold F. Puff and Cindy L. Moeckel, "Managerial Stress and the Woman Manager," *Industrial Management,* March–April, 1979.
12. Constance Backhouse and Leah Cohen, *Sexual Harassment on the Job* (Englewood Cliffs, N.J.: Prentice-Hall, 1981), p. 39.
13. U.S. Merit Systems Protection Board, *Sexual Harassment in the Federal Workplace* (Washington, D.C.: Government Printing Office, 1981).
14. Helen Rogan, "Top Women Executives Find Path to Power Is Strewn with

Hurdles," *Wall Street Journal,* October 25, 1984, p. 35; "Women Executives Feel that Men Both Aid and Hinder Their Careers," *Wall Street Journal,* October 29, 1984, p. 35.

15. "Stanford Physician Quits after Criticizing Pregnancy," *Chronicle of Higher Education,* January 18, 1984, p. 3.

16. See, for example, "Judge Suspends Sentence of Admitted Rapist," *New York Times,* January 22, 1977.

17. This example was provided by an anonymous reviewer, April 1985.

18. Carol A. Whitehurst, *Women in America: The Oppressed Majority* (Pacific Palisades, Calif.: Goodyear Publishing Company, 1977), p. 119.

19. Alfred Vogel, "Your Clerical Workers Are Ripe for Unionism," *Harvard Business Review* 49 (March–April 1971), pp. 48–55.

20. Ellen Cassedy and Karen Nussbaum, *9 to 5: The Working Woman's Guide to Office Survival* (New York: Penguin Books, 1983), pp. 164–167.

21. James A. Doyle, *The Male Experience* (Dubuque, Iowa: Wm. C. Brown Company, Publishers, 1983), p. 266.

22. This discussion relies heavily on Nijole Benokraitis, "Volunteerism–Ladies, Watch Out!" (Maryland Commission for Women, *Maryland Women,* Winter 1982).

23. Nijole V. Benokraitis, "Reentry Problems of Older Women: The Case of Displaced Homemakers," *Journal of Gerontological Social Work,* forthcoming.

24. Scott C. Brown, "Moonlighting Increased Sharply in 1977, Particularly among Women," *Monthly Labor Review* 101 (1977), pp. 27–30.

25. Kristin A. Moore and Isabel V. Sawhill, "Implications of Women's Employment for Home and Family Life," in *Work and Family: Changing Roles of Men and Women,* ed. Patricia Voydanoff (Palo Alto, Calif.: Mayfield Publishing Company, 1984), p. 161.

26. Sarah Berk, "Husband at Home: Organization of the Husband's Household Day," in *Working Women and Families,* ed. Karen Wolk Feinstein (Beverly Hills, Calif.: Sage Publications, 1979), pp. 125–158.

27. This discussion relies heavily on Nijole Benokraitis, "The Father in Two-Earner Families," in *Dimensions of Fatherhood,* ed. Frederick W. Bozett and Shirley Harmon Hanson (Beverly Hills, Calif.: Sage Publications, 1985), pp. 243–268.

28. Cited by M. Ferber and B. Birnbaum, "The Impact of Mother's Work on the Family as an Economic System," in *Families that Work: Children in a Changing World,* ed. S. Kamerman and C. D. Hayes (Washington, D.C.: National Academy Press, 1982), pp. 97–98.

29. Ibid.

30. See, for example, S. Yoher, "Do Professional Women Have Egalitarian Marital Relationships?" *Journal of Marriage and the Family* 43 (1981), pp. 867–868; J. B. Bryson and R. Bryson, eds., *Dual-Career Couples* (New York: Human Sciences Press, 1978); K. Walker, "Time Spent by Husbands in Household Work," *Family Economics Review* 4 (1970), pp. 8–11.

31. Betsy Morris, "Homes Get Dirtier as Women Seek Jobs and Men Volunteer for the Easy Chores," *Wall Street Journal,* February 12, 1985, p. 23.

32. Helen Rogan, "Executive Women Find It Difficult to Balance Demands of Job, Home," *Wall Street Journal,* October 30, 1984, pp. 33, 55.

33. U.S. Bureau of the Census, *Statistical Abstract of the United States, 1980* (Washington, D.C.: Government Printing Office, 1981), p. 87; Arlene Skolnick, *The Intimate Environment: Exploring Marriage and Family* (Boston: Little, Brown, 1978), p. 235.

34. Walter R. Gove, "The Relationship between Sex Roles, Marital Status and Mental Illness," *Social Forces* 51 (1972), pp. 34–45.

35. Walter R. Gove and Jeannette F. Tudor, "Adult Sex Roles and Mental Illness," *American Journal of Sociology* 78 (January 1973), pp. 50–73.
36. Jessie Bernard, "The Paradox of the Happy Marriage," in *Woman in Sexist Society: Studies in Power and Powerlessness*, ed. Vivian Gornick and Barbara K. Moran (New York: New American Library, 1971), pp. 145–163.
37. James A. Doyle, *Sex and Gender: The Human Experience* (Dubuque, Iowa: Wm. C. Brown Publishers, 1985), pp. 301–306.
38. L. Radloff, "Sex Differences in Depression: The Effects of Occupation and Marital Status," *Sex Roles* 1 (1975), pp. 249–265; Walter R. Gove and M. R. Geerken, "The Effect of Children and Employment on the Mental Health of Married Men and Women," *Social Forces* 56 (1977), pp. 66–76.
39. Joe R. Feagin, *Social Problems: A Critical Power-Conflict Perspective* (Englewood Cliffs, N.J.: Prentice-Hall, 1982), p. 164.
40. Ann Crittenden, "We 'Liberated' Mothers Aren't," *Washington Post,* February 5, 1984, pp. D1, D4.
41. U.S. Department of Labor figure cited in Mary Frank Fox and Sharlene Hesse-Biber, *Women at Work* (Palo Alto, Calif.: Mayfield Publishing Co., 1984), p. 201.
42. Margaret L. Andersen, *Thinking about Women* (New York: Macmillan Publishing Co., 1983), p. 154.
43. U.S. Department of Commerce, Bureau of the Census, "Characteristics of the Population Below the Poverty Level: 1981," *Current Population Reports,* Consumer Income Series D-60, No. 138, March 1983, Table 11.
44. Diana M. Pearce, "Farewell to Alms: Women's Fare under Welfare," in *Women: A Feminist Perspective,* 3rd ed., ed. Jo Freeman (Palo Alto, Calif.: Mayfield Publishing Co., 1984), pp. 502–515.
45. Barbara Milford, "Sex Stereotyping at School Faulted in Teen Births," *Evening Sun,* Baltimore, January 21, 1985, p. B12.
46. Nijole V. Benokraitis and Joe R. Feagin, *Affirmative Action and Equal Opportunity: Action, Inaction, Reaction* (Boulder, Colo.: Westview Press, 1978), pp. 44–56, 95–114, 154–167.

9

Getting Rid of Sex Discrimination: How Can It Be Done?

INTRODUCTION

In 1776, Abigail Adams wrote to John Adams, her husband the revolutionary, advising him about the new code of laws for the emerging United States:

> In the new code of laws which I suppose will be necessary for you to make, I desire you would remember the ladies and be more generous and favorable to them than your ancestors. Do not put such limited power in the hands of husbands. Remember, all men would be tyrants if they could. If particular care and attention is not paid to the ladies, we are determined to foment a rebellion.[1]

John Adams rejected her request, telling his wife to be patient and to realize that other issues were more important than women's rights. This view has been common ever since. Women have been told by men, and even by some women, that their rights are not as important as other matters. This has been true in the 1980s, with the emergence of a conservative president, Ronald Reagan, and his many associates opposed to many women's rights issues. Reagan took a stand against the Equal Rights Amendment (ERA), and in 1984 his Republican Party platform endorsed a constitutional amendment to bar abortion, opposed affirmative action programs as "reverse discrimination," and opposed the concept of equal pay for work of comparable value.

From Abigail Adams to today's women activists, the challenge has arisen again and again: "If particular care and attention is not paid to the ladies, we are determined to foment a rebellion."

In this book we have identified numerous discriminatory barriers facing women outside the home, especially in the work place and at school. We have seen women facing discrimination, and we have seen them fighting that discrimination. In this chapter we will examine strategies for change under three general headings: individual pressure for change, change through collective action, and broad societal changes.

INDIVIDUAL PRESSURE TO END DISCRIMINATION

Many women cling to misconceptions that perpetuate discriminatory attitudes and practices. First, they assume that if they work hard and do a good job, their talent and ability will be recognized and rewarded. Second, they assume that gender is irrelevant in the distribution of rewards and that "merit will win out." Third, they assume that someone else will fight the battles for them. Related to this, they assume that, over time, there will be sex equality. Each of these assumptions is wrong, and each maintains the status quo.

Every woman has certain rights under U.S. law. Knowing these rights, and pressing for them, is a major strategy for individuals. In the work place, for example, it is illegal for a woman to be fired for filing a sex discrimination complaint against her boss. It is illegal for a male employee doing the same work (even under a different job title) to be paid more than a similarly experienced female employee. It is illegal to force a woman to leave her job in the sixth month of pregnancy. And it is illegal to fire a woman employee who is talking to others about unionizing. In education, it is illegal to exclude women from government-paid work-study opportunities, monetary support through scholarships and fellowships, equal access to institutional facilities and athletic benefits, and entry into all areas of study. In domestic situations, it is illegal to rape a wife (in many states) and to deny credit, mortgage loans, or other financing on the basis of sex or marital status.

The first step to remedy some types of discrimination is for the woman to identify and recognize the discrimination. The second step is for her to stand up for her rights. Placing the burden of sex inequality on women might smack of reinforcing the "blaming the victim" syndrome. However, as we discussed in previous chapters, most men will *not* promote women's rights because of their personal and economic interest in maintaining discriminatory practices. Thus, women must take the initiative in fighting sex discrimination. At the individual level, these strategies differ depending on the type of discrimination.

Blatant/overt sex discrimination. One remedy is active intervention by individuals who do not discriminate. As one of our readers put it:

[There are] social/personal responsibilities of spouses, parents, teachers, legislators, friends, colleagues and others to act in behalf of victims *and* themselves. A lot of people won't *actively* discriminate, but they also won't intervene to prevent or stop discrimination (e.g., "You're a big girl. I assume you can take care of yourself." This translates to "It's really *your* problem, so it's up to *you* to find a solution.") There is really a lot to be said for the notion that if a person isn't part of the solution, he or she is part of the problem. . . . Men use this "non-intervention" reasoning mostly to avoid confronting one or more men (are they afraid, falsely, of looking "unmasculine"?).

Thus, *both* men and women should actively challenge blatant sex discrimination. Individuals in powerful positions can be especially instrumental in sending loud, clear, and public messages supporting sex equality. In 1983, for example, Mayor Richard L. Hillman of Annapolis, Maryland, sent a seven-page memorandum to department heads in city government outlining ways to eliminate sexual stereotyping and the use of derogatory and demeaning language and behavior toward women. The memo also included "threats" of disciplinary action in discriminatory behavior.

Another strategy is prevention. Some women accept jobs and enter educational institutions that they know have a well-established reputation for sexism. The motivations for such actions are mixed—the company might offer a slightly higher entry salary, the university might be in an interesting location, the applicant thinks that "my experience will be different" or that she will change the existing discriminatory practices. Invariably, such high hopes and idealistic expectations are dashed. If during the course of an interview or application process the applicant discovers the institution's discriminatory policies or practices, she should cite these as reasons for not accepting the offer (or scholarship) and send the rejection letter to the influential decision makers or leaders in the community, company, or institution.

Preventing sex discrimination on a more personal level is also important. In the last five or six years, law enforcement agencies, schools, and the media have been more willing to raise, publicize, and discuss such tabooed or neglected issues as rape, sexual harassment, and child abuse. Consequently, some states have set up rape crisis centers, shelters for battered wives, and fingerprinting programs in elementary schools. However, such responses are therapeutic or reactive rather than preventive. That is, they focus on what to do *after* the offense rather than on teaching women how to avoid or prevent violence, harassment, and discrimination. If more time and effort were spent teaching children and adolescents that physical violence and sexist behavior are *never* OK, some of our cultural acceptance of sex discrimination might begin to change.

Third, women should initiate legal action against the perpetrator. A woman can protest an insult. Or write a memo. Or discuss the problem with other workers who might be in a similar fix. All of these are real remedies for women seeking changes in the sex discrimination they face.

Gathering information on the organization's policies and records can be important in fighting discrimination. An aggrieved woman should collect data to back up her arguments. A company's poor record of past treatment of women or minorities can be important background data substantiating a claim of recent discrimination. Checking to see if other women employees have suffered similar discrimination can be useful, as can be checking court cases against the organization.

Companies themselves sometimes have data as well. For example, companies doing substantial business with the federal government must sign contracts requiring them to take affirmative action to correct discrimination against women in their organizations. Usually the company must prepare an affirmative action plan that spells out its weaknesses regarding the hiring of women and that lays out goals and timetables for hiring women to correct its deficiencies. This plan is kept in the files of the organization and should be available to employees. It is enforced by the Office of Federal Contract Compliance (OFCC) Programs.

If discussing the program with the boss does not work and internal grievance procedures are not available, an aggrieved woman can consider a court suit. The 1964 Civil Rights Act (Title VII) prohibits discrimination in employment—in hiring, firing, wages, promotions, and fringe benefits—on the basis of gender. And sexual harassment at work has been ruled by the courts to be illegal sex discrimination. The 1963 Equal Pay Act requires equal pay for substantially equal work. The 1978 Pregnancy Discrimination Act protects pregnant women capable of doing their job from being fired or demoted because of pregnancy. These laws are enforced by the Equal Employment Opportunity Commission (EEOC). An individual has six months after a discriminatory act to file a complaint with the EEOC. Unfortunately, the EEOC has a backlog, and it may take a long time for the agency to make a ruling in a particular case. But it is usually worth the effort if other strategies do not work.[2]

If the EEOC doesn't help, a woman can sue on her own. (In Chapters Three and Six we cited numerous examples of women, white and black, who have filed and won lawsuits aimed at eradicating discrimination in the work place.) For example, recently the assistant manager of a federal savings and loan branch in Washington, D.C., sued the bank and one of its assistant vice-presidents for sex discrimination. She said he forced her to have sex, and she yielded for fear of losing her job. The executive denied the charges, and the bank said it knew nothing about such charges. Although a district court ruled against the woman, the federal appeals court reversed the ruling, putting companies on notice that they are liable for such harassment by a supervisor. According to a January 29, 1985, article in the *Wall Street Journal,* "the court said the bank was legally responsible even if it knew nothing about the boss's conduct."[3]

Friends, family, co-workers, and supervisors should actively support women who are challenging sex discrimination. Interestingly enough, sex discrimination is still one of the areas in which we assume that the victim is guilty until proven innocent. We should supplant such cultural knee-jerk reactions as "Were you wearing something sexy?" with questions like "Has he harassed other women?" and "What's the procedure for filing an internal grievance?"

Related to this, working women should develop networks with the wives of offenders. Very often, there is a rift between women working outside the home and housewives. Working women and students are sometimes self-righteous about not being "just housewives"; housewives—however intelligent, well educated, and talented—may feel threatened by stereotypical images of young, attractive, and successful women who are out to seduce their hardworking, innocent, and devoted breadwinners. If such misconceptions were reduced on both sides, through seminars, lunches, and workshops, for example, women could reduce sex inequality more effectively in both the home and the work place. Such alliances might discourage the activities of the minority of women who are using sex to promote their career mobility.

Because of the pressures from women acting as individuals, some changes are taking place, especially in the more blatant forms of discrimination. By choice and out of economic need, women have moved into the work place in ever greater numbers. Work for pay has given many individual women greater economic independence. This outside work frequently changes relationships with men, since women can choose to divorce or marry with less concern for economic repercussions. The movement of women into the work place helps women build bonds with other women, whether it be over lunch or as part of a work unit. Working women increasingly interact with men in nontraditional settings as lawyers, accountants, doctors, and police officers. This gives women a greater sense of their own personal worth and identity, which, in turn, increases the willingness of some women to press against all barriers to achievement, be they blatant or subtle. In addition, men learn how to be equal rather than to dominate from these new women at work.

Subtle/covert sex discrimination. Implementing remedies to change subtle and covert sex discrimination are more difficult because, as we discussed in Chapters Four and Five, most of us are *not* conscious of these barriers. Also, because these obstacles can be difficult to measure and document, many people assume that subtle and covert sex discrimination issues are not worth pursuing.

Such assumptions are wrong. First, *it is critical to educate women and men about the existence, processes, and harmful effects of subtle and covert sex discrimination.*

1. Raise people's consciousness. Talk to each other. Compare experiences. Share supposedly confidential information about in-house politics and abuses of women. In doing so, assume that sex discrimination is environmental rather than "natural" or innate.

2. Reevaluate your definitions of stereotypically masculine or feminine behavior in mixed groups. For example, why do we penalize women for crying but accept male outbursts when both are acceptable forms for the release of such emotions as anger, frustration, or disappointment?

3. At the end of the day, think about the situations that made you feel angry, defensive, humiliated, or tense. Were such reactions based on your lack of performance or other people's treating you as a woman rather than a person? Were you treated fairly? Or were you exploited, manipulated, ignored, or demeaned? If so,

was this because you are a woman or because you "screwed up"? In answering such questions, compare your experiences with those of men in comparable situations or predicaments.

Then, *do something.*

To counteract subtle and covert sex discrimination, women (and men) can implement a variety of equally subtle and covert strategies.

1. *Help yourself.* Find out who the respected leaders are and solicit their help and advice on things like presentations, reports, and procedures. Ask them for tips about how to improve. Do some careful research. Compare your work loads and responsibilities with those of others (especially men's). If you are doing more, point this out—politely but firmly—to supervisors at every opportunity. Point out all your important accomplishments to your supervisor. Carefully compare your salary with that of men who have similar achievements. Volunteer to help colleagues, do the job seriously, and communicate that you wish to be acknowledged. Ask your "enemies" (male chauvinists and "Queen Bees") to evaluate your products, devise cooperative strategies to improve your work, and solicit their help in making your contributions known to others. In terms of committees or similar assignments, be selective: Devote your time only to important committees, volunteer to chair an important committee to avoid serving on two or three meaningless committees, and do your homework. Be active during meetings, don't be the first to speak to problems, be brief and well informed in your comments, don't take silly comments seriously, and don't be on the defensive. If you feel you'll be in the minority, especially when the majority of the opposition is male, don't start with a compromise. Argue for more than you expect; work toward a compromise and make it clear that you are compromising because you're willing to "carry the ball" in the "team effort." (Largesse is always more effective than pouting, sulking, or abusing colleagues.)

2. *Help other women.* Whenever possible, nominate women to prestigious or powerful committees, work assignments, and other visible and important responsibilities. If men are suspicious about a "women's bloc," throw them off guard by having the most outspoken, feminist woman nominate a male (especially if he is intelligent, albeit anti-feminist). Follow that nomination quickly, however, with women's names. If you are in a position to evaluate women, don't be shy about comparing the "double-day" obstacles of married women (especially mothers) with the lack of such responsibilities of single men, husbands, and fathers who have considerably more time to devote to employment activities. Also, be sure to encourage other women evaluators to do the same. Evaluate women honestly—encourage their accomplishments but be honest and constructive about weaknesses and limitations. If a woman suggests a worthwhile policy, procedure, or idea, reinforce her immediately—both in writing and informal communications. *Never* assume that the proposal is "obviously" too good, intelligent, or worthwhile to be ignored by decision makers. Also, never assume that feminists or women working in such female-dominated areas as social work, nursing, and clerical work are too unsympathetic, close-minded, radical, calloused, or successful to accept constructive criticism, sup-

port, or help. The men and women who work to improve women's rights may appear publicly to be very tough, independent, and strong. Privately, they are the most likely to feel embattled and isolated because they are often ridiculed and attacked. Give them your support—especially in public and in writing. Such support might motivate fence-hangers to get more involved in sex inequality issues:

> We had a "women's libber" in the department for about six years. She didn't get tenure—I'm not sure why—and left last May. I can't believe I'm saying this, but I miss her. I didn't agree with a lot of things she did—like lobbying for day care facilities and raising sex harassment issues—but she made me think. . . . Why do I put my wife down at parties even though I really love her? . . . I flirt with students. . . . I tell sexist jokes in class. . . . I have a lousy relationship with most women. . . . I'm glad she's gone, but, damn, if I don't miss her. (Male faculty member in an economics department)

3. *Recruit the help of men.* Develop alliances with liberated men. Solicit their support, communicate openly, and don't put them on the defensive. Work together, coauthor projects and papers, and encourage the involvement of men who do not have professional relationships with women. Also, become more aware of men who have good intentions but who behave in sexist ways. Very often, men who are fathers are concerned about daughters (but not wives, mothers, mistresses, or girlfriends) and are more open to discussions about sex inequality.

GROUPS ORGANIZING FOR CHANGE

The feminist movement: 1848-1960. The women's rights movement in the United States has been alive for no less than 140 years. In 1848 more than 300 people, including 40 men, attended the first major women's rights convention in Seneca Falls, New York. Led by Elizabeth Cady Stanton and Lucretia Mott, the convention represented women organizing collectively for change. The convention passed one resolution, in a close vote, calling for the "elective franchise," the right to vote. This convention marked the launching of a movement, whose impact was to be seen in many subsequent movements. From the 1850s to the early 1900s the women's movement, although small, was very active in demonstrations as well as legal and political activities. In numerous states in this period women attempted to vote; occasionally small groups were successful, even though their votes were "illegal." For example, women demonstrated for voting rights at the 1876 Centennial exposition in Philadelphia. By the early 1900s women's clubs were being created in increasing numbers, and there were growing numbers entering the job markets.

In 1910-1912, Washington, California, and several other states yielded to suffragist pressures and gave women the right to vote. Between 1910 and 1917 the number of members of the National American Woman Suffrage Association grew from 75,000 to over 2 million. Demonstrations and other protest activities secured passage by Congress of a full-suffrage constitutional amendment in 1919. After this major victory, the women's movement became relatively dormant, until its resurgence in the 1960s.[4] Yet the early movement emphasized one key concept: organize!

Organizing today. If individual remedies are not enough, one of the best things women can do is organize. In her analysis of sexual harassment in the work place, Lin Farley maintains that this sexist behavior has grown out of men's need to control women's labor. Sexism in the work place helps keep women in lower-wage jobs and puts up a barrier to women organizing. Farley argues that the solution is an integrated work force, with men and women sharing equally in job tasks and authority. The only way to meet this goal, Farley states, is for women to organize and act as a cohesive force.[5] Women in the United States have organized to fight for women's rights since at least the 1840s. In recent decades there has been an explosion of organizations, including women's liberation groups, political action groups, unions, and smaller groups of women in companies and government agencies.

Fighting in the courts. Small groups of women in companies are filing and winning lawsuits. Some recent lawsuits have involved women in the armed forces. In *Owens* v. *Brown* (1978) a federal district court ruled that the U.S. Navy could not discriminate against women by excluding them from serving on ships at sea.[6] Several women naval officers had brought this suit against the Navy to force a change in this policy. The prohibition on sea duty severely limited their careers in the Navy. The federal court ruled that the absolute bar on the assignment of women to sea duty abridges the equal protection guarantee in the due process clause of the Fifth Amendment to the Constitution.

Women in civilian employment have also joined together to fight discrimination in employment. In 1983 a class action discrimination lawsuit against the Allstate Insurance Company was settled in U.S. District Court. The case charged Allstate with paying women salespersons less than men, even though their records were superior to those of their male peers. Because the company paid people on the basis of prior salary history, most women were permanently locked into low wages. The company did not release the terms of the settlement, but it apparently met the women's demands for pay equity.[7]

In 1983 and 1984 women who worked in a coal mine in West Virginia complained that they experienced sexual harassment by men—the men pinched them and watched them dress and undress through peepholes in the bathhouse. Finally, seven of the women got together and filed a successful federal suit against their employer for negligence in not protecting them from harassment.[8]

NOW and other women's organizations. After a slow development in the 1950s, the women's movement for greater equality came dramatically onto the national stage in the 1960s. More and more women were working outside the home, but wages and working conditions remained poor, and male domination in the economy and in government remained entrenched. Women had previously joined in various movements for reform, such as movements for nonwhite civil rights, but now they pressed their own cause. Protesting women became the target of rage for many in the dominant male group, who ridiculed them as "libbers" and "bra burners." But the counterattacks did not stem the rise of this movement. Various organizations sprang up, ranging from the National Organization for Women (NOW), to the Women's Equity Action League, to the New York Radical Feminists, to the National Black Feminist Organization.

NOW, which was founded in 1966, has fought in recent years for a variety of anti-discrimination remedies at the state and national level. In 1984, NOW set up the National Committee to Support Women Strikers at Yale. It helped raise money to assist strikers with expenses and to pay for a nationwide publicity effort. The strike of women workers for equal pay for work was successful. In addition, NOW groups registered voters prior to the 1984 presidential campaign in the hope of defeating President Reagan's bid for a second term. NOW groups accused Reagan of actually stimulating discrimination against women by failing to protect women's rights and by reducing the effectiveness of civil rights enforcement programs.

NOW has also played a role in important court victories aimed at reducing gender discrimination. In 1984, NOW and the Women's Legal Defense Fund won a $246,000 settlement on behalf of women workers at a major grocery food chain in the Washington, D.C., area. The original complaint, filed in the early 1970s, documented that women managers in the bakery departments were paid substantially less than men in other departments. The chain agreed to improve its affirmative action program and to bring more women into management positions.[9]

Women's organizations have used a variety of strategies to bring about changes in society. One common strategy is to effect changes in the law. This was accomplished, for example, in the modest civil rights and equal opportunity legislation from the 1960s to the 1980s. New laws are often activated by court cases, some of which have led to improvements in the conditions of women. Normally a conservative force, the law has been used to expand the rights and opportunities of subordinated Americans. Other strategies used by women's movements to protest subordination include electoral strategies, nonviolent civil disobedience, and legal marches and demonstrations. Various women's organizations, including NOW groups, have regularly used picketing and leafleting to fight discrimination. For instance, in April 1984 a NOW group picketed the main Tucson post office over pay inequality for women.

Women in unions. Women have organized their own unions to fight sex discrimination in the work place. Such groups as the Women Office Workers (New York), Women Employed (Chicago), Union W.A.G.E. (Oakland), and 9-to-5 (numerous cities) are fighting for better conditions in the work place. These unions are concerned not just with the work place, but also with *women* in the work place. In addition, the number of women has increased in unions that have traditionally represented clerical workers, male and female. In recent years the number of women workers in unions has grown, even though union membership in the U.S. in general is declining. Women in unions earn a third more than nonunion women, and they have better working conditions and fringe benefits. Organizing has brought improved pay and conditions to many women employees. The unionization process is started by workers sharing a common grievance; the workers hold meetings, and then conduct a legal election to see if the majority of employees support a union. Under U.S. law, management must negotiate in "good faith" with the workers' association about wages, hours, grievance procedures, and working conditions.

The American Federation of State, County, and Municipal Employees (AFSCME), a union with a large number of women employees, has been a very active advocate of comparable worth. AFSCME, which has a special legal unit that works on employment issues, has been aggressive in getting comparable worth into bargaining sessions with public employers. In December 1983, federal district judge Jack E. Tarner ruled in *AFSCME* v. *State of Washington* that the state of Washington had violated Title VII of the 1964 Civil Rights Act by paying people in predominantly female jobs less than those in similar-skill, predominantly male jobs. Judge Tarner ruled that the discrimination against women "has been and is manifested by direct, overt and institutionalized discrimination." This case affirmed the principle of equal pay for work of comparable value that had been established in the Supreme Court case *Gunther* v. *County of Washington* (1981). However, in 1984 the Reagan administration's Department of Justice (Injustice?) quickly moved into the appeal process against the women and for the State of Washington. This AFSCME case was appealed to the Ninth Circuit Court, which in 1985 decided against the principle of comparable pay for comparable work.

Another major union with a large number of women members is the Service Employees International Union (SEIU). This union has also been aggressive in challenging institutionalized discrimination against women employees. On November 9, 1984, the SEIU local at the Equitable Insurance Company in Syracuse, New York, announced a contract settlement with that company, a contract that included a pay raise, new health and safety protection for women working on video display terminals, the redesign of work stations to reduce stress, and changes in evaluation procedures. A majority of the clerical workers had voted for the union in a legal election, but Equitable at first refused to bargain with the SEIU local. This refusal led to a successful boycott of Equitable by several AFL-CIO unions and the picketing of the company by women's organizations. Unions are beginning to cooperate in the struggle for employment rights for women employees.[11]

Women in education. Changing the behavior of male teachers and administrators in educational institutions is yet another major challenge. Women students can take action to improve the climate in educational institutions. They can, individually or in small groups, participate more actively in classroom settings. They can encourage women students to organize women's caucuses and other types of support groups for female students. They can organize informal seminars to discuss sexism in the classroom. They can conduct a survey of women students and faculty to ascertain the extent of sex bias and sexual harassment. They can circulate materials on sex bias and harassment of students and faculty. They can, with the help of women faculty, develop videotapes and other media for use in teaching about sex discrimination in education. Women students can also use the student newspaper to publicize sex bias issues, and they can demand the inclusion of women's issues in all courses.[12]

Moreover, working together with sympathetic male and female faculty members, women students can organize to pressure the college (or high school) administration to work to reduce sexism. They can pressure administrators to issue policy statements making it clear that sexist humor and sex discrimination in and out of the classroom by teachers will not be tolerated; to revise teacher evaluations to include an assessment of the presence of sexist language; and to implement a grievance procedure that will allow women students to pass along their views to male (and female) teachers who engage in sexist behavior.

Individual male teachers can also be pressured to change their own behavior: to avoid using sexist humor and disparaging remarks about women's professional and intellectual abilities; to forgo emphasizing a person's sex in evaluating his or her work; to avoid questioning a woman's seriousness in her educational pursuits; to make sure that women students are drawn into classroom discussions on an equal basis; to insure that women receive the time and professional attention that men receive; and to make special efforts to encourage women to consider traditionally male careers.[13]

SOCIETAL CHANGES TOWARD EXPANDED WOMEN'S RIGHTS

What have we, as a nation, attempted to do about sex discrimination? To answer this question we must examine government actions—including civil rights laws, executive decrees, and court decisions—as well as those of employers in the private sector.

The state and employment. Consider, for example, government action in regard to employment. In the twentieth century little government action was taken to deal with employment discrimination until the 1940s and 1950s, when a few state and local governments in the north adopted fair employment practices laws, usually with weak enforcement powers and relating to minorities but not to women. Until the 1960s little more than token action was taken by any branch of the federal government to desegregate employment situations. Several presidents did take a few steps in the direction of enforcing passive nondiscrimination—for example, Franklin Roosevelt's establishment of a Fair Employment Practices Committee in the early 1940s—but significant anti-discrimination action could not be observed at the federal level until the 1960s, when civil rights groups accelerated pressure on government.

Executive orders issued by President Lyndon Johnson in the 1960s required, at least on paper, government contractors not only to cease discriminating but also to act affirmatively to desegregate their labor forces.

In the mid-1960s enforcement of contract compliance functions came under the Department of Labor, the agency that supervises employers holding federal government contracts. According to Department of Labor studies, compliance reviews of contractors have had some impact in improving women's employment. The Office of Federal Contract Compliance (OFCC), the office within the Department of Labor directly responsible for supervising the implementation of executive orders, has issued regulations that, when built into contracts, require federal contractors to take affirmative action to eliminate discrimination in recruitment, hiring, and promotion procedures. Affirmative action refers to positive remedial practices going beyond passive nondiscrimination to bring in previously excluded women and minorities.[14]

Since the late 1960s federal contractors have been required to submit written affirmative action plans indicating the current representation of women in job categories and providing for affirmative goals and timetables for categories where underutilization of women exists. The OFCC has delegated compliance actions to other agencies, which are supposed to review federal contractors in their area to see if they are taking remedial action.

The effectiveness of the OFCC-fostered affirmative action has been seriously questioned, however. Compliance reviews by the U.S. Commission on Civil Rights and other agencies have indicated that few significant penalties have been applied to nonconforming contract employers. Grossly deficient anti-discrimination plans have been approved.

The 1964 Civil Rights Act, together with its amendments in the 1970s, prohibits discrimination in employment by larger employers. The EEOC was created to enforce Title VII of that act, primarily to deal with complaints of employment discrimination. The EEOC has the responsibility of investigating legitimate complaints, of seeking conciliation, and, failing that, of going to court to end discrimination. Because of the EEOC's management problems and lack of staff, a large backlog of cases has periodically built up, to the point where many complainants have found no practical remedy through this procedure.

There is no systematic evidence available on the impact of government enforcement activity on the economic mobility of women. What data we do have indicate increased pressure on employers, from small businesses to corporations and universities, to desegregate their work forces. However, the data on actual changes in the work force reveal a mixed picture. There have been some gains as the result of government enforcement, but the reasons for these gains are many, including women's protests and organization as well as government action.

Recent legislative action.   New civil rights legislation has been difficult to pass in the 1980s under the Reagan administration. In June 1984 the House of Representatives voted 375–32 for the 1984 Civil Rights Act, which would bar sex discrimination in all of a college's education programs if that college received federal aid in only one of its programs. The purpose of the act was to overturn the narrow *Grove City College* ruling (see Chapter One). However, following the desires of the White House, the Senate's conservative leadership killed the bill. If the bill is not resurrected in 1985–86, there will doubtless be even less progress in the future for women's education and athletic programs in colleges and universities. Also, in 1984, Representative Mary Rose Oakar's Federal Pay Equity and Management Act passed the House in a nearly unanimous vote. But again, the bill was blocked in the Senate by the conservative Republican leadership because it would require a study of the extent of sex-based pay discrimination in the federal government's pay classification system.

The Equal Rights Amendment. The original U.S. Constitution was a document reflecting racial subordination in its legitimizing of slavery and the slave trade, and it was not until the Thirteenth, Fourteenth, and Fifteenth Amendments that this legal recognition of racial subordination was removed. However, it is revealing of the sexist nature of the U.S. legal system that the Fourteenth Amendment speaks *only* of the right to vote of "male citizens" in the formerly confederate states. This first explicit reference to sex in the Constitution made it clear that no women, black or white, had the right to vote. Indeed, women got the right to vote in federal and state elections nearly half a century after black men, as a result of the Nineteenth Amendment (1920): "The right of citizens to vote shall not be denied or abridged by the United States or by any state on account of sex. Congress shall have the power to enforce this article by appropriate legislation." More recently, a Constitutional amendment has been proposed to give women equal rights with men. The wording is similar to that which expanded black (male) civil rights in the Fourteenth Amendment: "Equality of rights under the law shall not be denied or abridged by the United States or any state on account of sex. The Congress shall have the power to enforce, by appropriate legislation, the provisions of this article."

Still, as of the mid-1980s, this simple Equal Rights Amendment (ERA)—extending to women civil rights that black males received officially in the nineteenth century—has not been ratified by the necessary number of states, to a substantial degree because of the strong opposition of many state legislators (mostly male) who believe that the amendment will break down the traditional sex-role requirements for women. Attempts to resurrect the ERA in the 1980s have been difficult because of opposition from the right-wing male leadership (disproportionately Republican) in the Reagan White House and in the Senate. But additional efforts to put the ERA into federal law are critical to women's future progress. Challenges to the sex-biased character of law are essential to undermine the patriarchal underpinnings of our economy, our educational system, and our political system. Most women's organizations have pressed for the ERA, which, as many opponents clearly recognize, will indeed subvert the patriarchal character of U.S. work places, schools, and legal institutions.

Federal courts and employment. As we have seen, lawsuits brought by women and minorities have forced changes. The federal courts have, since the 1960s, become increasingly involved in finding remedies for employment discrimination, both intentional discrimination of the blatant sort and, less frequently, subtle and indirect discrimination. Court cases often have a limited impact, in that the remedies are case-specific and affect only one individual or, at the most, one plant or company. The courts' ability to reshape employment in an entire industry or other sector is thus restricted. A company or organization is first examined for the practices that must be demonstrated to be discriminatory, at least in effect, before court remedies can be imposed.

Once discrimination has been conclusively demonstrated in court, however, the remedies provided by federal courts have often been quite specific in attempting "to make whole" the injured parties. While there is probably no way in which a female victim can be completely compensated for the loss of status and money resulting from both discrimination and consequent delays in obtaining her "rightful place," some federal courts have made attempts to provide monetary compensation for injustice. In such civil rights cases as *Watkins* v. *Scott Paper Co.* (1976) and *Patterson* v. *American Tobacco Co.* (1974), the courts have used wage "circling" to freeze an employee's wages at the current level so that he or she will suffer no loss of pay while training in lower-paying (entry-level) jobs. In *AFSCME* v. *State of Washington* (1983) the court required large agency expenditures to bring the wages of women's jobs up to the level of comparable men's jobs. Moreover, in a number of civil rights cases, such as *Albermarle Paper Co.* v. *Moody* (1975), the victims have been awarded "back pay," calculated as the difference between the pay actually earned and what the individual would have earned without the effects of intentional discrimination.[15]

In *Owens* v. *Brown* (1978), discussed previously, we saw a federal court require the U.S. Navy to cease wholesale discrimination against women sailors seeking to serve on ships. In earlier chapters we have seen women win (and lose) cases charging male bosses with sexual discrimination. The judicial branch of government has been very important in improving the conditions faced by women in the work place.

The slow pace of change. Most change coming from the judicial branch has, of course, resulted from legal cases brought by women. Court action benefiting women is relatively recent. Not until 1971 did the U.S. Supreme Court rule against a legislatively drawn sex discrimination barrier. In recent years we have seen a slowing of progress in the federal court system. For example, a recent report by the U.S. Commission on Civil Rights found that 800 sections of the U.S. legal code had examples of sex bias or sex-based terminology that were in conflict with the ideal of equal rights for women. Many state laws are similarly sex biased. By the mid-1980s an increasingly conservative Supreme Court demonstrated a halting move away from equal rights for women in some areas. For instance, in 1984 the Supreme

Court ruled that an entire college is not subject to civil rights laws protecting women, even if one of its programs receives major federal aid. As we noted previously, congressional attempts to reverse this decision were opposed by the Reagan administration.

The legal difficulties faced by women are reflected in the slow pace of change in concrete political attainments. Women make up less than 15 percent of all officeholders in the United States. Although women are half the population, no woman has ever served as president, vice-president, or speaker of the house. Very few women have ever served in the U.S. Senate—only a dozen between 1920 and 1984—and only a handful have ever been members of the House of Representatives.

Employers in the private sector. In an examination of the relationship between gender roles and power, Lipman-Blumen states that eradication of sex inequality necessitates implementing new definitions and new solutions: "New decisions are needed about who can do what; who and what are valuable; what contributions are important; how and what resources are available to women."[16]

New solutions can be implemented by employers who can play an active role in changing written contracts, rules, job definitions, and procedures at the organizational level. For example—and this is consistent with Kanter's earlier study of corporations—Baron and Bielby propose that employers avoid tokenism, modify organizational rules to encourage women's career advancement, redefine "relevant work experience" to include women's nonpaid work experience, and give women more power in defining what characteristics are appropriate for hiring and promotion decisions.[17]

In addition to redefining and changing organizational structures to include women, employers should reduce job constraints to encourage men and single fathers who want to parent.[18] The number of single-male households is low—only 3 percent of all households in 1980. These rates, however, will increase in the future. By the year 2000, over 25 percent of all families with children will be single-head-of-household families. If employers in the private sector refuse to deal with the realities of a changing family structure, they will encounter even greater problems in the areas of absenteeism, turnover, drug abuse problems, and lowered productivity among both men and women.

Much remains to be accomplished by both government and the private sector in securing equal rights for women. There must be increased government and private action to eradicate sex discrimination, action aimed at covert intentional discrimination and indirect institutionalized discrimination as well as more obvious types. Civil rights laws need to be expanded beyond their present level to provide more effective regulation of, and more severe penalties for, discrimination against women in areas such as employment and housing. Government anti-discrimination penalties for intentional discrimination are either too weak or are applied only in token-to-modest numbers. Few government contractors, including both the private and the nonprofit sectors, have had their ties to the U.S. Treasury severed, even though sex discrimination by many of these contractors has been a routine way of life. Serious enforcement would doubtless mean loss of substantial government funds for hundreds of employers.

THE NEED FOR RESEARCH

Many women's groups working on employment, education, and housing issues are beginning to call for better research on patterns of discrimination. In many organizational settings there are numerous filtering points through which women must pass in order to secure high-status positions. Previous sections of this book began the task of tracing the mechanisms of discrimination that operate as barriers. But since many barriers are little studied, much research on such barriers as internal promotion practices remains to be done. Built into the foundation of this society, the direct and indirect mechanisms shaping sex inequality have for a long time been accepted as normal and just. Now researchers must get behind the scenes to identify the specific sources of this type of inequality.

Increasing documentation of and attacks on blatant forms of direct discrimination have characterized the period since the 1960s. It is time to focus on the more covert, subtle, and indirect mechanisms. In addition, researchers would do well to develop better indices of the effects of both direct and indirect discrimination. Existing statistical work, such as that of the U.S. Census Bureau, should be expanded in order to develop new statistical indices specifically designed to measure the consequences of such discrimination as the underutilization of women in many types of organizations. The limited applicability of existing Census Bureau indices results in part because they were not originally developed to measure discrimination. Research on and documentation of discrimination should be made public to help inform policy discussions. One reason for the apathy of some in regard to sex discrimination may be the misguided assumption that it has nearly been eradicated. Notions of "benign neglect" and attacks on such things as token affirmative action programs seem to be guided by the Pollyanna assumption that "liberty and justice for all" is reality, not rhetoric. A realistic appraisal, however, shows that only the surface has changed.

LOOKING AT OTHER COUNTRIES:
A COMPARATIVE VIEW

Some European nations have made greater progress in gender equality than the United States. It would be very beneficial if policymakers in the United States would take a closer look at some of the European programs. It is not easy to create a society with true equality between men and women after centuries of institutionalized sex inequality. But several countries, for example, Sweden, are committed to this goal and have made some progress. In the 1940s and 1950s legislative action in Sweden made it easier for women to combine work outside the home with family responsibilities. Leave of absence for childbirth was permitted, and an increased number of refresher courses and part-time jobs for housewives became available.

In the 1960s and 1970s the principle of gender equality became firmly embedded in Swedish law. Sweden has numerous government-financed day-care centers for the young children of working parents (but these facilities have places for only a third of the children who need them). The day-care services make it possible for women to develop careers outside the home. Moreover, according to a 1974 law, when a child is born or adopted, the parents are entitled to nine months of *paid* parental leave between them. While it is mothers who make the most use of this opportunity, fathers have begun to take advantage of childbirth leaves. The Swedish health and other social service programs apply benefits to individuals, not to family breadwinners. So women usually receive the same health benefits as men.[19]

In the 1970s and 1980s the progress toward greater sex equality in Sweden continued. There has been more discussion of human roles, not just of women's roles. The 1979–80 Act of Equality between Women and Men at Work bars sex-based discrimination in hiring, promotion, training, working conditions, and salary. The law explicitly allows affirmative action on behalf of women who are underrepresented in a job category. "Positive discrimination" to remedy pay wrongs was thereby legalized in Sweden in contrast to recent attacks on affirmative action programs in the United States.

Other countries, although considerably less wealthy than the United States, have implemented much more progressive policies regarding working women. Seventy-five countries have statutory provisions that guarantee a woman the right to leave employment for childbirth, guarantee a job when she returns, and provide a cash benefit equal to five months' full pay. Also, comprehensive day-care systems have characterized many European countries for years. For example, in France, West Germany, and Italy between 70 and 95 percent of preschool children are in free full-day public programs. Many European countries routinely allow parents to leave work to care for sick children. In the Soviet Union, China, East Germany, and Japan the school year averages 240 days, with a school day lasting six to eight hours; the American school year averages 178 days, with a school day of five and one-half hours.[20]

In 1978 the government-funded Women's Conference in Houston, Texas, articulated the goals of women fighting sex discrimination in the U.S. Its report demanded "as a human right a full voice and role for women in determining the destiny of our world." Among its goals were an end to violence against women in the home, federal government aid for women in business, federal government support for child-care facilities, and full employment for women who want to work.[21] It is interesting that greater progress has been made in meeting most of these goals in some European countries than in the U.S.

The example of child care. Many European countries have made more progress in the area of child care than the United States. This is true of companies, as well as of countries. Yet progress can be made. Although most American companies are unwilling to provide child-care services, those that have done so report that the services have helped recruit and keep workers. According to a September 10, 1984, article in *Newsweek,* Intermedics, Inc., a manufacturer of medical equipment based in Angleton, Texas, reports that it has saved more than $2 million in reduced turnover costs since it opened its own day-care center in 1979. Fel-Pro, Inc., a maker of auto parts in Skokie, Illinois, started a day-care center in 1983 (parents pay about half the costs—$50 per child per week). Fel-Pro found that the availability of child care reduced absenteeism, tardiness, and turnover and facilitated Spanish-speaking employees' learning English through their children. And, in New York City, a manufacturers' association, the city, and the International Ladies Garment Workers Union each contributed a third of the $300,000 first-year cost of day care, with parents paying on a sliding scale. These and other cooperative efforts are proof that affordable, quality child-care services can be provided with minimal costs and great benefits for American business, industry, government, and employees.

CONCLUSION

When looking at both old and new solutions for discrimination, one sometimes feels overwhelmed by questions. When one presses for moderate changes in existing patterns of economic and social discrimination, is one simply helping to perpetuate a corrupt system? Do women aspire to be controlled by bosses, male or female, for whom profit is more important than humane treatment of employees or safe, high-quality products? Working women who gain their independence must question the poor working conditions that many male workers face. They must begin to question the basic values that place jobs over families, the work place hazards that increase corporate profits, and the work tasks so closely supervised that workers' needs for autonomy and control are ignored. Susan Strasser suggests that pressure must be brought to bear to change radically the U.S. work place, to emphasize those human values that are thought to be distinctively "female"—compassion, kindness, emotion, concern with health—but that are really basic human values. Incorporating these changes might require a fundamentally new system of humanized economic democracy.[22]

Can remedies for subtle and indirect discrimination be implemented on a large scale without truly major changes in the structure of the existing economic and social system? The destruction of the mechanisms of gender discrimination on a really large scale might well begin to dismantle the built-in patterns of sex inequality that constitute foundation pillars of the society. Major structural changes, as in revising all-pervasive unequal pay systems so they do not have their present adverse effects on women, would certainly have an impact on the social system. Pyramiding a large number of institutional changes of this type might well alter the foundation of what is now a sexist-capitalist society. Thus, some argue that the basic socioeconomic system would be completely remade in this process. A humanistic, democratic socialism could result.

Others argue against this conclusion, suggesting instead that more vigorous anti-discrimination measures can be undertaken on an expanded scale, while keeping some system of capitalism in place. True, discriminatory recruitment procedures, unequal pay, and unfair real estate procedures could be eliminated without affecting the fundamentally capitalistic nature of the society—that is, the ownership of businesses and industries could still be in private hands. Yet at the same time, massive infusions of women into the organizational structures of this society, particularly the highest decision-making levels, probably would alter the shape of this particular brand of capitalism, for no longer could it depend on certain groups for the cheap labor and other subordinate positions essential to its operations. Seen from this viewpoint, capitalism in some form might survive a thorough purge of sex discrimination, but some of the fundamental structural and cultural supports of the system would likely be changed, with perhaps the entire system being humanized in the process. Greater power and influence for groups now in subordinate positions would necessitate a measure of toleration for diverse ideas, perspectives, and practices that the top white-male groups cannot now accept.

Critical for the future of major reforms seems to be the action of subordinate group individuals themselves. There are top-down pressures for change, and there are bottom-up pressures in the form of subordinate group individuals banding together in organized protest against oppressive conditions. Coalitions between subordinate groups will likely be required for future reform on a large scale. The likelihood of substantial future change depends on the willingness of women to keep the pressure on. When the entrenched system of institutionalized discrimination gives a bit, as in providing greater access to formerly off-limits entry-level positions in industry or government, that does not mean that discrimination—overt, subtle, or covert—will not continue in job benefits, promotions, and the like. Even hard-won advances can be rolled back, as has been the case in the 1980s. For that reason, protest against unjust conditions will need to be repeated over and over again.

NOTES

1. Quoted in Laurel Richardson and Verta Taylor, "Introduction," *Feminist Frameworks,* ed. Laurel Richardson and Verta Taylor (Reading, Mass.: Addison-Wesley, 1983), pp. 317–318,
2. Ellen Cassedy and Karen Nussbaum, *9 to 5: The Working Woman's Guide to Office Survival* (New York: Penguin Books, 1983), pp. 136–139.
3. "Companies Are Liable for Sexual Harassment by a Boss, a Court Rules," *Wall Street Journal,* January 29, 1985, p. 9.
4. Aileen S. Kraditor, *The Ideas of the Woman Suffrage Movement, 1890-1920* (New York: W. W. Norton, 1981); Eleanor Flexner, *Century of Struggle* (New York: Atheneum, 1973).

5. Lin Farley, *Sexual Shakedown* (New York: McGraw-Hill, 1978), pp. 208–209.

6. 455 F. Supp. 291 (1978).

7. Liz Nicholson, "Decade Old Allstate Employment Discrimination Case Settled," *National NOW Times,* vol. 17 (September-October 1984), p. 7.

8. William Serrin, "Women Are Finding Path to Power Lies in Collective Action," *New York Times,* January 31, 1985, pp. 1, 8.

9. Liz Nicholson, "Victory Won for Giant Foods' Female Bakery Workers," *National NOW Times,* vol. 17 (May-June 1984), p. 5.

10. "AFSCME v. Washington State Briefs Due Soon," *National NOW Times,* vol. 17 (September-October 1984), p. 5.

11. Liz Nicholson, "SEIU Organizes Clericals at Equitable," *National NOW Times,* vol. 17 (November-December 1984), p. 8.

12. Roberta M. Hall and Bernice R. Sandler, *The Classroom Climate: A Chilly One for Women?* (Washington, D.C.: Association of American Colleges, 1982), pp. 13–15.

13. Ibid., pp. 15–17.

14. This section draws on Joe R. Feagin and Clairece B. Feagin, *Discrimination American Style* (Englewood Cliffs, N.J.: Prentice-Hall, 1978), pp. 148–152.

15. *Watkins v. Scott Paper Co.,* 530 F.2d 1159, 1173 (1976); *Patterson v. American Tobacco Co.,* 494 F.2d 211 (1974); *Albermarle Paper Co. v. Moody,* 95 S. Ct. 2362 (1975); *United Paperworkers Local 189 v. U.S.,* 416 F.2d 980 (1969).

16. Jean Lipman-Blumen, *Gender Roles and Power* (Englewood Cliffs, N.J.: Prentice-Hall, 1984), p. 204.

17. James N. Baron and William T. Bielby, "Organizational Barriers to Gender Equality: Sex Segregation of Jobs and Opportunities," in *Gender and the Life Course,* ed. Alice S. Rossi (New York: Aldine Publishing Company, 1985), pp. 233–251; Rosabeth Moss Kanter, *Men and Women of the Corporation* (New York: Basic Books, 1977).

18. See Patricia Madoo Lengermann and Ruth A. Wallace, *Gender in America: Social Control and Social Change* (Englewood Cliffs, N.J.: Prentice-Hall, 1985), pp. 213–231.

19. Birgita Wistrand, *Swedish Women on the Move* (Stockholm: The Swedish Institute, 1981), pp. 5–20.

20. Ann Crittenden, "We 'Liberated' Mothers Aren't," *Washington Post,* February 5, 1984, p. D1.

21. Quoted in Zillah R. Eisenstein, *The Radical Future of Liberal Feminism* (New York: Longman, 1981), p. 232.

22. Susan Strasser, *Never Done* (New York: Random House, 1982), pp. 310–312.

Appendix:
A Methodological Note

Large portions of this book are based on interviews and written correspondence with 310 respondents (95 percent women) between August 1981 and December 1984. The interviews were largely unstructured and open ended. The typical interview lasted about one and one-half hours. The three or four major questions focused on whether the respondents felt that they were being treated differently because of their sex, under what circumstances, and by whom. The interviews probed for descriptions of differential treatment by sex.

The interviewees represent a broad spectrum of occupations and socioeconomic levels—domestic workers, laborers, operatives, craft, clerical, sales, professional, and managerial workers. Also, respondents include men and women who are employed in traditional and nontraditional jobs in education, business, and industry.

Each prospective respondent was told that all of the material would be confidential and presented anonymously and that the respondent's place of employment would not be identified. We have changed the names and places of employment. Because the data come from respondents in twelve states, anonymity is guaranteed.

Although many of the examples and much of the analysis in this book are based on our interviews, we also rely heavily on other sources of information—previous and ongoing research, media articles, and court cases—in such disciplines as law, social work, education, history, literature, art, science, and the social sciences.

Some of the studies cited, especially those in the area of overt sex discrimination, come from probability samples. Because our focus on subtle and covert sex discrimination is exploratory and we were primarily interested in developing conceptual typologies that would be useful in future studies, we relied on purposive and snowball sampling techniques.

Index